Crossing Fifth Avenue
To Bergdorf Goodman

SPECIALIST PRESS INTERNATIONAL

New York

Crossing Fifth Avenue
To Bergdorf Goodman

An Insider's Account
On The Rise of Luxury Retailing

Ira Neimark

New York

Specialist Press International books can be purchased for educational, business or sales promotional use. For ordering details, please contact:

Special Markets Department
SPI Books
99 Spring Street
New York, NY 10012.

For further information, contact:

S.P.I. Books
99 Spring Street, 3rd Floor
New York, NY 10012
Tel: (212) 431-5011
Fax: (212) 431-8646
E-mail: *publicity@spibooks.com*

10 9 8 7 6 5 4 3 2 1
First Edition

Library of Congress Cataloging-in-Publication Data available.
S.P.I. Books World Wide Web address: www.spibooks.com
ISBN: 1-56171-208-6

For my wife, Jackie, and our daughters, Janie and Robin, who lived with me through the many exciting experiences crossing Fifth Avenue to Bergdorf Goodman.

Table of Contents

Acknowledgments

There are many, many people who helped me along to a successful career; I hope that I mentioned them all and how they aided me to accomplish my objectives. There are also a great number of people, without whose help the book would not have happened.

I would like to thank, first, my wife Jackie, who should be listed as my collaborator since she over the years, collected and saved all of the articles and photographs that are shown throughout the book. In addition, she read, critiqued and cleaned up the pages as they were finished. I also want to thank my daughters, Janie Lewis and Robin Seegal, for reminding me of the many stories I told them that they remembered from when we sat around the dinner table after I returned from a busy days work at a very exciting retail career. My thanks also to my granddaughters, Hallie Seegal and Pamela Lewis, for asking me to tell them why the number 721 was so important to me.

My many thanks to Edward Nardoza, Vice President, Editor in Chief and David Moin, Senior Retail Editor, of *Women's Wear Daily,* for their early advice and encouragement, as well as making available to me the *WWD* "morgue", allowed me to research many of the stories that appear throughout the book. To Arthur Sulzberger Jr., after my spending a great deal of time at the NY Public Library, to no avail for what I was looking for, through one telephone call, was able to have his staff locate a Bonwit Teller advertisement that made such a major impression on me when I was a stock boy over sixty years ago. To Jeffry Aronsson, my friend and advisor, who guided me through the labyrinth of the technicalities involved in writing this book. Also to Phil Hawley, whose encouragement and confidence in me contributed mightily to the success of Bergdorf Goodman; to Randy Stambaugh and Jack Burke for bringing me back to Fifth Avenue; and to Isabelle Leeds for contributing her expertise and moral support in developing this project. Also thanks to Julian Bach, the retired legendary literary agent, who after I wasted over a year trying to find an appropriate literary agent and then an appreciative publisher, advised me to find a small, yet aggressive literary agent who would appreciate the potential of the story that I had written. This brings me to my good fortune of finding Maryann Karinch of The Rudy Agency. Thank you Maryann, for your enthusiasm and support. Thank you for always being at the other end of my many e-mails for your quick and wise responses. Thank you for being my editor, helping to make the stories as exciting as they really were.

Introduction

I was lucky to wander into retailing at the time when the successful department and specialty stores were enjoying the peak of their success. At a time when, in not too many years in the future, the major stores—so identifiable to their customers—would pass into oblivion like the luxury steamships of that era. I say lucky, since I was able to experience what it was that made the stores great to shop in as a family experience. No matter what the income level, from Klein's On the Square at 14th Street in New York, one of the very first large stores to sell lower-price merchandise, to the heights of Bergdorf Goodman and Bonwit Teller on Fifth Avenue, their customers were treated as valued assets to be treasured. I watched over the years as one great retailer after another disappeared from the scene. I was again lucky to have been involved with a few of the stores when they were considered the best in their cities, and from the distance and pinnacle of Bergdorf Goodman, watched their slow demise.

Three years ago, I was reminded of all of this when my oldest granddaughter, Hallie Seegal, asked me the significance of 721, my lucky number. I explained to her that my first job was at Bonwit Teller, 721 Fifth Avenue, and so the experiences that I remembered, and the hundreds newspaper clippings, saved over these many years by my wife, Jackie, gave me the impetus to write a retailer's memoir. Mine was an exciting career at an exciting time, meeting many important people along the way. I thought it only fair to share my prime stories for all those interested in retailing, particularly the excitement and the luxury of the fashion world. The stories explain, at a young age, my early awareness that something was out there that would fulfill my ambitions. Second, how Bonwit Teller gave me the vision of high standards and a taste level, to the New England experience, where I learned the sound Yankee basic principles of retailing. Finally, the story of my return to New York, and how I was able to combine my experiences to the culmination of bringing Bergdorf Goodman to the retail leadership in the world of fashion.

In retrospect, when Bergdorf Goodman was enjoying the height of its fashion reputation in the 1930s, '40s and '50s, no one could have known that a young man working across Fifth Avenue at Bonwit Teller as the "door boy" would one day, as Chairman and CEO of Bergdorf Goodman, revitalize the store to fashion leadership when it had fallen behind the leading fashion stores of the 1960s and '70s. Here I am.

Ira Neimark,
September, 2006

My Debut at Bonwit Teller 1

I s my retail career just a series of fortunate coincidences? Or is it like a ball bouncing around in a pinball machine, generally scoring points because some skilled hands flip it in the right direction?

Looking for a job in 1938 felt demoralizing since the country still suffered from the aches and fears of the Great Depression. Good jobs were scarce. Fortunately for me, either through instinct or luck, I found my way to the Hamilton Employment Agency in downtown Manhattan. Being the youngest and least qualified for a job, I sat there day after day waiting for an opportunity. When one finally came, I didn't even know where it was.

Hamilton sent me to Bonwit Teller at Fifth Avenue and 56th Street to be interviewed for the position of pageboy for the 721 Club. I had to ask a taxi driver for directions to the store, and then took the subway uptown. I even spent twenty-five cents for a shoeshine in order to make a proper impression.

The 721 Club was a unique concept set up to help men do their Christmas shopping in a store specifically set up to sell to women. Named for the store's address, 721 Fifth Avenue, the club occupied a room on the fourth floor. Most of the year it housed the Bridal Salon, but every Christmas, Bonwit's staff whisked all of the wedding gowns off to who-knows-where and transformed the space into an exclusive men's club, complete with leather, club-style armchairs, sofas, and walls discreetly decked in holiday decorations.

The key to my success in the interview was that the candidate had to fit a "Philip Morris"-style bellhop uniform with a tailored red jacket, black hat and white gloves. At one month short of my seventeenth birthday, I stood 5 feet, 8 inches tall and weighed a slim 130 pounds. I fit so I got the job!

My imagination reeled at the Christmas party where I performed my first major duties as pageboy. The guest list for this lavish 721 Club event contained names of some of the most successful businessmen in New York City. The cocktail party featured a long runway with beautiful models. Mary Martin, then the toast of Broadway, captivated the men with "My Heart Belongs to Daddy" from the Cole Porter musical *Leave It To Me*.

All I had to do was greet the men as they arrived, and at the end of the show, walk down the runway and present an extravagantly wrapped gift to Mary Martin. I remember walking down the runway and presenting the gift to her. But I also have a keen memory of what happened next. To exit the runway, I had to leave through the models' dressing room. Some of the models were not fully dressed. That was the first indication I had that I would like to be more involved in the fashion business.

While the 721 Club operated during the season, I stood at the club door welcoming men, and checked their coats as they signed a register. (A great mailing list.) I was also tasked with mixing cocktails if and when the men stayed late to purchase Christmas gifts after the bartender had gone. I learned how to mix manhattans and martinis. I didn't drink at that point, but I did like to eat the maraschino cherries.

The sales staff was made up of the most attractive saleswomen selected from around the store. They wore striking red dresses designed and made in Bonwit Teller's alteration department. Once a customer was comfortable, with a cocktail in hand, the sales person would bring an assortment of merchandise for his selection. The sales were great; however, I am sure the returns after Christmas were great as well.

The men were well groomed and rich, and the saleswomen, young and attractive. Needless to say, the interactions between these two groups produced more than just sales. A number of these young women had no problem remaining attentive to the young bachelors who frequented the club, and soon married well. I imagine they quite enjoyed their post-Christmas task of returning the 721 Club to its regular duty as Bonwit's Bridal Salon.

The store environment captivated me. I discovered that Bonwit Teller, despite being fifteen blocks from Broadway and 3,000 miles from Hollywood, was like show business. The display windows, glittering with elegance, projected drama like a stage set. The stunning interior décor immediately wrapped the clientele in distractions, much like a theatre lobby. And the employees—from the stylish sales people to the military-looking elevator operators to the consummate president—all seemed to be acting out carefully-scripted roles. The finery of the customers, scent of the cosmetic department, and luxury of the merchandise brought stories of opulence to life. I decided this was where I wanted to start my career. I was fascinated. I was determined to be successful. I was home.

As Christmas approached, I asked the personnel department if I might stay on after the 721 Club closed for the season. The answer was "yes," and I would next serve as doorboy at the 56th Street store entrance. Instead of returning to my high school, Erasmus Hall, I entered their night school classes. I got around the necessity of the required working papers by having my aunt Bert, who lived in Florida, send a letter to "whomever" that said I had come to live with her. Years later, I admitted to William M. Holmes, then the president of Bonwit Teller, that I lied about my age to get my first job at the store. Instead of firing me, he said, "Don't worry." He had lied about his age as well.

Lessons Learned

- To get the job, make sure you "fit the uniform" to get your foot in the door.

- It is important that the environment and atmosphere of the company, and the position suits your personality in order to maximize your ability.

Bonwit Teller made me a breadwinner at home, which meant a great deal because I'd lost my father at age eleven. My mother had supported our family after that—and done it with impressive success. We still owned our two-family home in Flatbush, Brooklyn, then an upscale middle class neighborhood.

You have no doubt heard the gripping tales from my generation of walking to school in rain, snow and gale-force winds. They're true. In the early twenties, there were no school busses. In fact, horse-drawn wagons still carried the milkmen and icemen, and oddly enough, even moved small homes. One of the highlights of the day was to hitch a ride on the back the iceman's horse-drawn wagon. Another was sitting on the curb with my friends and identifying the cars as they passed by: Pierce Arrow, Packard, Oldsmobile Buick. This might go on for hours.

My brothers and I attended PS 181. Until the seventh grade, my academic record hadn't earned any gold stars. Mrs. Schreiner changed that by expecting me to excel. When I entered the seventh grade, she asked all the students to announce their names. After I responded in a sullen tone, Mrs. Schreiner said, "Oh, you must be Lester's younger brother. He was a wonderful student." I went on to be the president of the seventh grade and the eighth grade as well as the valedictorian for the graduating class.

The only negative to this episode was the graduation suit. My mother had picked out a tan plaid suit with knickers at Stern's department store, where she was a salesperson. The suit cost $14, a lot of money during the Depression. I never let her know how I really felt about having my short legs stick out of those knickers.

At Erasmus Hall, I became president of my freshman class. Unfortunately, I did so well in math that I was promoted to the next class. The class was so advanced, that I got lost and fell behind. That problem combined with my poor performance in Latin class, and I was going nowhere. Why Latin? I think my father had planned on my following in his footsteps to be a lawyer. Somebody in my family decided that to be a lawyer, I should study Latin. Mistake.

During this Christmas holiday, I found the job at Bonwit Teller, where I wouldn't have to be a Latin scholar or mathematical genius. I left Erasmus day school for night school and never looked back.

It upset me to see my mother standing on the street at the bus stop in cold or rainy weather waiting for the bus. Only a few years earlier she has been riding around in her lavender Marmon. Back then, automobiles came in very few colors: black, blue, and maroon. My mother had the blue Marmon painted lavender. She liked the color, and that was that. When we went to visit, people often thought we were delivering flowers.

My mother was one of seven sisters—all popular beauties known as "the Brody girls." My aunts lived upstairs above us with my grandparents. Before each married and moved away, I would listen to them argue as to who went to a better beauty parlor, had a prettier dress, hat, and so on. As they told their stories, I learned how women thought about themselves and how they wanted to look. Each one worked in apparel stores before they were married, and their stories intrigued me. I have often thought this was one reason for my original interest in Bonwit Teller, and later, my understanding of the female customers at Bergdorf Goodman.

After my grandparents died and my aunts moved on, my mother rented the upstairs. As the Depression worsened, even with that extra income she found it difficult to pay for coal to heat the house. Instead of buying coal that we couldn't afford from a dealer, I made an arrangement with the janitor of an apartment house down the street. I bought coal from him for twenty-five cents a wheelbarrow. He had extra income, we had a warm house, and I discovered the entrepreneur in me.

I next relied on that part of me to finance my trip to Boy Scout camp. My friends who could afford it went for at least two weeks. Two weeks cost $15. It might as well have been $15,000—but I had an idea. I decided to have a raffle with a friend of mine. My uncle Jack loaned us $10 to have raffle tickets printed: "Send a Boy Scout to Camp for .25¢." The prize was $10. We went from door to door amassing the needed amount. At one of the last doors, a nice lady said, "What a clever idea!" Her son was a scoutmaster and she would tell him about it. We had a hunch the jig was up and quit soliciting before we were drummed out, or whatever they did to Boy Scouts who broke the rules. By coincidence, Uncle Jack won the raffle and got his money back. My friend Bob and I had two weeks at camp that we never forgot.

Lesson Learned

- Whenever the situation requires innovation, innovate.

1939–1940

As the doorboy, I became the newest addition to the Bonwit Teller parking service on Fifth Avenue and 56th Street. I greeted customers as they drove up in their own cars or limousines; some not only had chauffeurs, but also footmen. Not too long after I started this job, two ladies that I recognized as buyers for Bonwit Teller came out of the store. Buyers dressed as though they were the customers, usually wearing black dresses, hats, and gloves. These two women asked, "Are you Ira Neimark?" When I said, "Yes," they said I should know that at an executive meeting that morning, the president of the store, William Holmes, announced that if everyone on staff greeted customers as the young man on the door does, we would be a much better store. First reaction: I was glad I still had a job. Second: Surprise. I thought it was only proper to make eye contact with customers and greet them pleasantly.

Somewhere along the way I read Dale Carnegie's *How To Win Friends and Influence People*. This gave me on inkling that people liked feeling important and appreciated anyone from the doorman to the president who gave the impression of recognizing their importance. It seemed obvious to me that Bonwit Teller's customers expected and even required all the services they enjoyed in their social lives. As an example, when an older woman customer entered her limousine on a cold day, I customarily put her lap robe over her legs. Of course, if done slowly enough, it gave the customer time to fumble in her handbag for a proper tip.

Lessons Learned

- People like to be greeted with eye contact. To greet customers by their name has many advantages.

- Satisfying customers is and has always been the key to business success. To achieve success, it is critical whether it is greeting customers or being able to fulfill their needs for merchandise or service that is being offered.

Occasionally, my job redefined the dimensions of customer service.

Certain mornings during the week, limousines would arrive with the Whitneys, Vanderbilts, and other customers who owned racing stables on Long Island. They headed for the beauty salon, where they graciously answered questions about which horses were slated to run, and how well they were expected to run that day. Needless to say, many of the people in the beauty salon wanted to place bets on the so-called tips. They sent their money down to the 56th street door and I was asked as a "customer service" to take the bets to a drug store where George-the-bookie did business in a telephone booth, placing his customers' bets over the phone. On my first trip, I was surprised to receive a nickel on every dollar placed with him. On one trip, the bets were late in coming down. As I ran across Fifth Avenue to place the bets before the race would close, a thought occurred to me: If I didn't place the bets and the horses lost, I could just keep the money. The thought didn't last long enough to cross Fifth Avenue. I reversed my run back to the store, told the people it was too late, and returned their money. After a few weeks of this additional responsibility, the bookie asked me to cover the neighborhood for him. I reviewed this business proposal with my mother who responded with a negative response that could be heard by a deaf person within a mile.

Lesson Learned

- Always bet with other people's money.

As doorboy, my other responsibility was to relieve the doormen for their lunch break. The 56th street doorman, Pat Reilly was "the" doorman at the time. He was big with an Irish brogue you could cut with a knife. Before his lunch break, he would send me to a delicatessen on Sixth Avenue to buy him two quarts of beer. The rest of the day he was mellow. Whenever a customer wanted a taxicab, Pat would send me to the corner for a cab going north. (In those days Fifth Avenue had two way traffic.) I would flag a cab, jump on the running board, and deliver the taxi to the customer with a flourish. That usually generated a generous tip.

There were three events when I relieved the Fifth Avenue doorman that have stayed in my mind. One occurred daily— greeting Cardinal Spellman, who always tipped his hat to me as he walked up Fifth Avenue—and the other two rate as once-in-a-lifetime experiences.

One afternoon, a rather large man bounded out of a taxicab at the Fifth Avenue entrance. His long mustache, pointed up at both ends, gave away his identity. Salvador Dali glanced at the windows on either side of the entrance and rushed inside. About fifteen minutes later, I heard a deafening crash as a fur lined bathtub pushed through the plate glass window. Dali had designed two of the Fifth Avenue windows. One window showcased a mannequin wearing a fur coat standing in a matching fur lined bathtub. Sometime that morning, a customer wanted the fur coat, so a clerk replaced it with another. It seems that the self-proclaimed genius was incensed that the fur he had personally selected was changed without his creative input. Since I was a witness to this desecration, management directed me not to talk to the press about it. This served as my introduction to working with reporters.

The third incident involved an imposing limousine that pulled up to the Duveen Antiques Galleries across Fifth Avenue from Bonwit Teller. The word was out that the Duke and Duchess of Windsor were in the car. A large crowd gathered and I was among them. As the crowd grew larger, the star-struck mass of bodies pressed me tightly against the limousine. The next day the *New York Times* carried a photograph of the crowd. Lo and behold, there I was: A clear shot of my back. This was my first of many photos in the *New York Times*, but the only one of my back.

Lessons Learned

- When required to talk to the press, be as positive as possible about the subject.

After about a year on the door, the personnel director asked me if I would be interested in moving from being the doorboy to be the office boy in the office of the president. This presented a monetary problem. Although $17 a week was a modest salary, I made as much in tips, opening car doors, getting taxis, checking packages, and placing bets.

I brought this proposal to my mother. In a much quieter tone than the one she'd used in response to the bookie's offer, she explained to me the advantages to seeing and being seen by all of the important people in the store. And to learn as much as I could from the people I worked with. I accepted the position—the first promotion of my retail career. Years later when I saw the show *How To Succeed In Business Without Really Trying*, I felt Abe Burrows had read my script. Or I had read his.

Lesson Learned

- It is sometimes wise to accept a reduction in salary or position if it leads to a greater opportunity.

Act Two at Bonwit Teller   **2**

1940

Being office boy to the president held multiple benefits. For one, I got all of the stamps from foreign correspondence to add to my stamp collection. The most interesting prize of all was the last package to arrive from our Paris commissionaire, just before the fall of France to the Germans in 1940. The package was covered with 50-franc French stamps. I took the wrapping home, and soaked it in the bathtub to remove what must have been about twenty-five stamps. I had no idea of their value, and went to a stamp dealer at Rockefeller Center for an appraisal. He offered me $18 for the lot. Thinking back, I might have received a better price by shopping around. Clearly there was a good reason why I had been promoted to office boy and not the vice-president of finance.

Ever since I was a Boy Scout, and walked across the George Washington Bridge to go hiking on Bear Mountain, I wanted to have a canoe on the Hudson River. With the $18, I bought a fine second-hand canoe and kept it at a small boat yard a few miles north of the bridge. In those days, Bonwit Teller closed on Saturdays and Sundays during the summer, as all the uptown retailers did. This allowed me to canoe on the Hudson River throughout the summer of 1940. At the end of the summer, I sold the canoe—for $18—and bought a gray flannel suit to wear when I returned to work. I enjoyed the experience of buying as well as selling. This no doubt had an influence on my interest in becoming a merchant.

Another benefit was my close proximity to the advertising department. Many times when I walked by, the copywriters would hand me a piece of merchandise and ask me to name it. Once with a checked sweater, I said, "call it checkmate." It appeared in the newspaper! Other suggestions of mine also made it into the *New York Times* during my year in that position. My exposure to advertising convinced me I might want to pursue it as my career. I told Mr. Holmes of my thinking. He straightened me out in a hurry: "Advertising may seem like fun, but the big money is in merchandising." "Besides," he added, "when you become head of a store, advertising will report to you."

The war in Europe had intensified and many of the British nationals were returning home to report to their military units. When Mr. Oddy, the sales representative in America for Pringle cashmeres came to say goodbye to Bill Holmes, he was dressed in a splendid English officer's uniform, complete with a Sam Brown belt, and leather boots. Needless to say, I was in awe, and determined when it was time for me to sign up, this was the way for me to go. It seemed that whenever I observed people and situations that impressed me, I felt I could one day achieve the same lifestyle. When Bill Holmes arrived in the morning in his chauffeur-driven LaSalle, he was handsomely dressed with a bulging briefcase, newspapers under his arm, greeting everyone on the way through the store. I was impressed and decided that one day I would live and work the same way. Strangely, the young men I had worked with on the parking service had ambitions to join the police or fire departments.

Lesson Learned

- In planning a career, aim as high as you can. You may not hit the target at the top, but coming close is better than not aiming at all.

A third benefit I got as office boy to the president was insights into how a successful retail business functions. The most important of these—and probably the one that has served me best throughout my career—was Bill Holmes' belief in the value of building close relationships with key fashion designers and manufacturers. This may not seem like earth shattering wisdom, and taken as a stand-alone piece of advice, it's not. The brilliance of this approach was not that he believed in the worth of those relationships, but rather how he actively worked to build and sustain them.

I recall most of the nobility of fashion who visited his office. Designer Phillip Mangone, barely recovered from burns inflicted by the Hindenburg explosion on May 6, 1937, looked like the title character in *Phantom of the Opera*. Vincent dePaul Draddy, the new head of David Crystal, became famous soon afterward for introducing the Izod Lacoste golf shirt. Among the other visitors were Vincent Monte-Sano from Monte-Sano & Pruzan; Ben Gershel, head of the ready-to-wear company that bore his name; Archie Davidow, Sidney Wragge, head of the sportswear company B.H. Wragge; and Stella Sloat, later recommended to First Lady Jacqueline Kennedy by Diana Vreeland to help Mrs. Kennedy shake her image as a devotee of French fashion houses. These and many others were all important in building the foundation of the fashion business in New York.

As office boy to the president, I listened to conversations, and read memos and reports that fell into my hands each day as part of my job—and I asked a lot of questions. I was learning to look at the business from a whole new perspective. Lowly office boy that I was, I felt I was being encouraged to approach my job as if I were the president of the store.

One of my daily assignments that helped me gain this new perspective was to read *Women's Wear Daily* each morning and underline what I felt were the most important articles for Bill Holmes to read. Can you imagine what this did for me? Here I was, only eighteen-years-old, not only being encouraged to use my own judgment and initiative, but also being pushed to identify and address the concerns of the company's top executive. I had to learn to think like the president of a major department store. As I mentioned earlier, my mother urged me to take the office boy position to learn. At the time, I didn't know what she meant, but after only a few weeks in Bill Holmes' office, I realized that, rather than dropping out of school in order to work, I had merely exchanged one type of classroom for another.

Lessons Learned

- It is not so much in what you know, but in how you execute what you know.

- Opportunity is always all around you. Another key to success is to be able to identify and develop the opportunity.

This new management perspective also manifested in other ways. Going through the store each day, my observations of how we presented merchandise to customers puzzled me. In those days, mannequins on each floor stood by the wall between the elevators. This meant customers would see the clothes as they left the floor. I suggested to Bill Holmes that the mannequins be positioned a few feet in front of the elevators so customers could see the merchandise on display as they got off the elevators. A few weeks later all of the mannequins throughout the store were moved, and so was I.

Someone thought I was ready to be elevated to merchandising. I looked around Bill Holmes' office to examine where they would place my desk. However, that was not to be. Instead I was told my next step was to be the stock boy in the handbag department, in the basement. Not what I had in mind.

And that is the story of how I managed to move from Fifth Avenue all the way up to the executive suite, and then from there, directly down to the basement, thus ending up in a lower position than the one in which I had begun.

Lessons Learned

- The advice Bill Holmes gave me: "Sales people, designers and manufacturers—if you have them on your side, you will be a successful merchant." I always abided by it.

- To be able to put yourself in the mind of the customer—to understand his or her requirement—is half the battle. The other half is to meet that requirement.

The essential strategic lessons of retail came to me while I made the most of my promotion to the basement.

If Bill Holmes was known for anything as a merchant, it was his ability to have a buyer maximize the sales of an item. He insisted that each buyer have at least three re-orderable fashion items in stock at all times. He taught me early on: Most buyers left to their own devices will do relatively well, but unless they received the proper direction and support, they would not reach their full potential.

What is "proper direction?" Bill Holmes put a format in place that I became responsible for, and have used all through my career. It was, as all good retail principles should be, quite simple.

Each department had a folder with a form that vertically listed the style, price, and the sales by units for each week, the number of units on hand, as well as on order. Each item had a horizontal column that listed the number of weeks in the season. The buyer had to have at least three columns for "running numbers" or "best sellers," that is, the buyer had to have at least three items in stock that "ran" well. The format, in fact, was similar to a racetrack sheet.

Each week, I made sure that all the departments in the store sent the running-number folders to the president's office. A review determined whether or not the buyers were reordering enough of the style to keep it running. When the president thought not, the buyer heard about it. Most importantly, when a buyer said she didn't have a running number to report, she'd better go to the market and not come back until she had the required three. The running-number procedure was a very successful way to build a profitable business. I used the it every opportunity that I had throughout my retail career.

Another principle I learned at this time, was "don't buy tomb-stones." Over the years, I noticed that it was the custom for many buyers to buy as few pieces of a style as possible in order to buy many more styles. The logic was, the more items a buyer had, the more opportunities she had to reorder. Also many buyers weren't sure how well a style would sell, and thought they were playing it safe by stretching their options in this manner. In my opinion, if the buyer wasn't sure how well a style would sell, she shouldn't be a buyer. The best items sold fast, and being ordered as *one* in size 6, *one* in size 8, and so on, there wouldn't be a complete size range left for a second customer to choose from. A great many sales are lost because a customer sees something he or she would like to buy, and finds out the store doesn't have the item in the right size. So by playing it safe, the buyer lost sales. Worse yet, most of the left over sizes cluttered up the stock and were degraded to a rack of markdowns. I have often compared this problem to a buyer who went to the racetrack, and placed two dollars on each horse in the race, instead of betting to win, place or show. The buyer spent a lot of money, but had nothing to show for the effort.

Lesson Learned

- If you are going to be a merchant you have to gamble on your judgment. If your judgment is poor, so you will be.

One reason I was moved to the stock boy position was that the handbag department was experiencing unpredicted inventory short-ages. The difference between the inventory on the books and the physical inventory indicated either theft or poor paper work. I was expected to solve the problem. I suspect another reason was that this was the route of Bill Holmes' retail experience; he wanted me to fol-low in his footsteps. In fact, one day when he was taking a group of directors from Atlas Corporation, a financial investment conglomerate that owned Bonwit Teller, through the store, he stopped at my stockroom. He said to the group, which included the chief executive, Floyd Odlum, "This young man wants to have my job some day." I was extremely flattered and muttered some kind of thank you.

I placed threads at different locations in the stockroom night after night to see if someone was entering and stealing the merchandise, but to no avail. Eventually, I figured out the problem: The assistant buyer was charging back merchandise to manufactures at cost and retail prices that were different from the purchase price of the merchandise. She was confused with the sale prices versus the regular prices. There was only one major sale a year, so this price differential was considerable.

The stockroom held valuable information as long as I paid attention. For example, when the sales people came down each morning to select handbags to fill in their stock, they always asked for the handbags they felt were the best sellers. The approach, however, was not to allow them to have the best sellers without taking some of the slower models. Not unlike during WWII, to buy a bottle of scotch you also had to buy a bottle of rum and in some cases, two bottles of rum.

As I said, once a year the department had a major sale, with values so extraordinary, they caused a bit of a frenzy. The following advertisement is courtesy of the *New York Times*. Alligator, lizard, fine calf skins by the dozens, for $7.85 each. Unbelievable today. Bonwit Teller's major prestige handbag manufacturers, Koret and Pichel among them, cleaned out their stock for this annual event. Since I had to replenish the handbags from the basement stockroom every few minutes, and there two entrances to the floor, I would change from door to door each time in order not to have the customers stop me on the way to the department. One customer even offered me five dollars if I would tell her which door I would come out of on my next trip. I told her, but didn't accept the five dollars.

The buyer of the handbag department, Regina Hellman, actively supported my ambitions and had me meet the principal handbag

manufacturers of the day. In some cases, I was invited to lunch with them. One day, I was invited to the racetrack. Buyers lived by different rules then.

Six months after the memorable handbag sale and about a year into my stock-boy assignment, the Japanese bombed Pearl Harbor on Sunday, December 7th, 1941. Monday, as I listened to the stock-room radio, I heard President Roosevelt declare war on the Empire of Japan. We all knew life would never be the same again, but didn't envision the changes that were to come, both personally and in business.

On the personal front, my older brother, Lester, had been drafted the year before, so he was our immediate concern. People in the streets asked frantically, "Where is Pearl Harbor?" with similar concerns about their loved ones and neighbors. The initial reaction was that we would win this war quickly. We were all shocked when our lack of preparedness became known, and the enormity of our Pearl Harbor disaster sank in.

From the business point of view, price controls went on almost immediately, as well as rationing of strategic materials. This meant the leather merchandise in my stockroom became much more valuable, and purchasing new leather merchandise became nearly impossible. Regardless of that, each morning the sales ladies still asked for the best sellers.

Lessons Learned

- Salespeople can tell a best seller before the buyers. They can, in most cases, tell what isn't going to be easy to sell, and can also tell at what price it should and will sell for.

- If you have the salespeople on your side you will succeed. If the salespeople are not, you will increase the chances of failure.

A Retailer Goes to War   **3**

In 1942, I moved to the handbag merchandise control office. Where was each unit of merchandise located? How well did each style sell? These were the questions to which I had to have answers.

At the time, it seemed to me that there was no logical method for the buyer to determine how many styles to buy and how many units to buy of each style. This mystery persisted many years for me. In those days, it seemed a God-given gift for a buyer to make good decisions based on intuition, experience, and not much more. Fashion retailers at that point had not branched out as they did later on, however, so any buyers who had good sense constantly checked their stock and could usually come to a reasonable conclusion as to what was going on, and what action to take.

Eventually, I arrived at a formula that gave my buyers an advantage beyond a "reasonable conclusion." I will share this in Chapter 5 after relating a few formative experiences that occurred during and after the war.

Sara Pennoyer, Bonwit Teller's head of advertising and sales promotion, wrote a book called *Polly Tucker, Merchant*, one of many Dodd, Mead Career Books written by women "in the field" from the 1930's to the 1960's. The book generated royalties from apparel manufacturers using the Polly Tucker label. The royalties provided funds for the Polly Tucker Scholarship. I was one of the employees selected for the scholarship, and entered night classes at Columbia University, School of Business.

At that time, the war was six months old. I had just turned twenty, and enlisted in the Army Air Corps. On my last night of classes before leaving for my military assignment, since I was a bit superstitious, for good luck I touched the big toe of each of the statues at the entrance to the Columbia campus on Broadway. I pledged that I would return after the war and touch the statues again. I did.

Wartime experiences taught me a range of lessons that carried over well into my life as a retailer. I saw the rewards of setting specific goals, and the value of figuring out how to get closer to those goals no matter what life (or my country) asked of me at the moment. I saw examples of how "timing is everything," the pros and cons of stepping out of line, and the happy consequences of taking the time to keep up important relationships.

In early 1943, when I arrived at the Army Air Corps Cadet Classification Center in Nashville, Tennessee, we received our cadet uniforms and stood ready to be assigned for pilot, navigator or bombardier training. The first night as I prepared to go to sleep, I looked around our quarters. I saw all the hats with the wings on them and realized that I had achieved my boyhood dream of becoming an aviation cadet. Since I was twelve years old and had my first flight, I'd wanted those wings: It was one of the first goals that I had set for myself that I had been able to achieve.

As I traveled around the country during my flight training, if I saw an ad in a local newspaper that I thought had merit I would send it to Bill Holmes. It was my habit to write to him and Betty Vanderbilt, his secretary, fairly often in my travels to Air Corp bases around the country to keep them up to date and make sure they didn't forget me. Whenever I went into different cities— Nashville, Tennessee; Montgomery Alabama; Madison Wisconsin— I kept two objectives on my mind. One, I sent Bill Holmes my observations of the major stores in those cities. Two (equally if not more important), I dated the prettiest girls from those stores.

As a radar flight instructor, I was stationed at Boca Raton Airfield, near Palm Beach, where Bill Holmes had a winter home. He invited me to visit and bring him up to date on my experiences. When my visit was nearing the end, his butler announced the arrival of Adam Gimbel of the famous Gimbel family of retailers; I rose to leave. Bill Holmes asked me to wait so he could introduce me. He then proceeded to tell Adam Gimbel: One day this young man will have my job. I didn't need an airplane to reach the clouds that day.

Bonwit Teller, as many businesses did, had a patriotic policy of sending a check periodically to employees in service. One time when I was in a bar in Honolulu called PY Chong, I cashed my check at the bar. On reflection, I became concerned that Bonwit Teller would not appreciate my spending their generosity on gin. I was concerned even then with creating the proper impression. That incident stayed in my mind all these years.

Lessons Learned

- Drink if you will, but not on other people's money

- If you want to create a good impression, always let your management know that you are interested in and dedicated to your job.

- If you don't know how or why to make a merchandising procedure successful, keep your eyes and ears open until you find the person who has the answer.

At the end of the war, I was stationed on Saipan in the Pacific. By that time, most of us longed for things that connected us to home. My friend Paul Brown exploited that in a way that got him into a little trouble. Paul was selected to broadcast the Armed Forces Radio on the island—possibly the beginning of what today is called a disc jockey. Paul assembled a few household items near his microphone. He rattled tableware, clinked glasses, and announced, with dance music in the background, "Good afternoon, ladies and gentlemen, this is Paul Brown, broadcasting from the Marpi Point Country Club. It is a beautiful day and the music is playing for the dancers on the patio overlooking the bay." For hours after that, jeeps zigzagged all over the island looking for the country club. Even the commanding officer wanted to know what was going on. Paul was shortly relieved of his broadcasting responsibility. It came as no surprise to learn that, after the war, Paul went on to become a successful advertising executive.

When the war ended, I remained in Saipan for a time. The executive in charge of merchandise planning at Bonwit Teller wrote to me asking for a sense of how long to keep the job of his assistant open for me. I showed the letter to my commanding officer, who said that if he knew the answer to that question, he would give it. He had no idea when we would be returning home. I wrote back and explained my dilemma. When Bill Holmes heard about the letter, he was furious that an executive working for him could be so insensitive at a time when everyone was pleased the war was over, and wanted to show their appreciation to the people who had helped make victory possible.

As we waited on Saipan to go home—or so we thought—some of my buddies decided we should find souvenirs to bring home. Flying in for landings, we had always noticed a large cave at the end of the island that was pockmarked from the shelling of battleships sent to soften resistance prior to the invasion of the U.S. Marines. We felt that if we could get into the cave, we would find souvenirs left by Japanese troops who were in the cave when it was bombarded.

To get into the cave, we had to climb along a cliff around a bend about twenty feet above the ocean. Huge waves slammed against the cliff every fifteen seconds or so, allowing each one of us enough time to get around the bend before the next wave arrived. Norm Mattern wanted to be the first to go. He got halfway around the bend when the wave hit him, washed him off the cliff, and plunged him into the rough water below. We were stunned to see him sink; only his hat floated on the surface. We knew Norm was not a strong swimmer and feared the worst. Then his head popped to the surface and the next wave picked him up and brought him up to our level. I tried to grab him, but missed him on the first try. He slid and dropped back into the ocean, until the next wave threw him up again. With the other fellows holding on to my belt, on our second try, I was able to have him grab my left foot and get it under his armpit to haul him up. He was safe, although a bit cut up from the jagged coral. Needless to say we aborted our souvenir hunt—but the drama wasn't over.

About a week after this incident, we heard that a Japanese captain was going to surrender with ten of his Imperial Marines. Japanese Imperial Marines were selected for their height, usually about six feet tall. We attended the ceremony and, afterward, asked where were he and his troops had hidden on the island prior to their surrender? Imagine our shock when we learned they had hidden in the cave we had tried to enter before the wave swept Norm into the ocean. To this day, I wonder what would have happened if were able to get into that cave. Would we have been heroes with the Japanese captain surrendering to us? A more likely scenario is that the tall, able-bodied Imperial Marines would have turned us into casualties of war.

With the damn war over with, we became obsessed with: How do we get out of here? I was assigned to the 73rd wing compound, a tremendous area that had all the surplus material on Saipan that had to be either shipped home or destroyed. I had Jeeps, trucks, parachutes, radar equipment, and even two crated Piper Cubs. Since we didn't know when we might return home, a friend of mine and I thought of assembling one of the planes and flying to Japan, on to Russia, Europe, and then home to the U.S. Not a practical idea, but it captures the sense of desperation we felt.

Fortunately, I learned about an opportunity at the University of Hawaii. I applied and was transferred to an air sea rescue squadron on Oahu, so I could attend classes there. After a few months of enjoying Hawaii, I was qualified to return home.

Ira Neimark at Army Air Corps flight training school 1943

Many of us while waiting to return home were curious as to what were the current styles of clothing being worn by civilians. We wanted to dress properly to continue in our careers, or return to college.

I wrote to *Esquire* magazine. They were nice enough to answer: grey flannel suits, white or blue button-down oxford shirts, and a felt hat were the order of the day. (I wish today young people would be as conscious of their appearance as we were way back then.) A few days before I reported back to work at Bonwit Teller, John Wanamaker had an ad on grey flannel suits for $39.95. The store was mobbed. I was able to buy one suit. I was back in business.

Turmoil and Discovery

4

Returning from the war three years to the day to rejoin Bonwit Teller in 1946, I was assigned to the merchandise control office. My starting salary: $55 a week. It wasn't great, but the opportunity for exposure and growth appealed to me. How could I know that "exposure and growth" would involve watching and learning from the deterioration of the great Bonwit Teller?

In my new job, I monitored sales, markdowns, initial markup, merchandise receipts, and inventory levels for the whole store; determined deviations from the original merchandise plan; and made the adjustments up or down in order for management to direct the business. The position also required preparing merchandise plans for the next season far enough in advance for the buyers to plan accordingly.

I found the planning process fascinating. The arithmetic used to determine inventory levels that were required at the beginning of each month first intrigued me, and then bothered me. The procedure was based on a predetermined inventory turnover rate that could be adjusted in many different ways to give the same results. In other words, buyers could adjust their monthly plan to wishful thinking instead of a realistic level of inventory that their planned sales required. This was the beginning of my quest to find a scientific way to plan inventory levels related to sales.★

Lessons Learned

- The starting salary for a new job should be of secondary importance. It is the opportunity that the job offers for the future that is important.

- The single biggest reason for high markdowns and lower profit in many retail enterprises is the lack of professional planning practices.

At this formative stage of my career, the ownership of Bonwit Teller changed hands. I'll go back a bit to relate the original ownership of the store. The Bonwit Teller building on Fifth Avenue was built by Stewart & Company, then sold to P.J. Bonwit and Paul Teller in the early 1920s. Paul Teller dropped out at one point, and P.J. Bonwit operated the business until the stock market crash.

The story I heard was, after the crash, customers were lined up around the block to return merchandise. Mr. Bonwit was so discouraged, he left the store in 1934 by the freight elevator—never to return. He was quite the determined character. The foundation buyer told me when she made her first trip to Europe for the store, she made the mistake confusing American sizes with European sizes. P.J. Bonwit met her at the gangplank, and told her to get back on the boat and do the buy over. She also told me, when the second

---

★ In American retailing, turnover means the number of times it takes for the average monthly inventory to sell, or "turn over," to equal the sales for that season. This could be once a season (very slow) to many times that. The faster inventories sell, or turn over, the better. In the U.K., turnover refers to the sales for a season or a year whichever is being watched.

floor was being redecorated, Mr. Bonwit thought it was all wrong. He grabbed a fire axe and began hacking away at the construction.

Atlas Corporation headed by Floyd Odlum bought the business from the family. Floyd Bostwick Odlum was a very successful financier from Salt Lake City, who (according to insiders) wanted the store for his wife, Hortense. The Odlums asked Adam Gimbel, the head of Saks Fifth Avenue: Who did you think would be a good person to run the store with Hortense? They came up with William M. Holmes, the general merchandise manager of Chapmans, Milwaukee.

Adam Gimbel, a cousin of Bernard Gimbel, long-time president of Gimbel Bros. and grandson of the founder, said Bill Holmes was strong competition for Gimbels in that region and the family wouldn't be unhappy to see him moved to New York. Gimbels had a strong tradition in Milwaukee that stretched back to 1887 and desired to retain their preeminence. Later Bill Holmes and Adam Gimbel became strong competitors and close friends.

Hortense Odlum was initially president after the Bonwit acquisition, and Bill Holmes was the general merchandise manager. Her main contribution was to give the store "a women's point of view," not only in concept, but also in periodicals issued seasonally. She also started The Customers Advisory counsel. This consisted of a monthly luncheon for special customers to ask their opinions about how the store could improve its position as a top retailer.

When Mrs. Odlum finally withdrew from the business a few years later, Bill Holmes became the president. At that point, Bonwit Teller became "the fashion store of New York." With Bill Holmes as head merchant, Abe Schuel in finance, Sara Pennoyer heading advertising and publicity, and Ed Macdonald in operations, the store had an unbeatable combination.

At this time, the manager of the merchandise control office left the store. I was promoted to his position, reporting to Bill Holmes and Abe Schuel. It was a key step for me. I enjoyed the job tremendously, and it had an interesting side responsibility: I was expected to keep minutes of meetings with Mr. Holmes, Mr. Schuel, and Mrs. Pennoyer. I don't recall much about the meetings, other than Bill Holmes' Irish brogue, Abe Schuel's European accent, and Sara Pennoyer talking a mile a minute.

A interesting sidebar: A few years later, Floyd and Hortense Odlum divorced and he married Jacqueline Cochran, the famous aviator—whom he'd met (and purportedly fell for immediately) in 1932. Born into poverty in rural Florida, "Jackie" Cochran set her eyes on success, moved to New York City, and became a popular beautician at the Saks Fifth Avenue Salon. It was all part of a plan to realize her dream of becoming a cosmetics manufacturer. Cochran shared her dream with Floyd Odlum, who suggested she would "need wings" to cover the territory associated with a cosmetics business. She took him literally and earned her pilot's license. In her day, she set more speed and altitude records than any of her contemporaries, male or female, and the U.S. Postal Service issued a stamp in her honor in 1996. She also founded Jacqueline Cochran Cosmetics.

In 1948, Floyd Odlum sold Bonwit Teller to Walter Hoving, former president of Lord and Taylor. In the process, after more than twelve very successful years, Bill Holmes resigned from Bonwit Teller with a non-conflict contract for one year. After that, he became president of James McCreery owned by Associated Dry Goods. He struggled with that decision, asking the opinion of Dorothy Shaver, the new head of Lord and Taylor, also owned by ADG. He was concerned with the loss of prestige, going from Bonwit Teller on upper Fifth Avenue to a popular priced store on 34th Street. Her response was, "Profit is prestige." I don't think he was ever happy there.

A few years later, he left to become the president of Jacqueline Cochran Cosmetics. Moves like this within the industry were quite common and a constant reminder that important relationships merit consistent attention.

I was devastated when Bill Holmes left. Shortly after, Abe Schuel and Sara Pennoyer also left the store. I was now on my own. Fortunately, Hoving Corporation required a person familiar with many aspects of the merchandising and other areas of operation, and felt at that time that I could fit the role of merchandise control manager. The transition went rather smoothly.

Lesson Learned

- It is most important to know the history of the company where you hope to build your career. Understanding and appreciating the culture and the background of the successful executives you will be working with is imperative to "fitting in."

Hoving's previous success at Lord and Taylor partially hinged on his own method of merchandise planning. Fortunately for me, I paid attention when he did a briefing on his "weekly planning method," and thereby assumed responsibility for training the merchandise staff in its use. This particular form approached the planning of sales and inventory by week, instead of by month. None of us was familiar with this concept up to this point. It may sound ridiculous now, in an age when the Internet has supposedly reduced "a work week" to "three days," but this concept established a model that stores today should still follow if they want to reduce inventory problems.

Inventory management—or the lack of it—is and has been the single biggest reason for retailers to lose profit and often lose their businesses as well. Technology is not a solution to the problem: It helps those who are able to think through the problem. In many cases, technology just makes it obvious how badly a chief executive is failing.

First of all, it made sense to me to see sales of the previous year by week instead of month, as well as the inventory required to achieve those sales. However, with Hoving's formula, there was still one key element missing: how to understand what the most desirable inventory relationship to sales should be. As I indicated at the beginning of this chapter, I did not discover the answer to this important question until a few years later.

Hoving replaced Bill Holmes with the former ready-to-wear merchandise manager of Lord and Taylor, Roy Rudolph. A fashion merchant with a great sense of style, but he had a weak merchandising background. Fortunately for me. He did the logical thing and turned over much of the merchandising function to me. I was not exactly ready for this responsibility. Nevertheless, I set about to organize the merchandise office. Personnel sent a young man named Bill Cunningham to me to be trained in merchandise planning. Bright. Creative. Not comfortable with numbers. Bill went on to become the legendary fashion photographer for the *New York Times*, later described by Jan Reeder, the William Doyle Gallery Couture Specialist, as "a fashion historian, scholar, trend-spotter, cultural chronicler (fashion's consummate documentarian with a camera), who holds a unique position in the world of post-war fashion."

In the meantime, one of my more imaginative (if not enduring) ideas came by accident. Inventory management was very efficient, and shortages were at a minimum at Bonwit Teller until the controller died in an automobile crash. Without his supervision, shortages increased at an alarming rate. Shortages or shrinkage is the difference between the dollar amount of the inventory on the books and the physical count. I volunteered to find a solution. A friend of mine was a violinist; he recorded his music on what was then known as a wire recorder. One weekend listening to him record and playback, an idea came to me. I felt that if physical inventories were taken on a weekly basis instead of seasonally, the shortages could be isolated in order to determine the cause. Using the wire recorder a person could walk through the stock room reading the style and price of the merchandise into the recorder. This procedure would be easily five to ten times faster and more accurate than the normal way for a person reading the ticket to another person who had to listen then had to write the information on to an inventory sheet. The inventory sheets were then sent to an auditor to be processed, all time consuming. The wire recorded information was immediately sent to the IBM computer room in the store and key punched into IBM cards and run instantly. The results and the frequency of the reports helped to reduce the shortages significantly. For that time the idea was new, and successful. However, unfortunately for me, but good for IBM, IBM researchers eventually developed price tickets with a magnetic code that could be read by hand held scanners or at the cash register, relegating my idea to the dustbin of retail history. Management at the time was very appreciative of my efforts, and I was given the additional responsibility for inventory management. This was another step in my ambition to improve the management of inventories throughout my retail career.

Just about the time that I made these strides in understanding the fundamentals of profit, I saw the beginning of the eventual demise of Bonwit Teller due to the rapid expansion program introduced by Walter Hoving.

Previously Bonwit Teller had stores in Miami Beach, Palm Beach, and White Plains. They were customer conveniences more than viable businesses. None of these small stores was a drain on inventory or expense to the degree of the two large non-New York stores—first in Boston in 1948 and shortly after, in Chicago. The management of Bonwit Teller did not have the experience or background to undertake an expansion program of this magnitude in such a short time frame.

In 1949, Roy Rudolph appointed me Assistant to the President so he could concentrate on the fashion end of the business. His fashion concept would have worked for Bonwit Teller, except for the overwhelming project of the store expansion program. First, he sent me to Boston to help open that store, which had been the former Boston Museum of Natural History. A year later, he had me pack up and move to Chicago for that store opening. Neither store ever reached its potential. Excessive markdowns added to the detriment of the total company.

Helping to open both of these stores taught me a great deal of what not to do. Expansion for retailers is a necessary component for growth, but proper inventory management is the key to financial success. The demise of Bonwit Teller began slowly at this time as Walter Hoving took over as president from Roy Rudolph after his resignation.

After Walter Hoving, there was a long list of presidents until Genesco bought the store. Genesco had an even longer list including such well-known retailers as Mildred Custin, John Schumacher, and Helen Galland. At one point Maxie Jarman, chairman of Genesco appointed the former publisher of *Harper's Bazaar*, Bill Fine, to work with Mildred Custin, and then to replace her. As I understood it, Mr. Jarman's thought was that a good retailer has to be good at public relations, and this was one of the many good qualities of Bill Fine. About 1972, he interviewed me to consider working for him as president of Bonwit Teller. He then changed the invitation to general merchandise manager, which I declined since I had that position at B. Altman. Naturally, the thought of being named president of Bonwit Teller, where I'd started as a pageboy, intrigued me. But management there was changing too often for the situation to be a growth opportunity—for me or the store.

The situation at Bonwit Teller at this point spotlights how executive decisions can move a retailer to great success, as well as failure. In the mid-1950's, when Maxie Jarman named Geraldine Stutz to head up Henri Bendel, that was a brilliant decision with brilliant results. On the other hand, with so many senior management changes at Bonwit Teller, the store's character changed as soon as one executive left the building and another moved in. One major problem with the rapid change was that old inventory was put aside to be marked down at a later date.

The head liquidation buyer for Filenes Basement visited all the major New York retailers at least twice a year to buy left-over inventory. He told me that he put pencil marks on the back of some of the tickets of the old inventory in Bonwit Teller's basement, and found the same merchandise there season after season.

This story about my exposure to the rise and fall of Bonwit Teller is to point out that I was fortunate to be present at the successful years as well as an observer at its failure.*

Lessons Learned

- In many cases when a successful retailer, defined as a strong sales and profit growth company, with a growing customer base is purchased, the new owner is often too hasty in wanting the store to change to his concept. In more cases than not, this is the recipe for failure.

- Slow moving and old inventory will strangle any business, no matter how many management changes take place.

---

* Teri Agins observed in her June 26, 1989 article for the *Wall Street Journal*, "A Tale of Two Retailers: Bergdorf Rose, Bonwit Fell," that "Fifteen years ago, the two stores' situations were reversed. Bonwit was the mecca for wealthy, sophisticated shoppers, and Bergdorf was the dowdy rival. But while Bergdorf stayed small, concentrating on an eclectic mix of exclusive merchandise and turning its store into retail theatre, Bonwit Teller moved the chain's flagship store into cramped quarters, added branches in other cities and began focusing on mainstream merchandise."

My Fairy Godmother   **5**

To be a success, there are three main requirements. One is hard work; another is luck. As the father of Moss Hart, that famous American dramatist, said of his son: "The harder he works the luckier he gets." The third requirement is a fairy godmother (or godfather). The fairy godmother I had was the secretary to Bill Holmes, Betty Vanderbilt, called Betty Van. Betty Van told others and me—many times—that she was not related to the rich and famous Vanderbilts. In any case, it was Betty that I later found out who recommended that I be kept on as door boy after the Christmas of 1938, and the following year requested me to be Bill Holmes' office boy. Most important, it was Betty who told me the right time to approach Bill Holmes with any one of my dazzling ideas.

Moving the mannequins was one. Another was, since the 721 Club had a large gold knocker on the red door at the entrance, why not have the invitation to the 721 Christmas Party affix a miniature gold knocker on the cover? Then make it removable to be used as a pin for a lady? Betty told me when Bill Holmes would be most receptive to my ideas. Betty Van was not only right, but very bright.

When I had been office boy in the president's office, my small desk next to Betty's allowed me to see and hear what was going on in the nerve center of the store. I watched how different executives handled themselves when they came to the boss's office. One of the executives, whose family were florists, delivered a small vase of roses to Betty's desk every morning. Whenever

I smell roses, I remember the scent that welcomed me to the office every day.

After my rise through the ranks to merchandise control manager, I asked for the position of blouse buyer, which I got. I did not do well. I talked to Betty about my falling short of expectations, and once again, she took steps to help me.

But before describing how Betty Van influenced my next big move in retail, here is a glimpse of the sometimes humorous—not to the store, of course—highs and lows as a blouse buyer.

As merchandise control manager, despite my bright ideas and emphasis on plans, the buyers found it difficult to embrace the logic of my planning tools and to accept the goals to accomplish the profit objectives required. In many cases, the buyers would say, "If you were a buyer, you would see how difficult it is to meet these goals." I heard the complaint often enough to request the president of the store to appoint me the buyer of the blouse department. It didn't take me long to realize the buyers were right.

As blouse buyer, I most likely made every possible mistake—but salvaged a few of them with creative thinking. Perhaps my worst, and first, mistake was deciding that, due to the lack of specific buying experience, I would figure out the basics on my own. Among the errors I made:

Over assortment. Too many styles. My inventory was loaded with odd sizes and too many colors. Not being resourceful enough to seek out the answer to my problem from those who actually knew the answer, I asked an important blouse manufacturer, "should I buy a few styles with depth, or many styles without depth?" He gave the obvious answer that would benefit his business, not mine: "many styles."

I made my sales plan in accordance with everything I'd learned in merchandise control, but I recall staying late many nights, reviewing my cardex files trying to figure out how to resolve the problems that I had gotten myself into. The obvious answer was to markdown the old and left-over styles. This can be done periodically, but not at a frequent rate that will destroy the gross profit, as it did in my department.

As I said, however, I did maneuver out of a few failures by applying the same kind of innovative thinking that got me to Boy Scout camp.

One successful initiative reflected my lack of knowledge of the blouse market. Looking for new ideas, I would go to the better dress department at night and select styles that looked as though the tops could be copied into fashionable blouses. This idea distinguished our department in some small degree from the competition.

Geoffrey Beene, whom I got to know during this time, brought back a man's checkered shirt from his first trip to Paris that had a built in necktie. I adapted it for a women's style and sold large quantities. At that point I believe Geoffrey was a draper for Teal Trainer, but on the road to becoming one of the greatest American designers.

Since men's blue oxford button-down shirts were very popular, I ordered a shirt made up in silk taffeta, in pastel shades, with rhinestone buttons. They sold for $29.95 in reasonable quantities.

In the spring of 1949 I had a shipment on order from a manufacturer who produced handmade blouses in Puerto Rico. Easter was early that year, and the delivery was late. Three hundred long sleeve silk blouses arrived as the weather turned warm. I made a deal with the head of the alteration department: Remove the long sleeves for fifty cents a blouse. The short sleeve blouses sold out and I averted a disaster.

A few more successes in blouse buying occurred because of key insights to buying that I learned from Bonwit Teller's famous personal shopper, Bea Traub. She was one of the first to make this service important in all good retail stores. Mrs. Traub had the most impressive list of prestige customers one could imagine. Her office looked like a small living room, where lunch or tea could be served while she showed clothes to her society ladies. One day,

Mrs. Traub was in a panic: She had left her customer book in a taxi! That book held such value to the store that it was reportedly insured for $10,000. She called Bill Holmes. He called Jim Farley, then the post master general. Jim Farley called Mayor Fiorello LaGuardia. The book was located in a matter of hours.

Lesson Learned

- It is what you know as well as who you know that get results. It never hurts and is very helpful to know people in high places.

One day, Bea Traub called to tell me she had Gloria Vanderbilt in her office and was coming down to see me. When she arrived at my department, she quickly selected five or six of the newest blouses. As she ran off, she tossed a bit of wisdom at me: "It is easier to sell when a customer knows something is brand new, instead of being around for a couple of months."

An interesting sidelight, Bea Traub's son, Marvin, was attending Harvard University at the time. She would proudly tell me of his progress from time to time. Little did I know that one day we would become fierce, but friendly, competitors when he became the very successful head of Bloomingdales.

Lesson Learned

- A ready to wear inventory is only as good as its newest merchandise.

Back to Betty Van. Despite my random successes at blouse buying, my overall record impressed no one—least of all me. A call from Betty to Bill Holmes, then the president of James McCreery, resulted in my receiving an offer to move down to 34th Street to be the blouse buyer at McCreery's. I knew I would follow him to the end of the earth. In 1950, moving from upper Fifth Avenue to 34th Street seemed to be the equivalent.

Unfortunately, I didn't do well there, either. First of all, I suffered from a kind of culture shock. Except for being a woman, the main customer on 34th street was completely different from the one on 56th street and Fifth Avenue. On Fifth Avenue, customers generally wore sizes 8 to 16; on 34th Street, the range was 12 to 20. And at Bonwit Teller, the strong retail range spanned $19.95 to $39.95. At McCreery, my predecessor did a very strong business at $3.95 to $5.95.

The biggest lesson I learned in my year at McCreery was how to price a sale, both for a sell out, and not at a loss. At this point, buying for a special purchase sale was new to me because Bonwit Teller had only its semi-annual sales to clear out old stock. I asked the sales people what they felt would be the most desirable item to buy for the sale.

Since nylon blouses (not too sheer) were relatively new and in demand, we decided that would be our candidate for the major event. Unfortunately, they were distributed in rather limited quantities. Since the retail-selling price was $7.95 and the cost was $4.75, I decided that $5.00 would be the magic price—the price that would move every blouse in one day. The strategy, of course, was to be able to have a cost price low enough to not lose money at the $5.00 retail. To accomplish this, I found a resource that would forego a profit on the shipment in return for a promise of a long-term arrangement with me. That made it worthwhile for him to sell me the 500 blouses I required at his cost.

When the blouses arrived in the department, the sales women began buying the blouses for themselves—the indication of a sellout. I asked them to save the blouses for the customers, except for two each for themselves.

Needless to say, there was no reason to run an advertisement. When the blouses were put on the counter with a sale sign, women mobbed the blouse department. All the blouses were gone before the day ended. I repeated this concept in a number of situations in my career to great success, as you will read later.

Early on I realized, for a sale, customers are interested in desirable items at a special sale price. The best item at the best price brings the best results. Sales that are run today, shouting "50% off" are too general. They bring some results, but customers respond to specific items at a specific price, rather than having to do a mathematical calculation.

This rule applies to markdowns as well. When a department is overstocked for any reason, the buyer in more cases than not will mark the merchandise down to a price that the buyer would like the merchandise to sell for. This may work to a smaller degree than marking the merchandise to a price that is guaranteed to move the merchandise out in a day or two. In the long run, the buyer will have to take another markdown or two to arrive at the price the merchandise should have been priced at for the first mark down.

Lesson Learned

- There is always a magic price. The trick is to be realistic and determine at what price customers will really be excited. Too many times buyers decide what price would make their sale a success, not what price the customer will find exciting.

The one outstanding success that I had at McCreery did not even result from my creativity or expertise, but from Bill Holmes' listening to industry insiders at a wake. At this event for a key executive of Stern's Department store, some of the Stern's executives mentioned that they had great success with a new blouse fabric, Dacron. Bill Holmes recommended that I check it out. I reacted negatively, because I thought it was insulting for the head of the company to have to tell me about something that I was supposed to be the authority on. Over the years I have observed buyers being prejudiced in nearly every case when told by a superior to check something out. In nearly every case the buyer was wrong, including me.

After I got over my initial pique, I found the manufacturer, checked out the fabric, and wrote the biggest order of my career up to that point. The blouse sold, or so it seemed, to every airline hostess who flew into New York. With this success I decided I was more gifted as a merchandise manager, than as a selector of styles.

Nevertheless, I did learn what made a great buyer, even though I was never destined to join their ranks. The first thing is to understand and to know *your customer*. The second is to have the taste level necessary to select merchandise for *that customer*. The third is to know your wholesale market thoroughly, and to know the people who make it happen. This applies from cooking pots to couture. Where the organization is large enough, the buyer should select and the mechanics of buying should be left to the merchandise managers, who are there for guidance and direction, not for selection.

Lessons Learned

- In adjusting to a new position, examine carefully what the successes and failures of your predecessor were before embarking on a different strategy.

- Never appoint a person to be a buyer unless he or she has been a proven success as an assistant buyer. A rare exception may be made if the buying candidate is very bright, and has a smart merchandise manager to give direction and supervision.

Armed with my new regard for talented buyers and an understanding that I would always be better supervising them than being one of them, I decided to move on. Once again, Betty Van to the rescue. Betty recommended that I talk to Alice Groves, an executive recruiter. She had two positions to fill for a ready-to-wear merchandise manager. One was for the Blum store in Philadelphia, Pennsylvania; the other was for Gladdings in Providence, Rhode Island. At Betty's urging, I consulted with Bill Holmes regarding the opportunity to leave him and move up to be a divisional ready-to-wear merchandise manger at another company. He understood my decision and directed me toward Gladdings. Not enjoying his role on 34th street after being on Fifth Avenue made him relate to the fact that I did not enjoy mine either. Gladdings was the right decision.

I always knew Betty was behind me, available for good advise when I needed it. Over the years I sent many bouquets of roses to her. She deserved much more than that.

Lesson Learned

- Everyone benefits from a fairy godmother, or a godfather (sometimes called a rabbi) to guide you through the mine-fields of the business world and keep you pointed in the right direction to reach your goals.

The Magic Formula 6

Leaving home and New York for a new adventure was an exciting challenge. Except for a slight moment, I had few doubts that I would be successful.

The adventure began at Gladdings in Providence Rhode Island. Bill Holmes had advocated moving to that store, rather than Blum's in Philadelphia, because he knew the people at the Frederic Atkins Buying office, the N.Y. buying office for Gladdings. He felt I would fit in, in terms of personality and experience.

After my preliminary interviews at Gladdings, I met the chairman of the store, Frederic Aldred. He hired me as divisional merchandise manager and offered me the grand sum of $9,000 a year plus a guaranteed bonus of $1,000. I recall going home on the train thinking, $10,000 a year, wow, I was on my way to riches.

As one would assume from my experiences as a blouse buyer at Bonwit Teller and James McCreery in the past two years, I was not what would be called a notable success. However, I believe Gladdings executives were impressed with my merchandise control background, and assistant to the president of Bonwit Teller. Gladdings wanted to "trade up" and felt I could do the job for them.

I drove to Providence in my 1946 Buick convertible on Route 1, the main north-south highway at the time, and had to keep the top down since the malfunctioning muffler was blowing exhaust into the car. (Shortly after settling in, I bought a used Studebaker convertible to make sure I didn't asphyxiate myself.) When I finally arrived in Providence, I parked in front of the Biltmore Hotel, which

43

provided a slim connection to home since it was designed by the same New York architects who had done Grand Central Station. In front of me sat a large limousine that belonged to the new Governor, Dennis J. Roberts. I was impressed. Unfortunately, I had not made a reservation, so I was told to go down the street to The Narragansett Hotel. Very old, very unimpressive, but equipped with a great dining room. Soon, I found permanent lodging not far from the store, near restaurants where I could meet local people. I was the new bachelor in town, but that didn't mean very much at first. When I first came to Rhode Island, I would leave Saturday after store closing and make the long drive to New York. I spent every weekend in New York, and then went to the market all day Monday since the stores in Providence were closed on Mondays. I believe this was a holdover from the war when merchandise and employees were hard to get. The weekly drive took me past Hartford, Connecticut; in the distance, I could see G. Fox, one of the great stores of America. "One day," I thought.

After reporting to work on October 2nd 1951, I met the ten buyers who were to report to me. I had the thought, of course, that being in Providence, they couldn't be equal to the buyers I knew in New York. Shame on me! These ladies knew their way around their markets and manufacturers. They were pros who wanted me to help them move ahead.

Lessons Learned

- Adjusting to a new position, buying or otherwise, examine carefully what the successes were as well as the failures of your predecessor, before embarking on a different strategy.

- Deciding when to leave one position for another requires a great deal of thought for your career objectives. Additional advice from experienced executives should be part of the final decision.

One of the first steps that I took was to redo the merchandise plans for all the ready-to-wear departments with the aid of the Walter Hoving form. I couldn't wait to use my new-found skill. As happened then, and many times in the future, using this approach changed the peaks and valleys in the relationship between inventory levels and planned sales. In my opinion, an imbalanced relationship between the two is the single biggest reason for markdowns and erosion of gross profit in retailing. After I realized how to make the adjustment of inventory to sales, I felt I was getting closer to being on the right track.

At a crucial time, I had the good fortune to meet Sidney Stogel, the sales manager for a popular-priced line of dresses we carried. We both felt there must be a better method, not only for planning sales and inventory levels to reduce markdowns and improve gross profits, but also to bring about more balanced assortments of merchandise. We studied the buying forms used by all the retailers he did business with: Filenes, Jordan Marsh, *et al.* We studied them all, and came up with nothing new or different. I will never forget the day he came to my office and told me he had just gone through one of my dress departments and I was in trouble. I had too many styles, broken sizes and colors.

I was determined once and for all to put and end to this problem, since Sidney said he observed the same situation in all the stores he did business with. As with all new ideas, we started out with a simple concept, and then expanded it with variations. We asked ourselves, as buyers, using dresses as the example: what is the first thing we needed to know? We decided the buyer first had to know how many dress units were sold last year by week, and how many did they plan to sell by week for this year.

Fortunately, Sidney Stogel had come up with the form used by Steigers in Springfield, Mass. They were using an approach called "weeks of supply." Defined as such, the number of weeks was determined by the desired turnover. An inexpensive dress line, with relatively fast delivery from a manufacturer would be given a turnover rate of once a month, or twelve times a year. Since in

WEEKLY AND CUMULATIVE UNIT REPORT

SPRING 1992

DEPARTMENT: SEPERATES   DEPARTMENT NUMBER: 82   Revised: Month: 1   Date: 10   Time: 9 19

WEEK ENDING	NET UNIT SALES			MD UNITS		WOS PLAN 10	STOCK ON HAND		OUTSTANDING UNITS			TOTAL UNITS ON ORDER	PLANNED RECEIPTS	OPEN TO BUY UNIT	
	LY	PLAN	ACT	SOLD	OH		LY	TY	THIS MO.	NEXT	FUTURE			THIS MO.	NEXT MO.
FEBRUARY															
TO DATE	53	60				684		328				0			
TO DATE	49	60				713		327				0			
TO DATE	37	60				741		529				0			
TO DATE	39	60				770		729				0			
TO DATE															
PLAN / ACTUAL	178	240											386		
MARCH															
TO DATE	43	71				830		837				0			
TO DATE	47	71				879		855				0			
TO DATE	62	71				928		793				0			
TO DATE	54	71				977		589				0			
TO DATE	46	71				982		571				0			
PLAN / ACTUAL	252	355											512		
APRIL															
TO DATE	43	89				987		528				0			
TO DATE	54	89				974		906				0			
TO DATE	103	89				962		1081				0			
TO DATE	76	88				949		542				0			
TO DATE															
PLAN / ACTUAL	276	355											312		

this case the turnover rate had been decided to be once a month, the weeks of supply would be four weeks. Therefore, we would attempt to always carry on hand four weeks of dresses to equal the next four weeks of sales. A more expensive line of dresses or women's sportswear would be given possibly ten weeks of supply, and men's clothing that turned much more slowly, twenty weeks. We used the weeks-of-supply approach to relate the number of weeks of units (dresses) required to be on hand by week or month in order to accomplish the sales plan. I finally had the measurement technique that I had been looking for to add more expertise to merchandise planning.

The added benefit of this approach allowed us to measure any and all merchandise that was slow moving and not meeting the weeks-of-supply sales rate. If, for example, the weeks of supply for a dress department was six weeks, any style that would not sell out in six weeks was considered slow moving. This required the buyer and merchandise manager to make a decision. Conversely, if the style was selling faster than a six-week rate, another decision was to be made. This is where my expression the three R's of retailing came from. When the above decisions had to be made, I would advise, Reduce it, Return it, or Reorder it, but don't just sit there with your thumb in your ear.

The weeks-of-supply concept had to be computed manually using a comptometer, long before computers were developed for this type of work. However, I found using this approach, I could measure the selling and on-hand progress to plan for styles, manufacturers, sizes, and colors if I so desired. Over the years I have described this method of planning and analysis, a method designed by a simple-minded person for other simple-minded people to use. Making and following a buying plan, whether for inexpensive dresses or for top of the market fashion apparel should not have to require the brainpower of a rocket scientist. (The unit weeks of supply form and directions for its use follow in this chapter on pages 46 and 49.)

The requirement for determining the number of units on hand at that time required a physical count by the salespeople each week, preferable before store opening Monday mornings. This normally met with some buyer's resistance. I always countered with, I never heard them complain for the time it took to count and list merchandise for their markdowns that would show their shortcomings as buyers. An excellent by-product of this weekly count required the buyer to list merchandise that was one month, two months, three months, and older, in order to determine what action to take. This action would usually mean a decision to clear older merchandise in order to bring in new. Today computers are programmed to create all the information required to plan and execute the plan properly. Unfortunately today, even with all the modern tools that can give the needed information, many retailers, large and small are too slow to make the decision early enough to avoid the consequences of slow moving merchandise that will always erode gross profits.

With weeks-of-supply, I had the magic formula, but something was still missing.

Lesson Learned

- A good merchant should have an organized sense of urgency. Not taking the immediate steps necessary to move slow moving, unwanted merchandise, to make room for new desirable merchandise, has led to the demise of more retailers than I dare to count.

Guide to Using the WOS Report (either paper or digital):

A Proven Method for Planning Inventory in Relationship to Anticipated Sales

The Weekly and Cumulative Unit Report guides the user to a simplified method for planning the amount of inventory required at any given time to accomplish a sales objective. The procedure, in its simplicity, may be used to plan for whatever classification of merchandise is desired, from apparel to pots and pans. With experience, the user will find many uses, such as measuring the rate of sale and the steps necessary to increase the inventory. Or if sales were too slow to reduce inventory, the tool would be useful to maximize sales or to reduce losses. The concept can be compared to a sailor at sea, requiring navigation measurements to reach port safely instead of winding up on the rocks.

The key element in the procedure is the WOS Plan, or "Weeks of Supply Plan," determined by the desired turnover.

Example using sportswear separates:

(1) The user determines that a reasonable rate of turnover for that classification of merchandise should be twice a season (to be sold or marked down during that period). In this case, we define a season as six months—spring or fall—or 26 weeks; twice a season means a 13 week cycle. In the example shown, the user decided 10 weeks would be the desired number weeks for women's separates to be in stock, i.e., a turnover slightly faster that twice a season.

(2) The user enters the number of units expected to be sold each week during the season. It is helpful as a guide if the unit sales are available for the same period last year. If not, it is necessary for the user to estimate the unit sales by week to the best of his/her ability and adjust up or down as the season progresses. (When a buyer would

(continued on next page)

(continued from prior page)

challenge the requirement—How am I to estimate the rate of sale?—the answer was, How did you have the nerve to buy without anticipating how much you would sell?)

(3) And, as the example shows, after the unit plan sales are entered for each week during the first three months of the spring season, the 10 weeks' supply is applied to the sales forecast resulting in an opening inventory of 684 units.

(4) By making the same calculation each week, the unit plan shows the proper inventory required to achieve the sales goal, each week and the beginning of each month.

As the example shows:

With an opening inventory the beginning of February of 684 units, and anticipated sales for the month of February of 240, the user would be left with 444 units, therefore, the user must plan to receive 386 units during the month in order to have the proper amount of inventory on hand to achieve the sales objective for the following month.

At the beginning, the calculations for the inventory requirements were made by a clerical on what was then called a comptometer. Computers soon took over and the procedure has been use in various forms. The caveat, <u>no matter how the procedure is used</u>, is that discipline is required to take action to reorder when selling exceeds the plan. Equally if not more important, <u>remove the merchandise from stock by markdowns whenever the sales fail to achieve the plan.</u>

The Grand Prizes

7

---------- **1952–1953** ----------

" Success has many fathers, failure is an orphan" applies to my good fortune in meeting my wife-to-be in Providence. A number of people took credit for bringing us together. All of them may have the credit—I won the prize. September of 1952, a year after I arrived in Providence and established myself as an eligible bachelor, friends recommended that I call Jackie Myers. I called with a phone number that one of them gave me. A young lady answered, "T.W. Rounds Company." I said, "Sorry. Wrong number." I tried the number again, with the same reply. This time I asked to speak to Jackie Myers. "This is Jackie Myers," she said. This was the turning point of my life.

Jackie was the handbag buyer in her family's retail business, T.W. Rounds. This was a small group of prestige leather goods stores based in Providence. The stores later expanded under her father to a few other select areas, such as the Tennis Pavilion in Newport, R.I.

Early on in the courtship, we realized that we wanted to spend the rest of our lives together, but I didn't have the same optimism about my relationship with Gladdings. Initially, I felt I was not doing as well as I thought I should be doing at the store. And I wasn't sure that I would stay in Providence. The prospect of my leaving saddened my wife-to-be so deeply that, with her encouragement, I decided to stay with Gladdings. We married six months after we met. Her love and encouragement over the years have made whatever success I have achieved possible.

Jackie's family had a special bond with Providence. Her father had moved from Boston to Providence with his wife and three month-old Jackie to become the luggage buyer at The Outlet Company, the major department store in Providence. Harry Myers had a great eye for style and quality, and admired the Providence leather goods specialty store T.W. Rounds. He set his sights on buying it one day. The hurricane of 1938 devastated downtown Providence. Among the casualties: T.W. Rounds. The company that sold buggy whips, harnesses, and saddles since the Civil War came up for sale. Harry Myers had saved his money wisely, and was able to prevail over other prospective buyers since he could pay cash, whereas they wanted to pay in promissory notes.

With Harry Myers knowledge and acceptance in the leather goods market, he was able to assemble a sizeable and high quality inventory. T.W. Rounds became an even more prestigious company. The pinball of fate also bounced in his direction. The war had just started in Europe and America was building its armed forces. Newport Naval Base, Quonset Naval Base, and others, became very active and the Navy personnel brought business to T.W. Rounds that the Myers family had never dreamed of. Profits flourished during the war, and the company's success continued in the years to come.

About the time Jackie and I married, the merchandise controls and strategies that I developed at Gladdings began to effect measurable changes. Inventories became balanced; the weeks-of-supply model allocated proper inventory relationships to sales. However, since management wanted to trade up, I began concentrating on women's dresses as the trading-up effort. The prices we concentrated on—remember, this was 1952—were $29.95 and $39.95. The dress business did not respond. The controller at that time, later to become the chief financial officer and then the president, Leonard Johnson, took a keen interest in my strategies and concepts. Since the stores in Providence were closed on Mondays, he said, why not use the day to do a little fact-finding out of town? Management wouldn't even have to know. So I flew down to Miller Rhodes in Richmond, Virginia; Hochshild Kohn in Baltimore, Maryland; and Woodward & Lothrop in Washington, D.C. in order to study their priceline structure in women's dresses.

Comparing their pricelines★ with ours made sense because these stores were similar in quality and customer base to Gladdings. Each one also had very professional and experienced ready-to-wear divisional merchandise managers, who willingly shared their information with me. I returned in two days, not one, and had learned a valuable lesson: All the information I needed, in addition to what I had already learned, was out there if I would invest the time and make the effort to study it.

We adjusted the price lines downward to conform to the strongest pricelines of the stores I had visited—a shift of two price-lines downward. Business responded. Due to its list of fine member stores, The Frederick Atkins Buying Office became my learning ground and arena for developing relationships with the principals of the stores, some of whom were to determine my future in retailing.

About this time, the advertising manager of the *Providence Journal,* Charles Davis, introduced me to yet another resource. Learning of my curiosity for determining proper pricelines for various classifi-cations, he recommended I become familiar with *The Neustadt Report,* the product of a newspaper research group. This company measured all the advertising newspaper lineage of department stores in major cities by classifications and pricelines. This report and analysis gave me the ability to select the stores I felt to be most com-parable to Gladdings, and to compare and match their advertised pricelines, which were usually their strongest, to mine.

★ Price lining is a practice whereby retailers sell merchandise at a limited range of price points, with each price point representing a distinct level of quality. Source: *Retail Management: A Strategic Approach,* 9th Edition (Prentice Hall, 2003), by Barry Eerman and Joel Evans.

With the unit weeks-of-supply operating successfully and the price line studies bearing results, I was promoted to be the executive vice president and general merchandise manager of Gladdings. I finally felt qualified to be considered a merchant, but still had a lot to learn.

Lessons Learned

- Retailing does not exist in a vacuum. Any and all the information one needs to be a successful merchant is out there if you have the sense to know what you should be looking for, and where to look for it.

- Whenever possible associate with successful business executives. Smart executives are always looking for talented people. It is better to be known than to be a face in the crowd.

Now I knew I had the final key to merchandise planning that would give the answer to me or anyone else who was interested in their inventory problems. I had the same feeling possibly, as that of John Harrison, who in the 18th century discovered the way to measure longitude. He could guide sailors to safety; I could guide buyers and merchandise managers to profit.

In 1953, I had the feeling that the merchandising concepts I had been searching for were beginning to come together. The feeling was inspirational. Was it possible that by developing the weeks-of-supply concept, and being able to determine the proper price lines for a given market were the keys to being a successful retailer? Did I now have the answers for anyone who was interested in solving their inventory problems? Could I now guide buyers and merchandise managers to be more professional and profitable?

At that point, we had the ability to determine by classification, manufacturer, colors, sizes or prices what we required to make this year's sales plan realistic. The procedure I found could measure any one of these factors. If last year's sales were not available in order to give guidance, estimates were acceptable, since after a few weeks sales trends would show how accurate or inaccurate the estimates were, and corrections could be made. More important-ly, once the unit sales had been planned, the weeks-of-supply con-cept allowed for more accurate forecasting of inventory levels for any point in the season or a year. Better relationships of planned inventory levels to planned sales became my keystone to improved profitably. No matter where I applied the concept it worked. From here on out for the rest of my retail career, I was guided by this important merchandising principle. The question was always, no matter what the classification or item, "how many weeks of supply do you have on hand?" Or, "at what rate of weeks of sell-ing has that item been bought for?" In many cases over the years, whenever I asked a buyer that question for the first time, I received a blank stare.

Sidney Stogel moved into computers early on, and added a degree of sophistication and professionalism to the concept so that major chain retailers retained him for his expertise.

My enthusiasm knew no bounds. I felt like a scientist or doc-tor who, after years of experimenting, found the cure for the com-mon cold. I realized that no matter where I worked in retailing, I would have a merchandising technique to manage inventories that would put me and my companies ahead of the competition in sales and profits.

After teaching the procedure to my merchandising staff. I attempted to preach the gospel to my colleagues at the Atkins stores. In one instance, I had a small audience of Atkins store's general merchandise managers in the bar car returning from a convention at the Greenbrier resort in White Sulphur Springs, West Virginia. Possibly their judgment suffered from too much to drink: They were doubtful about using this new procedure. It was discouraging to me that everyone exposed to the concept did not accept this basic merchandise principle. At the begin-ning, of course, buyers didn't find it thrilling since it was a truer method of measuring their performance. Time after time, I've found that people do not like to be measured.

For the rest of my career, I attempted to convey the logic of this approach to all levels of management from buyers to store principals. My approach was to keep it simple, since buyers and divisional merchandise managers were not used to thinking this way. However, as time went on and the successful sales and profit results at Gladdings got the attention of some of the principals of the Atkins stores, I was finally invited to one these stores to explain the concept to them. It was G. Fox and Co., Hartford Connecticut. The invitation was a good omen of things to come.

Lesson Learned

- To convince people to use a different method from what they are used to is always a difficult task. To motivate them to change requires convincing them that the change will benefit them greatly. If they can't be motivated, they then must be directed. If they can't be directed they should be removed.

I needed to reach another threshold to management success at Gladdings by running a profitable sale. I had learned the basic principles of running a lucrative sale a number of years before this, first at Bonwit Teller with the frantic handbag sale, and then the nylon blouse sellout at James McCreery. The established formula was proven once again during Gladdings' first annual sale—one that would not only bring in extra revenue, but would also establish an event customers would anticipate each year.

With some outside direction from the retail consulting firm, Amos Parrish, we established the following criteria: (1) Select the most important classification in each department. (2) Decide on the "magic sale price," that is, the sale price that will move all the merchandise in one day. (3) Be able to make a reasonable profit on the transaction.

In order for the department to qualify for a full-page ad, costing $750 in the *Providence Journal*, the buyer had to sell enough units to equal ten times the cost of the ad. The first test ad ran on knit dresses, an important classification. The buyer for them had been asked, "What are your strongest pricelines?" Remember this was 1953–1954, and the prices were $39.95 to $69.95 from her most important resources, Kimberly and Guttman, two of the best known knit dress manufacturers, both long gone. She felt a sale price of $27 would move quantities to reach the unit goal. We knew then how most buyers think: "the triumph of hope over experience."

The next question was, what would happen if all the dresses were to sell for, say, $23? The buyer blanched and said, that would be crazy. They would all be gone in an hour. She didn't know how right she was. We figured we would have to sell over three hundred dresses to reach the goal to qualify for the advertisement! We nego-tiated with the Guttman Co. first for a cost price that would make a retail price of $23 marginally profitable. Once we accomplished that, it made it easier to convince Kimberly, since his competitor met our request, to do the same. We agreed that the manufacturers' names would not be mentioned in the sale ad, since both lines were sold to the major stores in New England, particularly in Boston.

The sale started, the ad ran, and so did the customers—to us. Since Gladdings had three small elevators and an antique wooden stairway that ran through the store, those customers who couldn't get on the overcrowded elevators ran up the stairs. As the buyer said, the dresses were gone in hours, not unlike the handbag sale at Bonwit Teller a number of years before, or the blouse sale at McCreery's.

An unfortunate part of this success was that the Kimberly name was inadvertently put in the ad. An honest mistake, it nonetheless cost Kimberly a lot of aggravation with their retailers throughout New England. The incident did yield some critical information, however: We had not known how carefully our competition was watching us. Many years later when I became the chief executive officer of Bergdorf Goodman, Kimberly was one of our major vendors. (Reportedly, the Duchess of Windsor favored Kimberly

knits and had more in her closet than we had in stock.) Jack
Lazaar, the owner of Kimberly, and I laughed about the Gladdings
episode. At the time it happened, he didn't laugh.

Lesson Learned

- The ability for the buyer to correctly find and negotiate for the
  "magic price" has always been the successful formula for moving sale merchandise. Filene's basement understood this concept better than many regular price retailers ever did.

It wasn't all a "numbers game" at Gladdings, of course. I also took
steps to elevate Gladdings' presence in the world of fashion. And, to
that end, developed good relations with the important New England
dress and sportswear manufacturers. In the process, I habitually visited their factories and selected "best sellers." I called ahead to say I
was driving to their factory, and then selected particular styles in
quantities that would fit in my car. The result was that I had prime
styles for Saturday's selling. This short cut saved going to their New
York showroom, ordering merchandise, and have it delivered a
whole week later—if the good styles were still available. Meeting
and getting to know the owners of their businesses on their home
turf was another distinct advantage. I remember particularly meeting
Carl Rosen and his father, the owners of Puritan Fashions in
Waltham, Massachusetts. His old father took great pleasure going
through stock with me to select what he felt were the most important styles for me to have. Carl went on to become one of the major
apparel manufacturers in the country, as did his son Andrew.

Lesson Learned

- Don't wait for desirable merchandise or opportunity to come
  to you. You must go after both.

Throughout my attempts to upgrade Gladding's fashion image and sales volume, I was not sure Mr. Frederic Aldred, the store's major owner and chairman of the board, ever noticed those successes. He did notice something else, however, and called me about it. He told me how impressed he was with my effort to maintain the store's integrity. One incident in particular caught his attention.

Gladdings took great pride in serving as the supplier for girls' uniforms for the prestigious Lincoln School. I was working with a reasonably reliable manufacturer who knew the delivery dates were tightly associated with the opening of school. He had every excuse in the book as to why he was delayed in his delivery. I ran out of patience and drove from Providence to his factory in Ossining, New York. Needless to say, he was surprised to see me and embarrassed that work on my order had not been completed. I told him I would sit in his factory all night if necessary until the uniforms were finished. It may have been close to midnight, but I got the uniforms, put them in my car, drove to Providence, and locked my car in the garage. The next morning, the uniforms were delivered to the school right on time as though nothing had gone awry. For me, this behavior was normal, but Mr. Aldred thought I went beyond the call of duty, and did honor to Gladdings. Shortly after, he elevated me to vice president.

Mr. Aldred was well on in age by the time I met him. Both he and George Ladd II, the company's somewhat younger president, captured a stereotypical New England style in their presentation. Mr. Aldred had a roll-top desk and wore pince-nez, spectacles popular in the 19th century that stayed put by pinching the bridge of the nose. When he went home at night, I speculated, he stepped back into the pages of a Charles Dickens novel from whence he emerged each morning. He was a fine gentleman, and as far as I'm concerned, will forever be the model of the gracious, circumspect New Englander. Also an unforgettable character, George Ladd looked like a New England sea captain. As a matter of fact, he claimed to be the grandson of a gentleman New

England whaler. Just as intriguing was the story that Gladdings was the oldest retailer in America. Established in 1766 "under the sign of the bunch of grapes," there was a wooden model of the legendary bunch of grapes under the marquee. When some of my contemporaries challenge the age of the store, I would kid them by saying; "We have enough old merchandise to prove it."

Frederic Aldred and George Ladd projected a very different persona from the retailers I knew in New York. They were extremely hospitable to me, and introduced me into their New England culture. I remember quite vividly the lunches to which they invited me at an old Providence institution, Miss Duttons, which happened to be upstairs from the main T.W. Rounds & Co. store. Many of the older Providence businessmen commonly had lunches there of clam chowder, clam cakes, and cod. I enjoyed the transformation from New Yorker to New Englander.

Jackie and I lived on Benefit Street, across from John Nicholas Brown's mansion and Brown University; that made a strong New England impression on me. I parked my car in General Ambrose Everett Burnside's former stable. Driving to New York each week, and being in the middle of the busy apparel market during the day, the transformation on arriving back at night to the peace and quiet of a gas-lamp lit street was something I will never forget. Over time, even my dressing habits changed to a more basic New England look: button down shirts, rep ties, and Hillhouse of Providence conservative suits.

(Years later, when I returned to New York, Leonard Lauder urged me to change my shirts and ties to his favorite, Turnbull and Asser of London. I eventually lost my New England look, but forever cherished what I found in Providence.)

Talent Shows and Falling Stars

8

1954–1959

Organizing good merchandising techniques is like building a airplane. After that's done, the key question is, "Who will fly it well?" The other half of the merchandising equation, then, is talent.

The ability to identify the potential stars of merchandising was one of the most rewarding benefits of being a divisional merchandise manager. Since selecting merchandise clearly was not my forte, I had to be able to spot merchandising talent in order to progress as a retail executive. As I mentioned, when I first met the Gladding's ready-to-wear buyers, I assumed they could not possibly be as up-to-date in buying and fashion as their New York counterparts. Gladdings had professional apparel buyers, however, who quickly convinced me that they would benefit more from my encouragement and direction than my New Yorker smugness.

As an example, one day the sportswear buyer came to me with a blouse and said, "I can sell fifty of these." But her unit open-to-buy plan* showed she did not have the flexibility to make this kind of buy. I asked her if she could sell fifty blouses, what did she need to sell five hundred? She said an advertisement, a window, and additional open-to-buy. The ad and window were easily arranged. We

---

* *Ibid.* Open-to-buy means the difference between planned purchases and the purchase commitments already made by a buyer for a given time period. It represents the amount the buyer has left to spend for that month and is reduced each time a purchase is made.

then adjusted her weeks-of-supply to accommodate an additional five hundred units. The promotion was a success. The reason I remember this incident? It was the beginning of another search for the rest of my retail career: to find talent, particularly buying talent.

This success not only made this buyer more aggressive—she recognized the unit plan would give additional open-to-buy when being assertive and less open-to-buy when being conservative—but also set a pace in merchandising strategy for other buyers. The key to success at Gladdings and the stores I was later associated with was determining which buyers knew their business well enough to back them, and which ones did not.

Many years ago at Bonwit Teller, Bill Holmes had a talented buyer of sportswear who found a designer called B.H. Wragge. She wanted to buy a few pieces from his collection. Bill Holmes said if the line is good enough to buy, buy it. She did, and the collection became one of the first sportswear names to gain national fame and Wragge became an exclusive fashion designer for Bonwit Teller. The buyer had a great eye for fashion, but succeeded almost in spite of herself. It was obvious she did not have the ability to grow a fashion line to its potential; she could handle only half of the equation. That experience never left me.

Walter Hoving once said, "There is no such thing as good taste or bad taste. You either have taste or you don't." The point here is that no matter what type of apparel is being bought for a store, buyers with a great eye are worth their weight in gold. Unfortunately, most buyers feel that they have the "eye." In many cases, their "eye" is blind. A successful retail executive who has the ability to identify a great selector, and then give the guidance and business support necessary in order to maximize a successful buy, has a winning—and necessary—combination. At least in-house.

Lessons Learned

- In retailing there are many important positions, but none as important as a talented buyer.

- Executives who can identify, develop and encourage talent are critical to a retailer's success.

That combination will go to waste if that same executive ignores the need to connect with manufacturers.

The Bill Holmes business philosophy of maintaining close relationships with manufacturers never left me. As I mentioned, I made it a point to travel to the New York market every week of the year after I moved to Providence. I programmed each trip with specific objectives to be accomplished with individual buyers and their vendors. Years later, Bill Blass once complained of me, "He wasn't a vendor, he was a designer." Happy to comply with that description.

The approach had many benefits. One was to give essential management direction and support to the buyers; the other, to give Gladdings in Providence, R.I. higher recognition in the New York market place. An ancillary benefit was that I kept myself up to date as to what the different stores in N.Y. were doing.

To make scheduling of New York meetings with buyers and vendors a priority, I ran a line through my calendar every Monday or Wednesday for "no appointments." The manufacturers often said it was a much more effective approach to vendor relations than the so-called straw-hat merchants. These were store principals who would visit the market once or twice a year, shake hands with their suppliers, mutter "How's it going" and go back home.

Another great advantage of the visits to New York was that Gladdings could inflate its benefits as a member of the Frederick Atkins Buying Office. With many of the top retailers from around the country also members of the office—G. Fox, B. Altman, The Broadway in California, Charles Stevens in Chicago, Miller & Rhodes in Richmond, Woodward & Lothrop in Washington—the visits gave me a chance to get acquainted with merchandising executives and principals of these stores. I learned their strengths and many techniques that made their stores so successful.

Later on I will explain how they all unfortunately missed the signals down the road that led to their eventual demise.

Semi annually, the Atkins Office staged meetings for principals of all the stores to attend. This also offered me a great opportunity to meet key players in the industry, and to have them explain their successes, and when they were willing, their failures. When I was promoted to general merchandise manager of Gladdings, I received my first invitation to an Atkins principals' meeting that was held in Dallas, Texas. It was 1955. Following this meeting all the future principals meetings were held in either the Greenbrier or Hot Springs, Virginia.

One incident stays in my mind. It was the first of many related to the legendary Beatrice Fox Auerbach, the president and owner of G. Fox and Co.

Jackie and I had just become the proud parents of our first born, Eugenie Beth, and I wanted to bring home a dress from Neiman Marcus for her. Picking up my nerve, I asked Mrs. Auerbach, since she was a grandmother, if she would help me select a dress for my daughter. She readily agreed and, after the meeting, off we went to Neiman Marcus. When we arrived at the children's department she quickly went through the children's dresses like the pro she was. Being disappointed in the selection, she asked the salesperson to get Mr. Stanley on the phone. When Stanley Marcus answered the phone, Mrs. Auerbach berated him: How could he, with a store as important as Neiman Marcus, have such a poor assortment of children's dresses? Would he please come down to the department so she could point out his failure.

Stanley Marcus came down to the department and, like a retailing student, he listened. And listened, while Mrs. Auerbach chastised him. If a customer comes to Neiman Marcus, she said, and Neiman Marcus reputedly carries a certain classification of children's dresses, then it was his personal responsibility to see to it that the customer had a selection worthy of its reputation.

Over the years, I heard the same speech many times, directed at me as well. I don't recall too much more about that Atkins meeting in Dallas, but I never forgot my first merchandising lesson from Mrs. Beatrice Fox Auerbach. I don't think Stanley Marcus did either.

Lesson Learned

- If a retailer has made the investment and commitment to be in business, the customer has a right to expect the retailer will also fulfill his responsibility of carrying as complete an assortment of whatever it is the store stands for.

In 1957, Jackie and I were blessed with our second daughter, Robin Margery. Like her sister Janie, she would later become involved in retailing—Janie as a fashion director at *Vogue*, and Robin, as an assistant buyer at Saks Fifth Avenue. (At Saks, senior management were so concerned that she would pass their merchandise secrets on to me that she left to become a buyer at the Atkins office.)

At about this time, as I put the new merchandising strategies and concepts into place, the sales and profits at Gladdings improved to the point where they attracted the attention of other retailers in Frederic Atkins Group. I had been appointed to serve on various committees with the general merchandise managers of other Atkins stores, and for the store principals' meetings of 1958 and 1959 at the Greenbrier, I served as chairman of the general merchandise manager's portion of the program. I was told that, to be selected from the smallest store in the group of major retailers to head up the meeting indicated very positive recognition and I should feel honored. I was.

In the 1958 meeting I introduced The Neustdat Report's retail advertising analysis that I had used so effectively in comparing Gladding's pricelines by classification with equivalent stores in New York. I also invited George Neustadt to explain his method and analysis that some of the major stores in the country relied on. Before the meeting, Mr. Neustadt asked me which general merchandise managers would take a negative position with his presentation. Undoubtedly, he had experienced such responses in his previous presentations. I gave him the names of the two that I thought would challenge his concept. Sure enough, the people I mentioned—the general merchandise managers of G. Fox and Miller & Rhodes—contested his views. Mr. Neustdat went to great lengths to prove his point and converted many in the audience. I mention this episode only to point out that in retailing, merchants must always be looking for ideas and techniques that will move them ahead of their competition. I was, and am still, puzzled at how some retailers can look no further than their noses.

In 1959, the Fredrick Atkins principals' meeting theme was "The Fabulous Sixties," and selected principals made presentations on their plans for the decade to come. Most presentations offered no surprises, sticking to popular themes such as branch store expansion. In preparation for my presentation, I toured the mill outlets in southern Massachusetts and in Rhode Island—and came away with a contrasting, and shocking theme.

It was apparent to me that I was seeing a major retail change taking place right before my eyes. The large, abandoned mills had plenty of parking spaces. The merchandise was reasonably presented on racks and tables, all self-service. Prices set at levels well below those in the department stores. And the mill outlets were busy, with not only "low-end customers," but also with mothers from the suburbs, the busy women we now call "soccer moms."

Going into the presentation, I had a grave concern: Since the threat of discounting was the theme of my first important presentation to some of the major retailers in the country, how would they receive it? I felt strongly that I had a responsibility to make my case for what I viewed as a threat to traditional retailers, particularly the privately owned Frederick Atkins family stores. With about one hundred people in the audience, from store

FREDERICK ATKINS, INC.

11 WEST 42nd STREET, NEW YORK, N. Y. 10036

564-0300

ADAM, MELDRUM & ANDERSON CO., INC. _____ Buffalo, New York 14205
GEORGE ALLEN, INC. _____ Germantown, Philadelphia, Pa. 19144
B. ALTMAN & CO. _____ New York, New York 10016
AUERBACH COMPANY _____ Salt Lake City, Utah 84110
THE BROADWAY _____ Los Angeles, California 90031
CARLISLE'S _____ Ashtabula, Ohio 44004
T. A. CHAPMAN COMPANY _____ Milwaukee, Wisconsin 53202
CLELAND SIMPSON CO. _____ Scranton, Pennsylvania 18503
D & L STORES _____ New Britain, Conn. 06050
DENBY'S INC. _____ Troy, New York 12180
DILLARD'S DEPARTMENT STORES, INC.
    BROWN DUNKIN CO. _____ Tulsa, Oklahoma 74102
    DILLARD'S _____ San Antonio, Texas 78213
    PFEIFER-BLASS _____ Little Rock, Arkansas 72203
M. EPSTEIN, INC. _____ Morristown, New Jersey 07960
GARFINCKEL'S _____ Washington, D. C. 20004
GLADDING'S INC. _____ Providence, Rhode Island 02901
HOCHSCHILD, KOHN _____ Baltimore, Maryland 21201
D. H. HOLMES COMPANY, LTD. _____ New Orleans, Louisiana 70160
J. B. IVEY & COMPANY
    IVEY'S CHARLOTTE _____ Charlotte, North Carolina 28201
    IVEY'S GREENVILLE _____ Greenville, South Carolina 29602
    IVEY'S RALEIGH _____ Raleigh, North Carolina 27602
    IVEY'S ORLANDO _____ Orlando, Florida 32802
    IVEY'S JACKSONVILLE _____ Jacksonville, Florida 32202
THE KILLIAN COMPANY _____ Cedar Rapids, Iowa 52406
LIBERTY HOUSE — California _____ San Francisco, Calif. 94108
LUCKEY, PLATT & CO. _____ Poughkeepsie, New York 12601
HARRY S. MANCHESTER, INC. _____ Madison, Wisconsin 53701
MARTIN'S _____ Brooklyn, New York 11201
McCURDY & COMPANY, INC. _____ Rochester, New York 14604
McRAE'S _____ Jackson, Mississippi 39209
MILLER BROTHERS COMPANY _____ Chattanooga, Tennessee 37401
MILLER & RHOADS _____ Richmond, Virginia 23217
MILLER'S, INC. _____ Knoxville, Tennessee 37901
MONNIG'S _____ Fort Worth, Texas 76101
PIZITZ _____ Birmingham, Alabama 35203
PORTEOUS MITCHELL & BRAUN CO. _____ Portland, Maine 04101
RHODES
    RHODES (California) _____ Oakland, California 94612
    RHODES, (Southwest) _____ Phoenix, Arizona 85016
    RHODES (Northwest) _____ Portland, Oregon 97205
THE SHEPARD CO. _____ Providence, Rhode Island 02903
THE ROBERT SIMPSON COMPANY, LTD. _____ Toronto, Canada
R. H. STEARNS COMPANY _____ Boston, Massachusetts 02111
ALBERT STEIGER, INC. _____ Springfield, Massachusetts 01101
PAUL STEKETEE & SONS _____ Grand Rapids, Michigan 49501
CHAS. A. STEVENS & CO. _____ Chicago, Illinois 60602
STONE & THOMAS _____ Wheeling, West Virginia 26003
TOWNSEND & WALL COMPANY _____ St. Joseph, Missouri 64501
TRIMINGHAM BROTHERS, LTD. _____ Hamilton, Bermuda
JOHN WANAMAKER — PHILA. _____ Philadelphia, Pennsylvania 19014
JOHN WANAMAKER — LIBERTY STREET _____ New York, New York 10038
WEINSTOCK'S _____ Sacramento, California 95803
ZOLLINGER-HARNED CO. _____ Allentown, Penn. 18101

owners, to presidents to general merchandise managers, I approached the podium with trepidation.

As I explained what I had observed and deduced, my words provoked surprise and disbelief. A relatively new retail phenomenon is springing up in the New England area, I told them, and it is likely to grow and spread. Eventually, it will threaten the very existence of the traditional department stores throughout the country, particularly the small independents. Some bright, entrepreneurial merchants in New England now use the large abandoned fabric mills to sell branded merchandise at discount prices. These so-called mill outlets are spreading rapidly. These retailers buy what we know as distressed goods, overcuts, and cancellations from established apparel manufacturers. With comparatively low overhead in those outlying locations, they can buy low and sell low. The mill outlets have been an instant success, and I predict they will spread to other areas of the country. I have studied one mill outlet in particular—Ann and Hope, in Pawtucket, Rhode Island. With more than adequate parking, large assortments of men's, women's and children's apparel, and very low prices it became an overnight sensation. As this type of retail outlet spreads, the threat to downtown department stores cannot be ignored.

The audience of my distinguished colleagues received my message poorly and with skepticism: "Ira Neimark, you worry too much."

I am sorry to say, my negative prophecy came true. About the only thing I didn't foresee at the time was that discount retailers would open large brick and mortar stores, and in some cases dominate the malls that were also growing rapidly at that time. From the list of Atkins member stores (Appendix A) from their meeting in the late 1960s, you can see that very few exist today. Reading the trade papers, I watched as slowly but surely, the stores disappeared one by one from the retail scene. Most of the traditional retailers of the day missed the signals of customer preferences. And so, they missed their future.

Lesson Learned

- Watch every trend in retail distribution. There are new concepts being developed every day. Some successful, some not. Analyze the successful trends to see if any part can be used to your advantage.

Wake-up Calls

9

1959

One by one, the calls came: Was I interested in making a change? No, I told them. I was happy at Gladdings. The owners and management gave me practical and moral support in my efforts to upgrade operations. I was even invited to a board of directors meeting to explain how the unit plan worked, not only in regulating inventories, but enabling us to predict a down or an up economy far ahead of normal forecasters. I recall doing some dance with my hands to illustrate how the required inventory followed sales trends. They nodded, as if they had confidence in my ability, but no idea what I was talking about. Their confidence meant far more to my career than their comprehension.

And then Leon Harris, the president of A. Harris in Dallas, called. Since his was also an Atkins store, Leon Harris had to ask permission of Gladdings' chief executive, Leonard Johnston. According to the Atkins Office rule, member stores were not to hire people away from each other unless there was discussion between the principals. Leonard Johnston told me about the call. Surprisingly to him, and to me, I felt so curious as to what was out there that we agreed I would visit and investigate.

At first, the thought of a position at A. Harris did not sufficiently impress me; the benefits to my family and my career seemed vague. The overture did, however, pique my curiosity as to what other opportunities were out there. Once again, I went to see Bill Holmes, who had become the president of Jacqueline

Cochran Cosmetics, to ask his opinion. Was it time for me to move on? I confided that I had outgrown Gladdings, and stores such as A. Harris, Associated Dry Goods, the owners of many department stores, and the executive recruiter Thondike Deland, were calling me. If a really good opportunity presented itself, he concluded, then I was ready to make the move.

Again the pinball bounced in the right direction.

He asked me to wait while he placed a few calls. First, he called the president of Bloomingdales, Jeb Davidson, who wasn't in at that moment. Next, he called Beatrice Fox Auerbach, the owner of G. Fox & Co. in Hartford. She had become president of the store when her father died, which was the same year I began my career in retail—1938. Bill Holmes told her he thought I was ready to move up to a larger position in a larger store, and wanted her to know about it before I made a move. Yes, she knew me. Yes, she would like to talk to me. I would like to think that he considered me a hot property and wanted to take credit for my being his protégé.

A few days later, Samuel Einstein called. The general merchandise manager of G. Fox and Co., Mr. Einstein said that Mrs. Beatrice Fox Auerbach would like to talk with me—confidentially. This call got my complete attention. I agreed to meet with Mrs. Auerbach.

The drive from Providence to Hartford should have been brief and painless, but a tire on my car blew out about twenty miles from Hartford. I would be late for my appointment. You don't have to be a graduate of Harvard Business School to know this is not the way to start a major career change.

I mention this incident as an indication of how much G. Fox Company's reputation meant in Connecticut. Not five minutes after I stopped the car to fix the flat, a big blue G. Fox delivery truck stopped. The driver asked, "Can I help you?" I was, to say the least, flabbergasted. After he fixed the flat, I told him I was on my way to a meeting with Mrs. Auerbach. He acted as though he did this all the time. In retrospect, knowing Beatrice Fox

Auerbach, it is possible she told her truck drivers to keep an eye out for a single driver with Rhode Island plates crossing the border at about ten o'clock. She was a very thorough lady!

The interview took place (alone) in her large office with a magnificent view overlooking the Connecticut River. She was rather a small woman who knew how to shift perceptions away from that. Her chair was slightly elevated, and in front of her desk were small stools. This conveyed the impression that she had much more height—no doubt an illusion she chose to perpetrate with many people. In contrast, the conference desk where our conversation took place involved no such special effects, although it was a bit long.

Our conversation centered on her frustration of not being able to have in stock what her customers wanted at all times. She felt that her customers should be able to buy basic items in the correct sizes as easily as they switched on an electric light. The merchandising performance of Gladdings, as outlined in the Atkins annual black book, impressed her. Even though all of the Atkins stores reported their figures, to be kept as confidential as possible, Beatrice Fox Auerbach felt her store performance was private. She did not want her figures spread all over creation. She often stated if anyone wanted to know her figures all they had to do was to call her and she would answer their questions.

Since I had explained the unit open-to-buy technique at the Atkins principals' meeting, and knowing of the reluctance of her merchandise people to adopt it to improve their performance, she asked if I would be interested in joining G. Fox and Company as assistant to the general merchandise manager? I would be able to install the procedure and supervise the merchandise division in its use. My answer was, of course, yes. She then said she would ask Leonard Johnston for his permission.

This is not he best way to negotiate a salary. For one thing, did Mrs. Auerbach know instinctively that, as I drove past Hartford on the way to Providence and saw the G. Fox building and her office lit up in the distance, I thought that, if I were ever asked to join G. Fox, I would walk barefoot from Providence to do so?

There are many interesting stories about B.F.A. that all added a great deal to my store of knowledge and knowledge of stores. As an example: When I was ready to leave her office, which was on the same floor as the toy department, I mentioned that I had promised to bring my five-year-old daughter Janie a harmonica. B.F.A. asked the buyer to come over and show us his harmonica selection. He had one for fifty cents. "What else do you have?" she asked. The buyer said he had another with music for five dollars. "What you do you have in between?" she asked. He blanched and said these were the only two he had. In a voice you could hear across the floor, B.F.A. declared: "I own this big store, but can never find what I want when I want it!"

I bought the fifty-cent harmonica before she skinned the poor fellow alive. As I was about to leave, she asked about my younger daughter. "Shouldn't you bring her a present as well?" My response was that she was only an infant and wouldn't know the difference. B.F.A. then proceeded to tell me that, no matter what age children are—particularly girls—they expect presents. This was the first of my many "Yes, Mrs. Auerbachs" for years to come.

We then saw small plastic telephones on display. I said this would be fine for Robin, my new baby daughter. The phones on display were white and blue. "We need one in pink," said B.F.A.

I could see the distraught buyer coming apart when he said, "We don't have the phone in pink, Mrs. Auerbach." Once again, she ranted and raved. I took the white one and made my exit before the very existence of my daughters caused any more damage. Nonetheless, this incident does spotlight the position she took throughout the store when a basic item was not in stock in size or color. I felt I had found the environment where I could make an important contribution.

But lest I leave the impression that B.F.A. went around striking fear into the hearts of employees, I should add a few facts.

Beatrice Fox Auerbach was a pioneer in instituting labor reforms for her staff, including a five-day workweek, retirement and medical plans, and financial assistance for employees facing emergencies. She also set a precedent in offering Blacks opportunities, not only for employment, but also advancement.

B.F.A. contacted Leonard Johnston. The rationale she expressed to him was that, at some point in the near future I would be moving on. So wouldn't it be better for me to be with her, connected to the Atkins Office, instead of a non-Atkins store? He didn't want to lose me, but figured if I had to go, then moving to a large store we all admired offered me more than staying with the small privately-owned Gladdings.

The next drive to Hartford was as memorable as the first. For some reason, I had to borrow Jackie's car, a good-looking red Chevy convertible—when it was clean. I met with B.F.A. and the general merchandise manager, Sam Einstein. I agreed to the position of assistant to Mr. Einstein, then in his late 60s, who seemed not too excited to have a young man climbing up his back. Perhaps as a not-so-subtle way of keeping me in my place, Mr. Einstein offered to match my Gladdings salary. I looked surprised (translate: annoyed). B.F.A. said no. They would pay me ten percent more than Gladdings. I accepted the position and the salary, as well as what followed: an invitation from B.F.A. to dine at her home. She then said she would send her chauffeur, Bill, home and she and I could go to her home in my car.

My car? How could I allow B.F.A—whose middle name could have been "fastidious"—in a convertible so dusty that I could write my name on the dashboard? I asked her if I could get to the car first to wipe it off. No luck, she said, "Let's go." Some lame excuse about the dust came out of my mouth. She sensed my embarrassment and, perhaps relieved that I knew the difference between clean and dirty, didn't say a word. I am happy to say the dinner that evening at B.F.A.'s beautiful home was the first of many visits Jackie and I had in her wonderful company.

Lesson Learned

- Whenever a job opportunity is offered, it is most desirable, if possible, to clear the decision with the former as well as the future employer. This will not be possible in all cases, but the effort should be made, if for no other reason than the executives will likely see each other over the years at social and business events.

Once I knew I would be joining G. Fox, I called George Neustadt. I asked him to analyze G. Fox's newspaper lineage *versus* Bloomingdales and B. Altman & Co., the two stores that I felt were similar. I wanted a good idea of G. Fox's strong and weak departments, as well as its pricelines, compared to the two New York competitors.

From the outset, it was apparent that B.F.A. was the lone executive who actually wanted me at G. Fox. My first assignment working for Sam Einstein consisted primarily of tedious tasks, mostly checking quantities on hand for mailing pieces and following up on customer wantslips. Wantslips were forms filled out by salespeople each day that listed customers' requests—wish lists. A good concept if it were not for the fact that salespeople hesitated to list too many wants, since it would reflect poorly on the buyer of that department.

The merchandising organization consisted of Sam Einstein, the general merchandise manager, and six divisional managers for basement, fashion accessories, menswear, ready-to-wear, children's, and home furnishings. Two of the divisionals, menswear and fashion accessories, obviously were competing to replace Sam Einstein when he retired. Could they miss the fact that I had been brought in to be a contender for his position? A position that, even at an age close to seventy, he didn't want to give up?

Oh, how the politics were about to play out in this cramped arena. The home furnishing divisional would retire before Sam Einstein, so he was out of the running. The children's divisional, Bernard Schiro, was B.F.A.'s son-in-law. He preferred to be a power behind the thrown. The ready-to-wear merchant, Amy Fagan, focused mainly on not having a new person interfere with her or her merchandise division. But the men's wear and accessory divisionals both wanted the job. I believe it was B.F.A.'s thinking that none of the above had the qualifications required to assume the top role. Armed with an ample background in merchandising, particularly in women's ready to wear, I had the credentials—or so she concluded—to survive in the pit with the lions.

The (Mostly) Fabulous Early Sixties

10

---------------------------- **1959–1962** ----------------------------

During my eight years at Gladdings, life had held joy, accomplishments, and surprises. I arrived in Providence a divisional merchandise manager, single, with no retail reputation. I left with my wife, two children, and a budding reputation as a merchant. Although leaving Jackie's family and hometown was sad in a way, anticipation drew us to Hartford. We knew that ending our new beginning was a formative move.

We shared the excitement of living in a new city because of G. Fox and Company—one of the most famous department stores in the country. On the afternoon of moving day, as Jackie and I drove down the Merritt Parkway and approached Hartford, a rise in the road gave us a brilliant view of sun setting behind the city. The car radio played the stirring last movement of Beethoven's Eroica symphony. It seemed like a magical moment and a good omen. As we arrived at the Hilton Hotel, a limousine drove up with Beatrice Fox Auerbach and a few G. Fox executives, all in black tie. As Jackie and I observed the group, we readily saw that G. Fox and Company was a class act.

We bought a new home in West Hartford that was being built on a golf course not far from the governor's mansion. At the time, the occupant of that estate was Abraham Ribicoff, who later rose to national prominence for a dignified show-down with Chicago

Mayor Richard Daley over the force he used to suppress protests at the 1968 Democratic National Convention. And although we didn't know it at the time, the home was only two streets away from Beatrice Fox Auerbach's mansion. The proximity later turned out to be quite beneficial since it was close enough for B.F.A. to ask me to deliver the day's sales figures to her home almost nightly.

Little Beach Park School was also a short walk down the street. I took Janie, and later Robin, by the hand and walked them down the street on their first day of school. Seeing other children clinging to their parents, I'd hoped they would want to stay, and they did. Beach Park was one of the first schools in the area to be integrated after the Supreme Court's decision in *Brown v. Board of Education*. When a little Black girl, Robin's age, entered the school and felt out of place, Robin brought her to our home for lunch. She also gave her a very personal gift when the weather turned cold: a warm coat. That particular act of voluntary integration was written up in *Newsweek*. We considered ourselves very fortunate parents.

Beatrice Auerbach helped make our transition from Rhode Island to Connecticut comfortable by making sure we received invitations to social functions, among them, opening night with her at the new Lincoln Center for the Performing Arts. She also welcomed our small family to her nearby farm on weekends. Janie and Robin loved seeing the farm animals, and especially enjoyed feeding the ducks. Being a smart business woman, the store had a small shop at the employee's entrance where dairy products from the farm were sold to G. Fox employees.

When I lived in Providence before meeting Jackie, I would sail on Narrangasset Bay, a great body of water that provided tests of skill and beautiful views. When Jackie and I married, I gave up sailing for golf to spend more time with her family at their country club, Ledgemont. After moving to Hartford, we looked for a comparable haven, which was Tumblebrook. It just so happened that B.F.A.'s husband, George Auerbach, was a founding member of that club. After waiting discreetly for a few years and gaining a promotion at G. Fox, I asked her if she would mind if Jackie and I applied for membership at Tumblebrook. She leaned backwards, took my phone and asked the operator to get Colonel Hartman, the president of Tumblebrook on the phone. When he answered, B.F.A. said, "Joe, Mr. and Mrs. Neimark would like to join. Would you please take care of the details." That was it. No membership committees, and no long interviews (other than, how much did we donate to UJA and Federation?). Beatrice Fox Auerbach's methods were from another time that is now long gone.

Lesson Learned

- A new position offers new opportunities. It is important to integrate slowly in order for people to feel they know you and what you stand for. Acceptance cannot be achieved overnight. As difficult as it may be, patience will always win out.

But aside from these short and long-term niceties, when I went to work, I was thrown into the lions' den. After about six weeks of snaps and jabs from the divisionals—after six weeks of being Sam Einstein's gopher—I asked to meet with B.F.A. As politely as possible, I told her that she was wasting her money and I was wasting my time. She said she had anticipated my frustration and had arranged to give me a division, as well as being the assistant to Mr. Einstein.

The way that B.F.A. arranged to give me a division showed that her wisdom was similar to King Solomon's. (When asked to settle an argument between two women claiming to be the mother a particular baby, he decided to cut the baby in half so that each could have her "share". The real mother begged that the baby be kept whole, so Solomon knew who should rightfully have him.)

In this case, B.F.A. separated a group of departments from their divisions, which she determined had not properly nurtured these departments. The orphan departments were quite an unusual mix. Daytime dresses; the lowest price dress department in the upstairs store; intimate apparel, a classification that required a great deal of detail work to maintain an in-stock position; and budget coats and dresses. The divisionals wouldn't admit it, but I am sure they were glad to give up their claim to the "babies"—but not to me. The other orphans were the Beauty Salon, piece goods, and the sewing machine departments. Was there a winner among them?

Turning them into winners became my challenge. Everyone from B.F.A. down kept me under microscopic scrutiny, mostly looking for flaws in my performance. In fact, I believe B.F.A. was the only one hoping for my success.

Nearly every action I took and every answer I gave provoked protests and contradictions. After six months, I asked Sam Einstein for a review of my performance. Since I was the newest member of the management board, I was required to keep the minutes of the meeting for distribution to the members of the board. These management board meetings took place quarterly in B.F.A.'s office after the store closed. Business followed a formal dinner, with B.F.A. always keeping her meetings on track and focused on productive discussion. So, during this six-month review, Mr. Einstein's first criticism of me was that I was very late in preparing and distributing the minutes of the meetings. Not true, and in my opinion, unrelated to the topic. His second comment was that my departments were not having increases in line with the total store. I realized he was looking at the wrong figures, whether intentionally or unintentionally. This reinforced my assumption that, whatever I did, he would not approve. Since time was on my side, I decided to use the old New England farmer's saying. "Saw wood and say nothing." I did not contradict him. Later on—after he retired—Sam Einstein reluctantly admitted that I was the logical choice for his position, even though our approaches contrasted sharply.

Since I was sure that B.F.A. was in my corner, I saw the challenge as winning over the divisional merchandise managers. After all, they were the executives that I had to work with. As best I could, I developed friendly, social relationships with each of the divisionals to show that I wasn't the wise guy from New York and Providence. In the process, without planning it or even knowing it at first, I began to recognize each person's strengths and weaknesses. It became apparent to me early on that, except for their fairly good taste levels, they had not mastered the basic merchandise techniques necessary for building sales and profit.

They inhabited a cloistered environment, working for the dominant retailer in Connecticut and benefiting more from the environment than from their own ability. B.F.A. recognized this, which is why, later on, she explained to me a main reason she brought me to G. Fox was my specialty store background. She believed specialty store retailers had to be smart to bring customers into their stores everyday, whereas department store merchants lived off customers who came routinely to buy pots and pans, and other sundries of everyday living.

Lesson Learned

- Whenever a new executive joins a company, the other executives at the same level, will circle like sharks (or lions) attempting to find his or her weak spots. Tact and superior knowledge will win out.

Being divisional merchandise manager of a diverse group of departments allowed me to flex my merchandising ability more than ever before. Five major situations stand out in my memory that helped me accomplish my objectives.

One. Since I lived near B.F.A., I dropped off the daily sales report at her home. The first evening I prepared to take the sales figures of each division by typing out a new envelope with B.F.A.'s name on it, Sam Einstein quickly corrected me. Don't ever use a new envelope for the sales figures for B.F.A., he cautioned. She prefers a used envelope, and we have many for this purpose. Another lesson on the prudent use of resources came from B.F.A. herself. The first evening I ran this errand, the maid answered the door and said, "Mrs. Auerbach would like you to come in." B.F.A. sat to the left of the fireplace with a small table in front of her. On the table and floor lay invoices. She welcomed me and asked me to sit down as she started to review the sales figures by division and by department. She asked a few questions about departments in my division, as well as my opinion of other departments in the store. She explained that the reason for having the invoices in front of her was to be sure the buyers negotiated the proper terms and discounts. I mentioned that Jackie's father did exactly the same procedure, but his business was very small compared to G. Fox. "My store would still be small if I didn't watch all the details," she said. Dropping the figures off each evening was the drill. Some evenings I would be invited in, other evenings I would leave the figures with the maid. Being able to have B.F.A'.s input and to share my thoughts with her was a highlight of my career.

Sometimes B.F.A. remained in her office after store closing and asked the divisionals to bring up their figures personally. If divisions didn't have a sales increase, she would demand to know why not, and would berate the divisional in front of his or her colleagues. I made sure early on to have an increase each day, no matter what.

Two. I introduced the unit open-to-buy plan to the buyer of daytime dresses. An intelligent man, he immediately grasped the concept and told the other buyers how easy it was to use. By realistically planning his unit sales going forward, higher or lower, it allowed him to adjust his on-hand inventory for the number of weeks of inventory he required to match his sales forecast. As an example: If his sales forecast was to sell 500 dresses a week for the next four weeks, being on a "4 weeks supply," he had to have at least 2000 dresses on hand at the beginning of the four week period. Depending on the dress sales for next four weeks, he again had to have the number of units on hand equal to the next four weeks, and so on. Needless to say, this was a fast-turning department. The average moderate dress department might be an eight-week department. Men's clothing at the other end could be as much as 26 weeks.

Another facet of this concept meant that any style in stock that was not selling rapidly enough to be out of stock at a four week rate, was subject to return to the manufacturer to exchange for a faster selling style, or marked down to make room for new merchandise. (Recall the three Rs of retailing in Chapter 6: Reduce it, Return it, or Reorder it.)

I mention that he was intelligent, since I found most buyers were more interested in additional open-to-buy rather than doing the detail work necessary to bring about current and fresh inventory. This buyer had been with the store for many years and B.F.A. enjoyed seeing that his work with me enhanced his success rate. He later told her that he had learned more from me in six months than in the previous six years.

In a short time, all of my departments adopted the unit weeks-of-supply plan. Weekly monitoring and supervision mitigated the buyers' tendency toward optimistic sales planning that wasn't balanced by an ability to recognize slow-selling styles. I found throughout my retail career that nearly all buyers believe in what Dorothy Parker called "the triumph of hope over experience." That monitoring and supervision largely occurred during buyers' meetings each and every Friday morning, a habit I started at Gladdings. I called that meetings "The Hour of Charm or Harm," depending on the buyer's performance that week. I held all meeting in the morning, since B.F.A. insisted that all merchandise executives be on the floor from 11:00 AM on. Since we were in

the embryonic stage with computers, we developed a crude manual fashion reporting system that gave weekly unit sales performance by style, as well as units on hand. Shortly after, we applied the
merchandising system to our IBM accounting machines.

In conforming to B.F.A.'s policy of being on the floor during
the day, I confiscated the floor manager's podium Saturday after-
noons. The podium sat at the foot of each escalator—more than
just a symbol of a floor manager present to ensure that customers
were taken care of. (Does anyone do this anymore?) At the
podium, I met with each buyer individually to review his or her
selling performance for that week, and how it compared to the
unit plan in order to make the proper adjustment to the sales plan,
up or down. When B.F.A. traveled the escalators, she could see I
was doing my work on the floor. This stands out as one of the
most enjoyable and constructive periods of my career. The ability to meet with each buyer individually, to review performance,
and to offer specific guidance on next steps that we would take to
reorder their best sellers and to get rid of slow movers—both sides
found the exchange energizing. The buyers actually waited at the
IBM printers to have the latest sales results for the review in order
to be prepared to go to the New York market first thing Monday
morning. My division's sales increased and gross margins
improved. Good for my image with B.F.A. Bad for gaining
acceptance by the other divisionals.

Three. Although the ready-to-wear departments were moving
ahead, we needed an exciting sale in intimate apparel, particularly in
January. We organized wonderful purchases from Van Raalte and
Vanity Fair, some of which required us to arm wrestle with the sales
rep to get the right discount but what else were we going to do in
January? The buyer of this department was not a particularly aggressive lady. For this sale event, I gave her some unusual reinforcement
to achieve a really special price. I asked her to please step outside
while I spent a moment with the sales rep explaining the "facts of
life," that is, if you can't help her when she needs you, she doesn't

need you. Thus, we arrived at a proper sale price and negotiated a full-page ad. As was her habit, B.F.A. wanted to see the merchandise before it went on sale. She always enjoyed a bargain. She liked what she saw and said, "I wouldn't put 'phone orders taken' in the ad." The ad was designed to have some expensive peignoirs as loss leaders, as well as best sellers at "magic sale prices." I waited for the latest weather report before approving the ad. The forecast called for rain and sleet the next day. I asked the advertising department to add "phone orders will be taken," to provide benefit to customers who couldn't navigate the bad weather to get to the store. The ad ran and, as I'd seen before, so did the customers. When the store opened, it was sleeting outside; they rushed up the escalators as well as the elevators, and mobbed the intimate apparel departments. The rest of the store was very quiet, but the telephone order boards lit up. We had a sell-out. Later that afternoon B.F.A. called me to her office. As I walked the length of her office, she shook her finger at me and hollered, "Didn't I tell you not to put phone orders in the ad?"

As politely as I could, I said, "Mrs. Auerbach, you said you wouldn't put phone orders in the ad. You didn't say I couldn't." She paused a moment, smiled, and then told me to make sure every customer who called in had the order filled. "The intimate apparel departments were the only place in the store that had traffic on this cold, rainy day," she added. "Good work."

Lesson Learned

- If for any reason you are going take the risk of contradicting the boss, be sure that whatever it is you do is going to be a success.

Four. About this time Beatrice Fox Auerbach made the decision to realize one of her main ambitions for the store: expand it to cover the whole block. I might add that, in the age of aggressive branch store expansion, G. Fox decided that the store's future would be the greater Hartford area, not in branch stores. In no small part, did this decision reflect an earlier branch store failure in selling farm equipment.

Merchandise managers heard the decision. B.F.A. asked each of us to submit our thinking as to how to use this additional space. Fortunately, I had had the experience of working with a retail developer, Flannery Associates of Pittsburgh, when Gladdings built their second and largest branch store in Rhode Island. Using Flannery's format of present sales, present sales per square foot and present department size *versus* proposed sales, proposed sales per square foot and proposed new department space, I put together a more professional presentation than the other merchandise managers. A few had merely written their ideas on yellow lined pads. I had the sensitivity to send a copy of the report to B.F.A. to the general merchandise manager, my boss, as well as our financial head. She called me to her office to explain my analysis and recommendations, which I did. Then she literally and figuratively pushed buttons to summon her senior executives and divisionals to her office. To my embarrassment and theirs, she began to berate some of the people there for sending scant information to her, instead of a detailed report like mine that made sense.

Lesson Learned

- When asked for ideas or suggestions from one of the highest executives in the company, it is important to keep the key executives in the loop. They will not like being upstaged, but appreciate that they were not kept in the dark. It also gives them the opportunity to be able to comment negatively or positively instead of just sitting there with egg on their face.

Five. G. Fox had an annual sale around Easter vacation, a time that made it easier to get extra sales help and to accommodate customers ready for spring and summer shopping. B.F.A. felt that the customers who bought from her all year round were entitled to a grand bargain at least once a year.

Aside from buying large quantities of merchandise for the sale, the store also had a contest among the merchandise managers and their departments. Each merchandise manager was assigned a comic strip symbol. I was Superman. The merchandise managers had sales goals for each department based on a percentage increase over the same period last year. Are you surprised that I was determined to be the winner? Each day the sales people in the departments that beat the others received silver dollars with a fanfare of bugles. Also, at the employee's entrance stood a large billboard with the comic strip characters drawn on a racetrack, so all the employees could see how their division heads had fared. Near the final days of the sale contest I led, with Bernard Schiro, Mrs. Auerbach's son in law, a close second. I asked B.F.A. if she minded my winning ahead of her son in law. "No favorites," she said. "Go for the prize." I did, and I won.

Lesson Learned

- If you are put in the position of competing with your peers publicly, develop a business strategy to make a good showing.

Having now described the five situations that helped me achieve my objective, I should mention one that didn't.

I noted in Chapter 9 that I had asked George Neustadt to analyze G. Fox's newspaper lineage *versus* Bloomingdales and B. Altman & Co. I thought it was a bright idea, but it backfired. The analysis I asked George Neustadt to prepare for me showed that many G. Fox departments were out of balance with their peer groups. The most glaring example was that G. Fox advertising in the ladies foundation department exceeded five times that of Bloomingdales or B. Altman and Co. I knew that G. Fox's sales were nowhere near those of Bloomingdales or B. Altman, so this baffled me. The reason: Playtex, one of the lower end bra and corset manufacturers of that time, gave as much advertising money to promote their product as the store wanted, even though the line was not compatible with the store's image. Bloomingdales and B. Altman recognized that fact, and so they didn't accept the offer. The general merchandise manager at G. Fox, however, couldn't resist the free advertising. Sam Einstein felt that since G. Fox was not a New York store, that I should bury that analysis. I was crushed, since this approach was one of my guides to comparing merchandising strategies with the best in the business.

Lesson Learned

- Never present the person you are hoping to replace with an analysis showing how wrong his strategy is compared to other leaders in the business.

What happened next perplexed me. I had made progress running departments and put reliable practices into place for buyers. Why then would B.F.A. insult me, or so I thought, by shipping me off to her "problem child," Brown Thompson?

The Problem Child

11

1962–1964

Hartford insurance companies influenced American business in lots of interesting ways, and ultimately played a significant role in the life of G. Fox and Company. The Hartford companies were the first to offer fire insurance, life insurance, auto and aviation policies, and so on, to help mitigate risks. During World War II, even the project to create the atom bomb had coverage through a Hartford company. But the management practices of the insurance industry also affected other businesses, particularly retail. The insurance companies were closed on Saturday and Sunday, which made it sensible for the department stores to also have two consecutive days off if they wanted to attract professional employees. B.F.A. was among the first to recognize this. She and other retailers chose to close their stores on Sunday and Monday.

The added benefit for the department stores being closed those two days was that all the sales people had the same day off; that allowed for a full staff every day to serve their customers. A full sales staff five days a week had the benefit of a customer's favorite salesperson being there to serve her, instead of as it is today. Today, with most stores being open seven days a week and almost every night, it is impossible to maintain a full sales staff. But this same practice of staggering work hours and using part-time help that may aggravate regular shoppers has provided a clear benefit to retailers. They quickly found it offered a way to reduce selling costs. This approach reminds me of another New England story.

A farmer running into hard financial times decided to feed his horse one less oat each day, and assumed the horse wouldn't know the difference. It worked fine, until one day the horse fell over dead from starvation.

It seems peculiar and illogical that department stores today run full page sale or clearance ads in a paper such as *The New York Times* at the cost of $50,000 or more only to have customers respond, and then search the floor angrily for someone to help them. Fewer sale ads, with the money spent on more professional sales people on the selling floor is what customer service is all about. Successful retail businesses are built with great sales people, not heavy advertising. This emphasis on personalized and professional customer service has value that retailers today seem to have either forgotten or never recognized.

The service at G. Fox achieved a superior standard. When I first arrived at the store, I ordered grass seed and a spreader. The next day, a G. Fox truck brought the lawn seed, but no spreader. I called the store and, within hours, a G. Fox motorcycle arrived with the spreader. Reportedly, G. Fox would send a truck to pick up a spool of thread that had to be returned, and the store would be open even during a blizzard. The standard was that the store was always there for the G. Fox customer.

As my Superman and other stories suggested, my first two years at G. Fox involved strong performance. B.F.A. was pleased, Sam Einstein reluctantly accepted me, and the other divisionals realized I had brought a degree of professional merchandising to the store that they hadn't seen before. To my dismay, this happy state did not last long.

One Monday in 1962, shortly after winning the G. Fox annual sales contest, I was in my office catching up on paperwork. Jackie called to tell me that B.F.A would be picking me up in her car. When I got into B.F.A.'s limousine, a thunder storm overtook us. I should have considered that an ominous sign. On the drive to her home, she told me that the president of Brown Thompson was retiring, and she wanted me to take that position. How appropriate that thunder and lightening provided the backdrop for this unnerving invitation.

When the car reached her home I expressed my deep disappointment. I had given up a perfectly good position at a top store in Providence, and moved my family to West Hartford to be at G. Fox, not a slumping, second-rate store like Brown Thompson.

When I got home, I slammed the front door and promptly called Bill Holmes who, at this point, was not well. He suggested that I meet him at the Westchester Country Club, in Harrison, New York, where he lived. The insight he provided once again gave me perspective on a thorny situation. B.F.A. most likely had a problem, he concluded. The old man at Brown Thompson wanted to retire. She had one person she felt was qualified to replace him. "Do it," he urged, otherwise as I continued to work for her, she would always remember that I wouldn't help her when she needed me. I took Bill Holmes' advice—the last advice he ever gave me. He died six months later. I attended his funeral in New York surrounded by many of the people that I started with at Bonwit Teller. I felt as though I had lost a close relative.

When I next met with B.F.A., I told her I would accept the position—with a caveat. When I bring Brown Thompson to a profit, I wondered, would I return to G. Fox as the general merchandise manager, succeeding a retiring Sam Einstein? B.F.A., of course, had her own caveat. She said for me to bring it to a profit, and then find an executive to run the store after me, and then we could discuss my future. I had great faith in the lady, and I wanted the general merchandise manager's position.

Lessons Learned

- No matter how undesirable a request from management may be, consider the long-range implications. As in many situations in life, you must consider if the gamble is worth taking.

- Seeking good advice from people with successful experience
  will help to arrive at the correct decision.

And so, I plunged in at Brown Thompson, despite the fact that my skills might not be enough to overcome some of the hurdles. Specifically, the divisionals at G. Fox had the ability to help or hurt me. They could shine their loyalties in my direction or go against me. If I succeeded at my new appointment, I would then be the next general merchandise manager of G. Fox and they would have to report to me. If I failed, they might have a shot at promotion to the senior post. They also knew they could sabotage my efforts to save Brown Thompson by directing their manufacturers not to sell to the store.

Knowing the history of G. Fox gives an interesting insight into how Brown Thompson became B.F.A.'s problem child. That history will also make it clear why my association with G. Fox represents a momentous phase of my career.

Gershon Fox, B.F.A.'s grandfather, built his dry-goods store on Main Street in Harford in 1847. From the earliest days, he laid down many of the basic business principles later used by his son, Moses Fox. The store on Main Street flourished, allowing the family to make steamship visits to Europe, pay for tours for their daughters, and sustain business for their father. The Fox daughters, Beatrice and Fanny, as the story was told to me, met the Auerbach family on one of these steamship trips. Both daughters married Auerbach brothers and moved to Salt Lake City, where the Auerbach family had a store. Legend has it they moved West with the Mormons, and were told by Brigham Young himself, "You will build your store there." George Auerbach, Beatrice's husband, had charisma and a knack for success, and reputedly could have gone far in business or politics in Utah. As Moses Fox grew older, however, the couple decided to move to Hartford. The plan was for George to take over the store from Moses Fox.

In 1917, the original store on Main Street burned down as Moses, Beatrice, and George watched the fire from across the street. They vowed to build a bigger and better store. During the fire, the G. Fox employees asked the head of the store next to theirs, Brown Thompson, for help. Brown Thompson's chief executive refused. Years later, when Brown Thompson fell on hard times due to the G. Fox dominance, the Auerbach family—with justified satisfaction, I'm sure—bought the store and treated it like a uncomely stepchild.

To replace the fire-ravaged building on Main Street, the Fox and Auerbach families built a magnificent eleven-story department store so large that it earned the moniker "Fox's Folly." The original store may not have been insured enough to cover the cost of the new store, but the family had invested wisely in the young Hartford insurance companies themselves, which generated income that they used to fund the new enterprise. The store was so large for the initial inventory that B.F.A. instructed the employees to put merchandise on the shelves and also to put empty boxes on them to give the impression of a store with a hefty inventory of products! The store succeeded instantly—some Fox, some folly.

Shortly after the new store was built, George Auerbach died, reportedly from a mistaken medical diagnosis. Since Moses was getting on in years, it fell to Beatrice to take her father's place. She always said that from the neck up, she was the same as a man. Her only weakness was arithmetic. She told me she had pockets sewed in all her dresses so she could use her fingers to count without anyone seeing her do it. Her retail concept was quite simple, but very effective. She wanted the store to be run as she ran her home: clean, neat and orderly. She carried this out with aplomb and dedication, not lip service. Let any employee, at any level, violate her standards and B.F.A. immediately struck down that person's lame notion of what was acceptable. Day after day, year after year, I lived with and tried to meet those standards. They gave me a refined sense of how a retail store should be run. With the fashion background I gained from Bonwit Teller, the merchandising

concepts developed at Gladdings, and the store management of
Beatrice Fox Auerbach, I felt I was ready to be promoted to
general merchandise manager of G. Fox and Company.

But first, I had to tackle the Brown Thompson project.

Lesson Learned

- It is important to become familiar with the background and
  culture of the company you become associated with. The
  owners and principals appreciate, and require, that interest be
  shown by executives as a matter of pride and understanding of
  the business principles used by the company.

My presidency of Brown Thompson was like Hercules' cleaning
the Augean Stables. Could anyone take a place suffering from so
much neglect and transform it overnight? The store really was an
ugly stepchild, literally and figuratively. An ancient building, no air
conditioning, a selling basement for toys and hard goods with a
chicken rotisserie that could be smelled throughout the store, and
a large leased shoe-repair department. It reeked. The merchandise
mix and presentation were secondary in every respect.

My objectives: to position the store for the lower-end G. Fox
customer to bring it back to profitability; to find a replacement to
run the store when I was to return to G. Fox. Even if I achieved
them, my future with G. Fox was not certain.

Over the next two years, I realigned the merchandise by concentrating on basic budget and moderate-level manufacturers.
Meanwhile, the devious G. Fox divisional merchandise managers
took special care to inform their manufacturers that they would not
think kindly about them if they were to sell to Brown Thompson.
To counter their strategy, I notified my contacts in the market: I will
remember those of you who help me and those of you who don't
when I return to G. Fox. (I stuck to that promise, much to the dismay of some of the players.) At one point I made the decision to

exterminate the losing toy department in the basement and open a basement off-price floor. I hired a key basement buyer who had to buy through jobbers, as the discount stores were doing, since the prices were so low. Later in my career, I brought this experience to people who accused me of understanding only how to move expensive merchandise.

For opening day, we ran a four-page sale section in the *Hartford Courant*. I don't think we made a lot of money, but the basement store was a mob scene. After that, by following the same track and appealing to a well-defined customer base, Brown Thompson became marginally profitable. After about a year, I found a bright, young aggressive merchant from Litt Brothers in Philadelphia, Alvin Richer, to help implement the strategy. We worked together for about a year before I returned to G. Fox, when he then took over as president of Brown Thompson.

At the unfortunate time of President John F. Kennedy's assassination, the store had a $70,000 increase going for the month of November. Compared to G. Fox, that would had been $700,000—a substantial number. However with the tragedy, and the closing of the store for the presidential funeral, we lost most of the sales gains we had. What it did, however, was quantify the store's limited potential.

During my struggle with Brown Thompson, I had a call from Stanley Marcus's office. Mr. Marcus was at the Pierre Hotel in New York and wanted to talk to me. He was looking for a general merchandise manager for Neiman Marcus. "Come to Dallas. Meet the executives," and so on. That never happened. Stanley and I kidded each other over the years. I said that the reason I considered the position was it would have been fun to answer the phone and to say, "Neiman Marcus, Neimark speaking." The negative, I jokingly told Stanley later on, was that he wanted to pay my salary in Neiman Marcus gift certificates. Being the perfect gentleman that he was, many years later at a Good Guys luncheon in his honor, he said one of the mistakes he made in his career was not to hire Ira Neimark.

The experience at Brown Thompson taught me humility. Throughout my career, whenever someone complained about his or her store, for whatever reason, I reflected back to Brown Thompson and said, "You don't know how lucky you are." If I could do it over again, I would have transformed the store into a shopping haven for young buyers, similar to the shops in London like Biba or Way In at Harrods. However, that trend was still four or five years away.

Lessons Learned

- If management wants you to take on an unpleasant assignment, as difficult a decision as it may be, do it with the understanding that the risk may exceed the reward in the long run.

- No matter what type of store you are involved with, decide who you want to be, and what customer you want to appeal to.

- Motivating an organization when the past and present were bleak requires enthusiasm and courage. Make everyone in the organization know what the plan is in broad detail. Outline to the managers of the business the overall plan in greater detail. And be "consistently consistent."

Take-Overs, Inside and Out **12**

---------------- **1964–1967** ----------------

M y return to G. Fox was inauspicious and an unsettling *déjà vu*. My small office was in a corridor near Sam Einstein's office and, once again, I held the title of assistant general merchandise manager. I felt like Lew Ayers portraying the soldier who tried to resuscitate a mortally wounded man in the movie *All Quiet on the Western Front*. When he returned from the "dying room," no one seemed to care. In this case, the only one who appeared interested in my return was Beatrice Fox Auerbach. She sent a plant to my office, with a note, "Welcome back." I was assigned to merchandise some of the better apparel departments. By again applying the merchandise principles that had proven effective for me, the performance of these departments improved dramatically, much to the consternation of Sam Einstein.

Finally, in early 1965, a year after returning to G. Fox, Sam Einstein retired to work on special assignments for B.F.A. At long last, she appointed me general merchandise manager of G. Fox and Co.

Resentment, perhaps salted with a bit of anger, fed the attitudes of the divisional merchandise managers. The merchandise manager of the men's departments was the most disappointed at failing to secure the position long-held by Sam Einstein. To ensure he wouldn't feel left out, when I was invited to my first Frederic Atkins general merchandise manager meeting, I asked him to come to with me. He did, and that simple act turned him into a supporter. His family told me many years later, how much that gesture pleased him.

The other divisionals possessed enough self-interest and good sense to realize that the merchandising techniques I recommended improved their performances as well. Merchandising at G. Fox and Company was running smoothly. The store had wonderful customer acceptance. It dominated Connecticut both by appealing to customer loyalty and offering superior service. When R. H. Macy opened a large branch in nearby New Haven, we advertised that we would make same-day deliveries to New Haven, just as we did in Hartford, and effectively blunted the new competition.

One of the major benefits of being general merchandise manager was my close association with B.F.A. Other retailers held her is such high regard that once, when she attended the National Retail Dry Goods Association meeting, all of the hundreds of attendees stood and applauded her as she entered the auditorium. When it came time for me to make my first European trip for G. Fox, B.F.A. had her own ideas as to how and where I should travel. First of all, I should fly first class in order to sit next to the type of people she would like to think of as her customers. And in order to understand her lifestyle, and taste level she had developed over the years, she wanted me to stay at the hotels she and her family had enjoyed. In Rome, I stayed at the Hotel Hassler. In London, The Connaught. In Paris, the Ritz. To this day when my travels take me to Paris, Jackie and I stay at the Ritz. On one trip in the late 1990's, a new desk clerk was on duty and didn't recognize us. Jackie asked gently, when he had a moment would he please let us have a copy of our past room statements over the years for a souvenir. When he produced the records (and saw how frequently we stayed there), everything changed. We got back our favorite junior suite, and I might add, at the right price.

Back in Hartford, B.F.A. and I met in her office every Saturday for a brief lunch, and then toured the store from the eleventh floor to the basement store. We visited nearly every department every week. As a matter of course, she questioned the buyers, sometimes about minute details of their operation. She expected an answer, if not on the spot, then soon after, and followed through to see who remembered to get back to her without her having to call them. One of her secrets was to review the "want slips" previous to her tour; these were records of consumer requests for unstocked or out-of-stock merchandise. She would also ask to have each department send their customer special order files to her office once a month. She wanted to be sure customers' special orders were given the proper attention. Termbooks, showing the arrangements that departments had with each of their suppliers, also went to her once a month to be sure the buyers maintained them correctly.

Two age-old procedures of B.F.A. were honored like religious rituals: maintaining basic stock books and old season reports. Basic stock books showed the number of units required to be on hand in order to serve customers properly. To be out of a basic item was heresy, and treated accordingly. Old season reports indicated the age of merchandise in stock. The fact that merchandise managers had to submit their reports for the president's analysis puzzled me. I sent my first report to B.F.A.'s office noting that I had marked down the merchandise that I felt should be out of stock, and didn't think the president of the store had to take her valuable time to tell me how to get rid of old inventory. If I felt so strongly about this issue, B.F.A. declared, then I would have the responsibility to monitor the age of inventory reports for all the departments in the store with her each month. This procedure also became a religious ritual for the rest of my career.

Not all procedures struck me as positive, however. One that her father passed on to her was that all the mail that came to G. Fox— addressed to anyone at any level—was opened and sent to her office. I became aware of this procedure when I first joined G. Fox because I hadn't received any letters of congratulations from business associates, particularly those from the market. A week or two after I arrived, B.F.A. called me to her office and handed me a large group of letters. Hiding my surprise was impossible. All mail addressed to G. Fox was company business, she asserted. If someone wanted to write to me personally, they should write to me at home. I politely labeled her business practice an invasion of privacy. She countered that such correspondence told her more about what was happening in her store than anyone could imagine. This practice of opening employees' mail was ultimately declared illegal. Who would have imagined that decades later, the same issue would arise with e-mail, but with the reverse decision in terms of employees' rights?

The next few years brought growth in sales and profits. I felt my future with this family owned company was assured.

Lessons Learned

- Beatrice Fox Auerbach inspired anyone who came in contact with her. The ability to motivate people by her loyalty to each and every employee when that person performed to her standards was legendary. Not meeting her standards meant reassignment to a lesser responsibility, which also inspired loyalty.

- It is most important to articulate what your standards are, and to be sure that the standards are monitored frequently and consistently in order that there be no question of employees understanding what is required.

- Whenever a question arises, say regarding a customer service, no one should have to go to the company manual for an answer. Everyone should say, "What would management expect me to do in this situation?" and act accordingly. It will work many more times than not.

- In a retail store and many other types of businesses, maintaining basic stock books, now computer programmed, is a given. Just like brushing your teeth at least twice a day. No imagination required, but it has to be done. When you turn on the light switch, you expect the light to go on; when a customer asks for a basic item, the customer expects it to be in stock. The alternative is not only a lost sale, but also the potential loss of the customer.

- In a department store or a specialty store, age of inventory has always been to me the equivalent to water moving through a pipe. Merchandise always has to keep moving. Slow moving inventory clogs the store's pipes. If slow moving merchandise is not cleared one way or the other the whole system breaks down.

- The taking of markdowns can be developed into a profitable way to do business if the markdown is taken early enough, allowing money from the sale of the reduced merchandise to be reinvested in new merchandise. Experience shows most buyers and very few divisionals know how or care to do this, hence, lost business, lower gross margins, and eventually red ink on the bottom line.

As happens in all businesses, nothing stays the same. One day in 1966, an article appeared in *The New York Times*. Federated Department Stores bought the I. Magnin and Bullocks stores, two prestigious West Coast retailers. The Federal Trade Commission had given approval with the provision that Federated would not purchase another retailer for a certain number of years. B.F.A. called me to her office that morning. She found it disheartening that the Lazarus brothers, who headed up Federated, bought these two companies. It had been her feeling that if she were ever to sell, she would have preferred working with the Lazarus brothers, whom she respected as retailers and knew quite well. With the FTC order in affect, that would not be possible.

Six months later, she summoned me for a confidential conversation. She was in the process of negotiating to merge with the May Co. Department Stores, but if word got out, the negotiations would end. One reason she had selected May Co. was that the head, Lincoln Greise, was a relative of hers. That means that G. Fox and Co. would (sort of) remain in the family. Again, the triumph of hope over experience took over.

After our discussion, I went to the latest issue of *Women's Wear Daily* to see the buyers listed from retailers visiting the New York markets. (In those days buyers visiting their buying offices in New York were listed.) I was not familiar with the May Co. stores, and when I reviewed the listings, I felt disappointed. Whereas, G. Fox and Co. had a national and an international reputation as a class retailer, in a league with Kaufmann's in Pittsburgh and Famous Barr in St. Louis, May Co. stores company were largely unimpressive except to those people who thought "bigger" and "highly promotional" constituted class. Our fate seemed certain.

After reviewing May Co. annual reports, I had no doubt that they were much more profitable than G. Fox and Co., but G. Fox had a uniqueness that May Co. was unlikely to appreciate. We would become another Hecht Co. or O'Neil's of Akron. Good retailers, but highly promotional.

If May Co. were to pay their good money in May Co. stock, they had a perfect right to impose their management strategies, and at some point their management. They also had a responsibility to their shareholders to boost profit performance. On the downside, retail mergers involving huge sums of money invariably stripped stores of their identity, and in the process, eroded their position in their markets.

After the sale to May Co. was finalized, and before we announced it to the press, B.F.A. called a storewide meeting on the main floor, as she did whenever she had an important message for everyone. She told the employees of her decision to merge with May Co.; most importantly, she would continue to run the store.

By a strange coincidence, Sam Feinberg, a senior reporter for *WWD* had a long-standing appointment with B.F.A. He was outside the front door when he saw that something important was going on before the store opening. As he told me many years later, he was a successful reporter more for being in the right place at the right time than for any other reason. That day, he was at the right place and broke the story.

Lesson Learned

- Nothing is forever, good times or bad. Be aware and always be prepared for the possibilities of change, as you would be for any natural disaster.

Life, Of Sorts, and Death 13

Tenuous as it was, the family connection between G. Fox and The May Co. evaporated shortly after the merger when Lincoln Greise retired. Stanley Goodman, then president of Famous Barr in St. Louis, replaced him.

My first recollection of Stanley Goodman was his call to B.F.A. requesting an appointment to visit with her and to see the store. I happened to be in her office at the time. She told him she was not interested in his meeting her employees, since he had committed the grave indiscretion of allowing the newspapers to publish his salary.

The merger had made B.F.A. one of the largest stockholders of May Co. Department Stores. I suggested to her that, because Stanley Goodman was the new chairman of the company that now owned G. Fox, perhaps it would be to her benefit to have a smooth relationship with him instead of a confrontational one. On some level, that probably did not occur to her. B.F.A. suffered from the same presupposition held by many other retailers who sold their businesses. They deposited their payment, money or stock, and then thought they could continue to run the store as they did in the past. This was the situation I observed with B.F.A., and later Andrew Goodman at Bergdorf Goodman and Stanley Marcus at Neiman Marcus. It is possible, of course, that the companies who purchased the stores emphasized the concept of merger, and the sellers of the stores naively believed it.

I had no doubt at this point that family-owned stores would soon be relics. Their relatively small profits didn't generate the needed capital required to expand their operations to compete with major retailers. Within a relatively short period of time, most of the other Frederick Atkins member stores were either absorbed by large chains or went out of business. And superimposing an alien corporate culture on what made the family-owned stored successful, in many cases, helped to move the family stores to their eventual demise.

Stanley Goodman did visit the store and charmed B.F.A. and everyone else in sight—superficially. With her gift for knowing people, B.F.A. quickly concluded that Stanley Goodman was a truly vain man. And what could be worse, she mused, than a vain woman? A vain man. Unfortunately, the chemistry with Stanley Goodman and me was not good. He seemed aloof; I could not feel comfortable with him. I suspected he had a strategy for G. Fox that involved moving some of his May Co. executives to the store. B.F.A. confirmed my suspicion by telling me that Stanley Goodman wanted to have one of his May Co. people replace me as the general merchandise manager as soon as the merger took place. B.F.A. was in position at the beginning of the relationship to veto this idea, however. Many years later when Bergdorf Goodman was a retail success story, Stanley Goodman at a National Retail Merchants Association (formerly National Retail Dry Goods Association) meeting gave a speech that named me with a group of other retailers who were his protégés. Now that's vanity.

In my opinion, B.F.A. had the right idea. G. Fox needed a merger, now known as what it actually is—a sale. Whether it was to be Federated Department Stores, May Department Stores or Associated Dry Goods, which all wanted to buy the company, it was just a matter of time which one did. The May

Co.'s swift change in culture that undermined her control and standards made B.F.A. physically ill. Within a year after the change in ownership, Beatrice Fox Auerbach died. She was never sure if what she did was for the betterment of G. Fox and Company and its many loyal employees.

Previous to B.F.A.'s death, she appointed one son-in-law, Richard Koopman, to the position of chairman and Bernard Schiro, her other son-in-law, became president. I was promoted to executive vice president while retaining the title of general merchandise manager. The May Co. principals told me it was their plan to have me eventually take over as president. Meanwhile, I was to recruit a successful retail executive to be my replacement as general merchandise manager when I moved up. I lured a bright young man from Bloomingdales, Robert Suslow, who was their divisional merchandise manager of women's sportswear. I knew he was a winner from the moment I met him. Bob went on to become the CEO of Saks Fifth Avenue, and head of Saks Holdings owned by the British American Tobacco Co. He achieved remarkable marketing and merchandising success in repositioning Saks Fifth Avenue.

About a year later, complications caused by May Co. management derailed my plans and hopes. The president of Kaufmanns, Pittsburgh, was set to retire within two years and management informed me they wanted him to be president of G. Fox during that period. After he retired, I would assume the presidency. Moving the aging president of Kaufmanns to G. Fox would allow them to promote David Farrell, a most competent retailer, to the top position at Kaufmanns. But what could a soon-to-retire May Co. executive do to help G. Fox progress? On a more personal level, the thought of having to prove myself all over again discouraged me. This action reinforced my uneasiness with the May Co. management, and I don't believe they ever felt comfortable with me, either. Their approach of moving management around may have benefited their total organization, but it left too many executives vulnerable to the vagaries of their decisions.

Was there anything positive about the sale of G. Fox to May Co.? Three things, actually, with the first two interrelated. The first one was the New York buying office, which had a few more forward thinking concepts than Frederick Atkins. And the second, which made the first one possible, was Dawn Mello. In addition to May Co.'s merchandise staff in New York, they had a fashion staff headed by Dawn. One day after May Co. had taken over, the senior executive at the May Co. New York office visited G. Fox with her. I could tell walking through the store together, that Dawn Mello was a knowledgeable fashion merchant, more so than any of the other May Co. executives who had invaded our life at G. Fox.

In meeting Dawn, I remember that, years earlier, B.F.A. had retained Tobé Davis, a fashion consultant. Tobé's job was to visit the store once a month to critique the fashion image and content of stock. After Tobé herself was no longer active, B.F.A. had me involved with Tobé Associates, which became the top international fashion and retail consulting service. My feeling was that possibly Dawn Mello could fill this position in some official capacity. Dawn and I agreed that our buyers visiting with her and her staff each week during market trips to New York could upgrade G. Fox's fashion image. What was interesting, and typically unfortunate for the May operation, was that the fashion office of May Co. recommended different resources to visit and to buy from those recommended by the merchandise office. It also became obvious to me that very few of the May Co. stores used the fashion office effectively, since many of the stores were more promotional than what we later called "fashion forward."

The third positive outcome was a series of sessions that May Co. set up to teach the management of the stores how to write our job descriptions, train our executives, and develop methods to measure performance of desired objectives. At one session, David Farrell, then general merchandise manager of Kauffmann's; Howard Goldfedder, his counterpart at Famous Barr, and I were asked to write down our responsibilities in order of importance.

I have never forgotten what followed. None of our job descriptions agreed with each other. We all listed the same responsibilities, but in different order.

The management group directing the seminar led us through the steps necessary to line up our priorities. The exercise of drawing up a job description has limited value if the priorities listed conflict with the chief executive's thinking. The disagreement, however, does give the two parties a chance to negotiate and discuss, which should lead to a much more satisfying job description. The second part of the sessions explained the need to have standards in place to measure performance in relationship to a job description.

The management consultants recommended that job descriptions start with the chief executive and work their way down through the organization. It was interesting to see how many executives conceived of their job differently from their superiors. But the opposite was true as well. When it came down to words on paper, the way chief executives would describe their jobs offered surprises to the people who reported to them.

Without question, May Co. operated professionally, but their business culture undermined the potential of their stores. They micromanaged to the point of calling each week to find out the markdowns for that week. And when corporate executives would visit the store, they would comment on everything from the lighting in a department to how many stripes should be in a rep tie. As a result, executives from May Co. stores generally thought they were being second-guessed on most decisions.

Regardless of their responsibilities as a public company, the business methods used to stimulate growth also proved to be the source of a major weakness in American retailing. They involved an efficiency that led to homogeneity in all the stores. Nevertheless, May Co. succeeded on one level, growing impressively after appointing David Farrell to head the company. He helped make it one of the leading retailers in the country.

Lessons Learned

- In all difficult situations, as highlighted above, there are things to learn and good people to meet.

- No matter how professional and successful a company might be, particularly in a takeover, if the new business culture is different enough to make you feel ineffective and untrue to your potential, consider how to move on. Otherwise in the long run there will be unhappiness and frustration on both sides, which is a double negative not worth enduring.

While B.F.A. held the reins at G. Fox, I enjoyed many happy, productive years. Other retailers had contacted me while I worked for her, but I had offered a "Thanks, but no thanks." Now it was time for me to say, "Tell me more."

Lesson Learned

Whenever there is a change in ownership in any business, the new owner will invariably have in mind management changes. Executives at different ages have different challenges:

- The young executive is usually protected by lack of seniority and can ride out and may benefit from the change.

- The senior executive is usually most at risk. Be prepared for a change in your position, either for someone to replace you or an executive above you who will want the change.

- In the case of the senior executive, keep your options open by always being aware and discreet for the opportunities that are available to you in other companies.

A Retailing Facelift

14

──────────────── **1969–1970** ────────────────

R eturning from a European buying trip in the spring of 1969, I had a message from Randolph Stambaugh, the president of B. Altman & Co. He wanted to meet for lunch. The Frederick Atkins office needed a new general manager, so I presumed that motivated his call. One of the major stores in the Atkins group, B. Altman held a lot of influence over selecting a new head for the office. I had no interest in that position, but I did have a high regard for Randy and would see him regardless of what he wanted to talk about.

I met Randy at the Union League Club. He had just moved up from general merchandise manager to president. He told me that he had recommended me as his replacement. Could I say "yes" fast enough?

Once again, the bouncing pinball hit the target. Soon after that lunch, I gave Jack Burke, the chairman of B. Altman, my formal acceptance. I knew Jack from the Atkins meetings and both men openly admired B.F.A. Both of them reminded me of the time, a number of years prior, when B.F.A. had invited them to take a tour of G. Fox. She told me to show them whatever they wanted to see, including the figures she didn't submit to the Atkins black book. They even said that the tour and my merchandising performance influenced them, and that one day, they would like me to work with them. They felt B. Altman and G. Fox had many similar characteristics.

B. Altman & Co. had a reputation as an ultra-conservative store, guided by generations of ultra-conservative merchants.

It also had a large, loyal following, and one of the best sales forces in the city. Jack Burke's father had taken over from Colonel Friedsom, Benjamin Altman's nephew. As I heard the story, when John Burke, Sr. turned B. Altman over to John Burke, Jr., he told young Jack, "Don't change anything." Young Jack, heeding his father's advice, steadfastly resisted change. John Burke, Sr. was so conservative, he had the display windows closed on Sundays and prohibited showing lingerie in the windows. A few years later, our new display director, Bob Benzio, did Fifth Avenue windows using fur-trimmed bathroom fixtures as backdrops. Jack Burke ordered me to remove the display. I objected: "You will never be able to hire creative people if the word got around we are still so conservative." The display stayed.

An unjustified reason for B. Altman's reputation as an-ultra conservative retailer stemmed from the rumor that the Catholic Church owned it. A lot of bizarre extrapolation led to that gossip. Jack Burke's father, chairman of the B. Altman Foundation, was one of the higher laymen of the Catholic Church in New York, as was John Coleman, one of B. Altman's Foundation board members. The store also offered members of the clergy a discount on purchases, which was not uncommon among stores. But the discount combined with the fact that B. Altman was a complete department store made it especially attractive to priests and nuns on a restricted budget. It was not unusual to see priests in their collars and sisters in their habits shopping at B. Altman, thereby giving the impression of the Church's involvement.

My challenge was to bring this grand old, conservative store into the mainstream of retailing—to build an up-to-date men's and woman's fashion business, while maintaining its great reputation in home furnishings, as well as a store renowned for its dedication to customer service. After eighteen years of learning my profession in New England, returning to New York with this clear goal fueled my confidence that I would be successful.

I relished telling Frank Chase, the new president of G. Fox, that I was resigning and would appreciate his notifying Stanley Goodman.

Ironically, when Chase was a divisional at Bloomingdales years earlier, he had expressed a desire to be the general merchandise manager of B. Altman. It didn't happen for him. I doubt that he was pleased that it had happened for me.

Jackie enthusiastically supported my decision to leave G. Fox and the forked-tongues of May Co. management. She and our daughters loved the thought of moving to New York and of my moving to B. Altman. Jackie and I drove to New York from West Hartford the night before I was to report to the store. We entrusted the B. Altman night watchman with my lucky desk set that Jackie's father had given me when I received my first promotion at Gladdings. I then touched each corner of the building for good luck. Not that I was superstitious, but a bit of good luck can't hurt. Ah, the joy of being back in New York!

Lesson Learned

- Keep your nose to the grindstone. Working hard and long to achieve your objectives is bound to be recognized by your superiors, your colleagues, as well as by your competition.

When Jackie and I moved to New York, Beatrice Auerbach's sister, Fan and her second husband, Les Samuels, took us under their wing. The association with them was a highlight in our lives after leaving West Hartford. They invited us many times to their fabled dinner parties at their magnificent triplex apartment on Park Avenue. They even hosted an engagement dinner party for our daughter, Janie. It was at one of these dinners that Les Samuels said to me that B.F.A. was wise to sell G. Fox. This, he explained to me, stopped B.F.A. from pouring money into the store and finally gave the family the benefit of the May Co. stock.

I must describe the Samuels' extraordinary apartment in order to tell the story how, after Fan died, Imelda Marcos entered the picture.

The building at 660 Park Avenue is at the North West corner of 67th Street and Park Avenue. The private entrance on 67th Street lead to a splendid winding staircase that took us to the first floor to a small foyer that opened on to magnificent fifty-foot, seventeenth-century English pine-paneled drawing room that rose two stories. The dining room was equally as impressive. A one-piece Alençon lace table cloth adorned the dining room table seating twenty. I was particularly impressed with the table cloth since a number of years ago, as a blouse buyer at Bonwit Teller, I had an Alençon lace blouse that was the most expensive blouse ever carried in stock—Alençon lace deserving the reputation as "the queen of lace."

Les would never discuss money, or what it would buy, but one evening he took me aside and told me a secret. While we were having cocktails, he pointed out a most beautiful antique (c.1760) English commode. He whispered with pride, "This commode cost more than Beatrice's mansion in West Hartford."

Years later after Fan died, when Les moved into the Waldorf Towers he retained Sotheby's to show his outstanding collection of English antiques from the Georgian period, as well as French antiques from the same era. These pieces that furnished the four-teen-room (as I recall) apartment, minus what he was moving with him to the Towers, would be available to selected customers.

He told Jackie and me that, when the first of Sotheby's clients, Imelda Marcos, came to the apartment, he watched her eyes very carefully to gauge her reaction to each collector's item. If she got excited about any one piece, he concluded, that would help him to decide whether or not the price should be higher. He was stunned. She never batted an eye throughout the visit. As Mrs. Marcos was leaving, she invited Les to one of her high profile din-ners for Adnan Khashoggi. He expected her to comment not only on the magnificent priceless antique furnishings, but also on a desire to take over the triplex apartment. She never brought the subject up.

About a month later, a check arrived for the antique furnish-ings. Jackie and I believe Les told us the amount was $6,000,000 from the Kenmarc Corp. Imelda Marcos got the antiques, but not the apartment at 666 Park Avenue.

At one of Les Samuels' last dinners—black tie, of course—after he moved to the Waldorf Towers, he placed me next to the delightful Mrs. Douglas Mac Arthur, the widow of General Mc Arthur. (I had taken the reins at Bergdorf Goodman by this time.) At one point, she asked where I had served during the war. "In the Pacific," I answered. "Are you one of the young men who got us out of Bataan?" she asked.

"No," I replied, "I was in the Air Corps."

She then asked, since the General was in charge of the Pacific Theater, "How were you treated?"

I laughed. "He didn't pay very well."

We chatted comfortably after that, to the point that she explained that she was having great difficulty in finding a silk raincoat in her size—a very small size. I told her that I would be pleased to see that she had what she wanted from Bergdorf Goodman and contacted one of our "can do people," Jack Cohen, to follow through with a coat as a gift from me. She responded with a gracious note thanking me and Bergdorf Goodman for such a wonderful present. I felt that the General would be pleased as well.

We had made the formal move to New York on July 20, 1969, after watching the astronauts land on the moon. Perhaps this sight inspired the divisional merchandise managers to think of me as an alien invader. They strongly disliked the fact that an outsider got the position of general merchandise manager, just as the divisionals at G. Fox had rebelled against it. This time, it was the home furnishing divisional who felt slighted. Unfortunately, he knew almost nothing about ready-to-wear, the store's major merchandising weakness.

Jack Burke and Randy Stambaugh recognized that B. Altman had a well-deserved reputation as one of the best upscale home furnishings stores in the New York area. (B. Altman furnished the White House during the Truman presidency, and sent linens to General Mc Arthur when he returned to the Philippines.) Previous to becoming the general merchandise manager, Randy Stambaugh had been the divisional merchandise manager of home furnishing, and before Randy, the legendary collector James "Archie" Keillor. Both built B. Altman's tremendous home business. With no fashion reputation, however, B. Altman could not overtake the competition, namely, Bloomingdales on 59th street and Macy's on 34th street, which had aggressive, experienced merchants building their women's and men's apparel businesses. My priority for B. Altman, therefore, was to upgrade its fashion image.

One day prior to the public announcement of my joining B. Altman, I was in the market with Dawn Mello and took her aside. "What do you think of B. Altman?" "A great store waiting for someone to wake it up," was her response. Based on the help Dawn Mello was to me at G. Fox, and her understanding of the retail landscape, I had set my mind that she would become the fashion director for B. Altman, but I could never have predicted how circumstances would fall in line with my plan.

Lessons Learned

- Try not to show your frustration when management changes take place that you have no control over. Do your job to the best of your ability, and keep an eye open for opportunities at another company that will appreciate your talents.

- Always look for smart people. The way to tell if they are smart is to see how sincere they are in describing their personal ambitions. If their ambitions are similar to yours you will be able to tell how sincere they are by your understanding and relating to their goals and objectives.

Shortly after this, the May Co.'s New York office had a change in management with Lee Abraham, Dawn Mello's husband, becoming head of it. They felt it was not appropriate for a husband and wife to work in the same office, which gave me the opportunity to offer Dawn Mello the position I'd had in mind. First I had to convince Jack Burke and Randy Stambaugh that we needed a fashion director. Stores with fashion directors generally used them as advisors to the merchandise staff, so they influenced merchandise people more than directed them. Buyers, divisional merchandise managers, and some general merchandise managers as well, tended to concentrate on sales volume and markdowns—and they should have. This created a blind spot in the organization, however, since no one focused on fashion merchandise that was new and exciting. My proposal to Jack and Randy was to put the fashion director above the divisional level for the sole purpose of having divisionals and buyers report to her on how they were following her direction on buying fashion lines. All the normal reporting on buying plans, markdowns, and so on, would continue to go to the general merchandise manager. This idea represented a radical departure for a retail store. I believe it still is in most cases. Jack and Randy, not necessarily grasping the ramifications of what I proposed, agreed to implement my strategy. The rewards followed.

Lessons Learned

- It is always important to make a good first impression with your peers and superiors. In merchandising, to demonstrate that you know how to present and to move fashion merchandise is a good way to start.

- To find and to be able identify talented merchants is critical to success. Therefore it becomes necessary for potential talent to demonstrate their fashion ability. This can best be done by observing how aware the merchant is to current trends, not too attached with what was, but more interested in what will be.

The hunt for talent that could turn around B. Altman did not end with Dawn. In some cases, it was right in front of us. Under the fashion office was the accessory fashion director, Caryl Sherman. She had a great sense of style as well as being a good merchant— an unbeatable combination. Prior to Dawn's arrival, she had reported to the merchandise manager of fashion accessories. He was a grand old man of many years at B. Altman, and had his ideas about what the fashion director job should be. His ideas and mine were quite different, but he could see the changes taking place and graciously went along. In contrast, Caryl's creativity exploded under the new model. Later on, I helped her establish the buying office for Bergdorf Goodman, Neiman Marcus, and Holt Renfrew in Paris, London and Milan. She was another great success story from this era.

Before I officially joined B. Altman, Randy sent me a folder of projects under consideration. The list covered B. Altman's direct mail program, a private label program, and a woman's shoe warehouse. The first two made sense, but a woman's shoe warehouse didn't. When I arrived on the scene, I reviewed the project with the merchandise manager of women's shoes and the shoe buyer. Their rationale for the project was memorable, if not logical. They had convinced management, that even though they had to mark down "fashion shoes" at the end of each season, they should be able to carry basic styles over to the next season. Since there wasn't room in the shoe department for the so-called basic styles, they requested a warehouse. What is a basic style, I wondered? We went through boxes and boxes of shoes they defined as basic styles; at some point, the saying "in the eye of the beholder" popped into my head. These shoes could not be described as basic styles. They were dressy shoes that possibly could be sold the next season to customers who didn't know better, but their presence in inventory limited the ability to bring in new styles. Their strategy to cover up having too many shoes in stock was to relegate them to a warehouse of "basic styles." The phrase I used for this type of merchandising was "amateur night at the follies." I cancelled the warehouse project and brought in a professional shoe merchant, Saul Kaplan, a good friend whose opinions I respected.

Saul was one of the positive memories of my unhappy stint as president of Brown Thompson. He managed a shoe company that leased shoe departments in department stores throughout New England, including Brown Thompson. Saul and I envisioned putting in a Pappagallo shoe department for younger customers. Under Saul's supervision, the shop succeeded instantly. (My daughter Janie got her fist retail experience in the Pappagallo department.) Saul next become the merchandise manager of all the shoe departments, as well as the Men's division, and remained a good source of counsel for years to come.

Lesson Learned

- If you can help it, never deal with amateurs, or people who don't know how to maximize their responsibility. Find a professional; it makes life easier and more profitable for everyone.

Although not trendsetting, the men's and women's fashions at B. Altman were up to date, but presented in a dreary manner. I set out to revamp the fashion floor. Potted palms occupied floor space that should have been used for merchandise displays, almost as if they were hiding something. I made it clear they had to go, but the display people worried about Jack Burke's reaction. "What will he say? The plants have been here for years?" No doubt, they had. In fact, they looked like they had been there since the store opened in 1917. As reluctant as he was to change the store, Jack Burke was also smart enough to know that, if someone knew what he was doing, he should leave him alone. As a corollary, Jack figured that, if the person did not know what he was doing, then he would find out soon enough.

As I walked through the store, the problem of pathetic, or absent, displays surrounded me. An example: Suede apparel was popular in the junior departments around town. B. Altman had the right suedes, but in no special location. The solution: A dominant display, with merchandise located next to the display, spurred sales at a brisk rate.

Introducing the basic merchandising programs I had used effectively at Gladdings and G. Fox felt rather painless at B. Altman. Walking through the store with Jack Burke one day, we came to a dress department made up primarily of Izod Lacoste dresses. He felt that department never had enough stock to do business so I showed him, Randy Stambaugh, and the ready-to wear-merchandise manager the unit open-to-buy procedure. It illustrated that Jack was right. The unit plan projected sales plans could increase dramatically, if supported with the proper amount of inventory. I made three converts on the spot.

The next step was to identify the talented people within the organization, since I'd already attracted outsiders like Dawn and Saul. Aside from the home furnishing divisional who had wanted my job, talent lurked behind the racks, but no one had been around bring it forward. An assistant buyer named Barbara LaMonica had received a promotion to buyer of casual sportswear—a dormant department, and that wasn't her fault. When we turned it into a Calvin Klein department, the volume surged and B. Altman became a principle Calvin Klein account. Barbara went on to great success, both at B. Altman and later at Bergdorf Goodman. We did recruit one or two more outsiders, however, including the better apparel buyer from I. Magnin, Corinne Coombe. Again, she succeeded at B. Altman and later at Bergdorf Goodman.

Having identified talent, I was in a much better position to work with people who could help identify the apparel opportunities under our noses. One centered on B. Altman's steady cashmere sweater business, known to its regular customers, but not known to the general public. Instead of including cashmere sweaters in a small fall sale brochure, we ran a full-page sale ad in the *New York Times* that featured all the important Scotch cashmere names: Pringle, Ballantine, Lyle and Scott. Year after year, that sale provided a winner and proved, once again, that desirable merchandise with a magic price assures a sell out. The cashmere sale set a pattern for many of the other retailers.

Due to our instant progress and exceptional team at B. Altman, I was thinking of 1970 as a year of energetic success. And then one small hitch upset my optimism. James Brady, then the Editor and Chief of *Women's Wear Daily*, sent a reporter to interview Randy and asked something like, "Now that Best & Company closed, is that the future for B. Altman & Co?"

WWD had changed a great deal from 1940 when I had the responsibility as an office boy to underline stories of potential interest to Bill Holmes. John Fairchild had taken over from his uncle, and turned a successful trade paper into a "must read." It was a flourishing trade paper, to be sure, but its allure was the unique glimpses of New York social life and insider views of the retail stores and the personalities running them. With most of the time their stories being accurate, it even had credibility. Once in a rare while, however, a story based on speculation crept in and caused problems. One was the October 1970 article on Best & Company, the fine Fifth Avenue children's store, which had just closed its doors.

Randy Stambaugh, one of the finest gentlemen I've ever known, seldom lost his temper. But this reporter pushed him to the brink. He refused to continue the interview on Best & Company as soon as he realized it was a set up. Soon after, *WWD* came out with a featured article entitled, "Stambaugh takes the fifth on Fifth." A great headline for a newspaper, but the story caused nearly endless problems. Concerned employees, manufacturers who sold to the store, countless customers–they all took *WWD*'s story as the scoop on B. Altman's imminent demise. Randy and I wrote a letter to our employees, another letter to the market, and a third letter to our charge account customers explaining how B. Altman had been on Fifth Avenue and 34th Street since 1914, and we darned well intended to stay there, regardless of *WWD*'s hints of impending doom. *WWD*'s story was correct, but about fifteen years too early.

Shortly after this fiasco, James Brady left *WWD* and Michael Coady replaced him. I liked Michael as soon as I met him. He struck me a persistent, thorough newspaperman who was interested more in news than rumors. Michael may have irritated some people with his critical observations early on, but knew his business and eventually reached his potential as a fine editor. He also excelled as a businessman, eventually becoming the president of *WWD*.

Michael also became a supporter of my efforts to upgrade the fashion image of B. Altman—or so I thought. When I left B. Altman in 1975, he was asked about my accomplishments. He said, "Neimark moved the store an inch."

"An inch?!" came the question.

"If you moved the sphinx an inch," he said, "that would be an accomplishment."

Lessons Learned

- Newspapers, like all businesses, have knowledgeable and ambitious people (and sometimes they are the same.) If you help them they will help you. Helping does not mean leaking confidential information. This may be considered a favor, but doesn't garner respect. Give the story to the newspaper that will reach your audience. The caveat here is to be sure you explain to the newspaper that didn't get the desired story first, it will be made up for the next time.

- Releasing the same story to all the press at one time may be safe, beneficial and diplomatic, but again newspapers like all businesses, want to be first. You must select the medium that best serves your market.

The New, and Old, Worlds **15**

V incent dePaul Draddy—his amazing generosity and presence—represented every reason why I aspired to return to New York and to have a collegial relationship with the retailers I greatly admired. I first met Vin Draddy in 1940 when I was Bill Holmes office boy. He had married the daughter of David Crystal, the sportswear manufacturer, and was their leading salesman and later president. Known forever as the man who paired Londoner "Jack IZOD's" reputation for quality with the name of legendary tennis player René Lacoste, he was first a great athlete, and later, a great businessman. Famous for his achievement at college football, he was also a skilled golfer. He often played with Bill Holmes and would stop by the office to pick him up on their way to the Westchester Country Club; hence, my first introduction.

In the late 1960s when Vin took over the running of David Crystal, he had a brilliant idea to have lunch with friends. Not just any friends. Instead of running an ad in *Life Magazine* to reach the retailers, his customers, he could spend the same amount of money on a lunch at the 21 Club restaurant, inviting the top retailers from New York and other cities, such as Washington, Boston and Dallas. Then he could reach the retailers directly and develop great relationships. And that he did.

Vin called the group "The Good Guys Club," and held the lunches every year during the last week of November, just before Thanksgiving. He invited not only top retailers such as Andrew Goodman, Stanley Marcus, Harold Krensky of Bloomingdales,

Allen Johnson of Saks Fifth Avenue, Jack Burke and Randy Stambaugh, and Geraldine Stutz of Henri Bendel, but also important magazine and fashion newspaper editors. Carrie Donovan and Nancy White from *Harper's Bazaar* were among those who made the list. The format was a roasting of the retailers by Vin Draddy, who emceed the event as he went around the table introducing the guests and their particular retail and golf weaknesses.

Each guest was expected to send a small, inexpensive gift to the lunch for each of the other guests. The Good Guys Lunch eventually encompassed about forty people, each of whom required a large plastic bag to transport the "loot"—excellent stocking stuffers for our children during the holidays. Another expectation was humor. Each guest provided a not-too-risqué joke. Stanley Marcus, a great storyteller, habitually called me a week before the lunch to see if I had a new joke for him.

But I wasn't part of this retail fraternity from the beginning. It was only after I joined B. Altman that Vin asked Jack Burke and Randy Stambaugh if they would approve of his inviting me to be a member. Their agreement meant that B. Altman & Co., in a frothy expression of retail dominance, had three Good Guys. Vin always found a way to make things work.

Vin proved that time and again, showing his good heart and ability to "connect the dots" in myriad ways. When Jackie and I were looking at what eventually became our home in Westchester, New York, Vin was visiting a friend nearby. I spotted him on the street. He went through the unfinished house with us, and always claimed that he'd helped us envision how that house would work perfectly for us. When it came time for our daughters to attend school, we hoped for admission to Rye Country Day School, but were told "No. There are no openings." Knowing Vin had very good connections in Rye, I called him. "Give me a couple of days," he said. Within a week, he called to say that Janie was all set to attend, and Robin would be admitted the next term. A number of years later Jackie and I drove my 1973 Jaguar to Palm Beach. Jaguars being what they were then, we barely made it. We

Ira Neimark and Vincent dePaul Draddy

wanted to take the Auto Train home from Florida, but it was filled. Again, I called Vin. He had a winter home in Palm Beach, and I asked if he could help us. Vin rescued us by calling Ernie Sabayrac, the head of FootJoy. Ernie found out who owned the railroad and which golf club he belonged to. He called the golf pro at that club, asked him if he would ask the member for the favor of getting our indisposed Jaguar and us on the train. Done. This was Vin at his best. And when Jackie and I wanted to join Century Country Club, he added his good word. Tubby Burnham an old friend of Vin's told me years later: "Vin called his golfing buddies at Century, and told them that Neimark is a good guy, he wants to play golf, so what's the big deal?" That was Vincent dePaul Draddy. I was one of his many friends who said, when he called, "Whatever you want, you've got it."

A few years after Vin died, Marvin Traub suggested to me that we should bring back the Good Guys Club. We did. Marvin Traub, Burt Tansky, Arnold Aronson, and I carry on in Vin's stead, and the new group profoundly honors the older merchants and welcomes the new.

Fun as it was, a Good Guys luncheon didn't distract us from our work as merchants, it reminded us of what it took to excel. These gatherings, and the ongoing exchanges with colleagues throughout the year, sharpened us as competitors. I'd like to think that customers were among the prime beneficiaries of this interaction.

And so, filled with new ideas and possibilities, I looked for more ways to improve B. Altman. In 1973, I recommended moving the men's clothing department to the main floor. What would be displaced? The food and gourmet department. My thinking was that a dominant men's clothing, sportswear, and furnishings department on Fifth Avenue would be a destination location for men. The tactic worked. B. Altman became a more important factor in the men's business. This was the time when Ralph Lauren sold his merchandise exclusively to Bloomingdales and I felt that Ralph Lauren should have a major presence in B. Altman. After a meeting with Ralph, I explained my interest, and puzzled at the exclusive arrangement with Bloomingdales—New York was, after all, a large city. To make my point, I offered to hire a helicopter so we could clearly see how far apart Bloomingdales was from B. Altman. Ralph declined my offer, but did sell to B. Altman and every other major retailer shortly after that.

Lesson Learned

- As in all businesses it is important to know and to be familiar with the major players. Being able to discuss and have entrée to their expert thinking will always broaden your knowledge.

After some effort, Randy and Jack convinced me that it was important for me and the store to get a view beyond New York— far beyond. They wanted me to meet our market representatives by literally going around the world to visit them. I had never been away from my family for any length of time, and this trip was to take twelve weeks. I agreed they were right in principle, but there was too much to be done at the store to stay away that long. I negotiated them down to six weeks.

My first stop: Hawaii. I recall having dinner on the veranda of the Royal Hawaiian hotel overlooking the Pacific Ocean, and thinking of the time I'd spent in Hawaii and the Pacific during the war. Very different experience from this adventure.

I visited with B. Altman's exclusive bathing suit maker, which produced quality suits, but in my opinion, not up to date. But that was for the new fashion office to evaluate, I concluded. I also visited George Ladd III, who had been a divisional merchandise manager at Gladdings when I was the general merchandise manager. He was working for Hawaii's Liberty House, a young and growing group of stores that Federated ultimately absorbed in 2001. The son of George Ladd II, the Gladdings president when both of us worked there, George III struggled to reach his potential under his father. I mention George because one of the negatives in my career was my inability to maintain relationships with so many previous associates. Maybe I had outgrown them, or maybe I was moving too fast to maintain a close relationship. This problem repeated itself a number of times and it has always bothered me.

Next stop: Tokyo. Mr. Ando met me. He was possibly in his 90s at that time. As a young boy, he had worked for Benjamin Altman, who had passed away sixty years before this! No matter where he took me to meet our suppliers, I was greeted as Mr. Keillor, B. Altman's most famous merchant.

The exposure to the Japanese artisans and makers of decorative home merchandise—suppliers to B. Altman for so many years— opened my eyes to a wonderful new experience. The great regard all these people showed for the expertise and professionalism of our management and buyers was inspirational.

My responsibility was to maintain the traditional relationships of Benjamin Altman, Archie Keillor, and Randy Stambaugh that had been in place many years before me. On our first day, Mr. Ando invited me to lunch at the Okura Hotel. "Do you like Japanese food?" he asked. I think so, I told him. We went to the sushi bar and I ate, as the expression goes, "like an out of town buyer." He commented that most Americans didn't like raw fish. I speculated that, because my father's family came from Holland where herring is a key part of the diet, I had a natural inclination to like it. As the proliferation of sushi bars illustrates, American tastes have certainly changed since then.

After Tokyo I traveled with him to Kyoto, an impressive city. As we continued to visit artisans and manufacturers, I became knowledgeable to some degree about Far Eastern decorative home merchandise. I am sure this is what Jack Burke and Randy Stambaugh had in mind.

Taiwan, Hong Kong, Thailand—I tried to meet as many of our suppliers as possible to maintain continuity for the mutual benefit of the manufacturers and B. Altman. In each case, I remembered a pointer Bill Holmes had offered to me many years before:

"At least once a year do something that will more than justify your salary."

I had that in mind with each country I visited. A particular instance that more than paid for the trip was my visit to Bangkok. I was to meet our agent, a woman, whom I'd envisioned as someone out of a Somerset Maugham novel. Landing in Bangkok, I looked for a middle-aged woman wearing a bemberg print dress, a black patent leather straw hat, and long white gloves. Instead, a very attractive blond in her late thirties, dressed in something akin to American sportswear, greeted me. She was not only the B. Altman agent, she was also a partner with a Thai woman in a teak factory producing table wear. By eliminating the middleman's fee, we worked out a very satisfactory wholesale price that enabled B. Altman to sell large quantities at a pleasing profit. I did spend part of a day sightseeing while sailing down the filthy Klong River viewing beautiful temples.

On to India. Of all the countries that I visited on this trip and others, India appeared to be one the greatest potential markets for exports to America. I felt the same way thirty years later when I went as an advisor to the Modi Company of New Delhi. With such a large pool of intelligent labor, and a colorful culture, someone should have been able turn this country into a fabulous market. Alas, this did not happen with me then, or even by the beginning of the new century. Somehow, the Indian bureaucracy has inhibited great growth potential in merchandise. There may be more to it than that, but it has been one of my disappointments to see such possibilities remain unrealized, even while some of India has dramatically improved their economy through computer technology.

Mrs. Sahni, our agent in India, had excellent contacts and was a wonderful hostess. Over the weekend she invited me to play golf with her and two other friends at the New Delhi Golf Club, formerly an Indian cemetery. Somewhere in the 19th century the English Army converted the cemetery into this unusual golf course. There seemed to be a tomb remaining on each tee. In addition to the foursome and two caddies, we also took two ball boys in order not to lose any balls since they were so expensive. At one of the holes, we chased monkeys from stealing the balls hit onto the fairway. At Mrs. Sahni's home, one of our buyers who met me there was so concerned about the water that he took pains to avoid drinking any. As he lifted a scotch on the rocks to his lips, I pointed out that the ice cubes were from the local water, which kept him sober all evening. I was to make many trips to India, but never forgot my first visit to New Delhi, Agra, Jaipur, and small towns in between.

After India, I went on to Israel, where B. Altman had an exclusive arrangement with a small costume jewelry company. In touring Jerusalem, I saw how the temples had been desecrated before their liberation in the 1967 war. The security at the Tel Aviv airport was also a harbinger of things to come. Among other requirements, I had to disassemble my pen and pencil set and unload my Minox camera.

After Israel, I proceeded to Frankfort, Milan, Paris and lastly, London. It wasn't until my later trips that I visited Ireland to meet with the executives at Waterford Crystal and Wedgwood. The European part of the trip for home furnishings held some interest, but I was really taken with the creativity of what we now call the Pacific Rim.

About a year after returning from my whirlwind tour of the world, I got a call from two of our buyers in New Delhi. Three families in Hyderabad had pooled their blue and white imari ware, which can be various types of fine porcelain, and wanted to sell the whole package for one million dollars. If they deemed it a good value, they should buy it, I said.

They felt the buy was too big for them, and wanted me to fly to India to help make the decision. I flew out of JFK Airport on Pan Am 001, arrived in Tokyo, left Tokyo for Saigon—the peace offensive was on at the time—and then was off for New Delhi to meet Mrs. Sahni, our Indian agent. Our gift buyer, Archie Keillor's daughter-in-law, came from Florence to meet us, and the three of us headed to Hyderabad, a large city with a remarkable cultural heritage.

When the plane door in Hyderabad opened, heat poured at us as though we faced an oven, and this was early evening. It was so hot that the city had to ration electricity. Each of the city's three zones had electricity for eight hours and when we arrived, everything in our zone was blacked out except for the airport. We saw people sleeping on the sidewalks in front of their houses to get some gasp of fresh air. Our driver may have had a foot brake, but he seemed far more proficient with his horn. If someone got in his way, he would simply drive on the other side of the road, blowing his horn all the way to alert oncoming drivers and pedestrians. Surviving that, we arrived at what we in the States would describe as an antebellum mansion. An elderly Indian man dressed in a long white toga carried a lantern and waved us through a large gate. The run-down house was lit only by candles. In each room, tables were covered with chinaware stacked high. The people representing the three families said there were over 500 pieces, and wanted no one to know this merchandise was for sale. Their other condition: Every thing had to be sold in one lot. We scanned the inventory and told them we would be back in the morning. For some reason, as I went around the rooms, I had a strong feeling we were looking at less than 500 units. The next day when we returned, I asked the Indian security guards if I might take pictures of the imari ware with one of the newest Polaroid color cameras. "No," he said. I then asked if they would like their pictures taken? "Certainly." In fact, they were very pleased to pose for me. In the one minute it took for the color Polaroid to develop, and while they were amazed watching their pictures take form, I walked around the rooms with my miniature Minox camera, and photographed the whole collection. Reviewing the collection, we discovered one family had exquisite taste. The second family had nice chinaware, and the third family had the type of merchandise you would find in a commercial roadside English hotel.

We offered to buy the first third. They insisted it had to be sold together. My retail experience indicated that you make your profit with what you sell and take your loss on what is not sold. Selling only one third of the collection would be a loss to B. Altman. We declined the offer. Soon, I was on my way home by way of Europe, going around the world in two days.

Why was this experience significant? The big problem in India was to receive exactly what you ordered and the problem persisted. At B. Altman, and later at Bergdorf Goodman, we had Indian extravaganzas. Big, showy, good for public relations, but not the foundation for any long-term arrangement for the stores or for India.

Lessons Learned

- Travel will always broaden your experiences. It is important to always explore every opportunity. The best opportunities may come from the most unexpected places.

- Remember, one transaction each year that will cover your annual salary will be rewarded and appreciated by everyone involved in your future.

Rewards and Hazards of Good Taste

16

The neighborhood of Fifth Avenue and Thirty Fourth Street suited a store with the exquisite detail of B. Altman. Built to Benjamin Altman's specifications, the store was completed in 1914 shortly after his death, and it reigned for many years as the premier retail entity on Fifth Avenue. The main floor of B. Altman was magnificent. Parquet floors stretched from Fifth Avenue to Madison Avenue, with large crystal chandeliers along the same distance. At Christmas time, each chandelier bulb was capped with a small red shade.

The setting begged for merchandise that matched its opulence and departments with high standards. After raising the women's ready-to-wear and men's departments from the dead—or at least a deep sleep—it seemed to me the best classifications to develop next were fashion accessories and cosmetics.

The cosmetic department had the same fixtures in place for many, many years. It seemed dreary and out of date. Neither customers nor the cosmetic industry considered the business dynamic. Turning that perception around would require creative energy.

The strategy was to present each cosmetic company with a new planned layout, and to invite them to contribute to the cost of the construction of their dedicated space. When we presented Estée Lauder, Charles Revson, Richard Saloman, and the other

Ira Neimark, Lyn and Charles Revson

cosmetic executives with the plan showing the location of each of their departments, it seemed like negotiating the Peace Treaty of Versailles. Finally, all the executives had established areas they wanted and were happy—except Estée Lauder. She insisted on having the exact spot she considered the ideal location and nothing less.

To gain her ground, she asked to meet me on the main floor with her husband Joe Lauder, and their sons, Leonard and Ronald. It was as though she had her troops ready for battle. She wouldn't budge in her request for the space allocated to Richard Salomon's Charles of the Ritz. Naturally, she got what she wanted, after I made Richard Salomon happy with a larger space adjacent to Lauder.

The opening of B. Altman's new cosmetic department was a black-tie event with cocktails on the grand main floor, and dinner served on the new third floor. Every cosmetic executive involved with B. Altman was invited, as was the press. Jack Burke and Randy Stambaugh reveled in the success.

During the course of the evening Charles Revson asked me where the nearest phone booth was located. As I took him to the phone across the long floor, Estée Lauder asked me to tell her where he was going. I had heard they watched each other very carefully, but until that incident, I wasn't aware how carefully.

I had first met Estée Lauder in 1965 when I was the general merchandise manager of G. Fox. She and Beatrice Fox Auerbach were two of a kind. Both had style and class; both had strong wills. They nearly, if not always, got what they wanted. One day Estée Lauder was visiting G. Fox, and told me she was surprised at how many customers left the store carrying only their handbags. "If you was [sic] running the store properly," she scolded, "the customers would be leaving with G. Fox packages, not just their handbags." Her barb certainly had merit, but she may have also looked for such opportunities to remind G. Fox executives that they had made a mistake years before in not carrying the Estée Lauder line when it was new. At the time, the divisional merchandise manager decided it wasn't for G. Fox, so Estée Lauder sold it to Sage Allen, a smaller competitor down the street. It took years of courting to get the line into G. Fox. That same merchandise manager kept Charles Revson waiting for such a long time when his line of special nail polish was new that he left the store in a huff. When B.F.A. heard about the rude handling, she drove to New York and invited Charles Revson to lunch to apologize. She also shifted the responsibilities of that merchandise manager.

Lessons Learned

- Always look for the opportunity to be exposed to the thinking of smart women in the retail world. This can be a major benefit to the understanding of the woman customer.

- Whenever a resource selects your store (no matter how large or small) for the introduction of a new product, the executives concerned must notify the senior executive so the product can be judged by more than one person.

During these first years with B. Altman, throughout the store, one fashion department after another rose up to achieve a higher level of aesthetic excellence—and profitability. The next logical step, or so B. Altman management thought, was adding another branch store to the group already operating. These were located around New York City, namely, White Plains, New York; Short Hills and Paramus, New Jersey; St. David, Pennsylvania; and Manhasset on Long Island. In keeping with B. Altman's traditional approach to management, the branch stores were conservatively run. Senior management in all the stores comprised operating people, which raised serious questions for me. My thinking went toward dual management, similar to how major retail companies divide their top level positions today; a CEO and a president. One is a financial operating specialist and the other, a merchant. As a direct consequence of their dominance by operations executives, B. Altman branches were boring. And instead of building another boring store, I pushed to make the existing branches more exciting. This was not to be.

In joining B. Altman, I had reunited with the Frederick Atkins office and some truly remarkable executives. Initially it was through my association with Atkins that I met Beatrice Fox Auerbach, and later Jack Burke and Randy Stambaugh. This time around, I met Philip Hawley, who had become head of the Broadway-Hale Stores in 1972, and Hart Lyon, the general merchandise manager.

Lesson Learned

- Whenever the opportunity presents itself to meet the leaders of the industry that you are involved with, do so.

Broadway-Hale Stores scored impressive financial victories and were on a growth track, so naturally Jack Burke, Randy Stambaugh and I kept close watch on them. One day, we were reviewing the figures in the Frederic Atkins black book and couldn't help but notice that their profit performance was much better than B. Altman's. Since our gross margins were in their range, as were our expenses, they were puzzled as to why Broadway Stores were so far ahead of us in profit—until I pointed out their credit card income. Broadway customers were helping to bankroll the rapidly expanding business by paying close to eighteen percent annually on their unpaid balances. This is something Jack Burke didn't want to do to B. Altman customers. His father said don't change anything. He didn't.

Broadway-Hale soon became Carter Hawley Hale, incorporating the names of the three principal architects of the business, Edward W. Carter, Phillip M. Hawley, and Prentis Cobb Hale, a major shareholder and former owner of the Hale Department Stores. Phil Hawley took over as chief executive of the new corporation and Hart became president of the Broadway. Shortly after this change in management, the head of the Atkins office asked me if I would consider becoming the general merchandise manager of the Broadway Stores. Although complimented by the offer, I was happy at B. Altman and not interested in moving to a store as promotional as the Broadway. I also saw no benefit to uprooting my family and moving to Southern California.

Under Phil's leadership, Carter Hawley Hale aggressively acquired several retails chains and prominent stores, including Bergdorf Goodman. Even before that, in the late sixties, Phil showed his taste for acquisition by buying Neiman Marcus. This was a radical departure for them, since specialty store retailing is as different from department stores, as a private jet is to a commercial airliner. The CHH executives also had a history of opening branches, which grew out of Ed Carter's keen eye for real estate.

Not long after Carter Hawley Hale bought Bergdorf Goodman, a plan emerged for Bergdorf Goodman to open its first branch store. Not coincidentally, Andrew and Nena Goodman had a weekend home in Rye, not far from White Plains and felt that area would be a hospitable location for Bergdorf Goodman's first branch store. While CHH did have a good track record with branch stores on the West Coast, they repeatedly acted on the belief that, to be successful, a branch store couldn't be large enough. Unfortunately, this concept shaped the planned Bergdorf Goodman branch—a specialty store, not a department store like the Broadway. For the branch, Bergdorf Goodman management selected property owned by B. Altman & Co. that was adjacent to B. Altman's White Plains store. B. Altman sold it to Bergdorf Goodman at a reasonable price, since management felt that having Bergdorf Goodman next door and Saks Fifth Avenue across the street would entice Westchester upscale customers.

Every Saturday, I visited two B. Altman branches, which meant I saw all the B. Altman branches once a month. I reviewed how stores were covered on merchandise classifications, observed displays, and collected input from sales people. One Saturday shortly after Bergdorf Goodman began construction in White Plains, I met Randy at B. Altman's White Plains store. We went to the roof to see how the Bergdorf Goodman construction was progressing. The excavation seemed enormous. I asked Randy, "How large is that store going to be?" One hundred and forty thousand square feet! I knew then that Bergdorf Goodman was building itself a problem. The store's selling space on Fifth Avenue occupied that much space; why would a branch in an upscale suburb require the same footage? The store turned out to be prohibitively expensive to build. This was not to be just another branch store—this was Bergdorf Goodman's taste level taking up residence in the suburbs. Months of delays and cost overruns ensued. At great expense, the marble was flown over from Italy to meet the passing deadlines. The night before the store finally opened, White Plains got a real treat: A gala the likes of which the suburbs had never seen before, and possibly will not see again. It was a black tie affair, with a fashion show featuring models in couture clothes riding the escalators.

During the course of the evening, Phil Hawley asked my opinion of the store. Looking back, I must say I was out of order in telling him—the very night of his gala—that I believed he had a big problem. Too late, I remembered the story of the groom asking a friend of his before he walked down the aisle, "What do you think of my bride?" As I predicted, sales on opening day were dismal. There is an old retail expression that would apply here: "The two biggest days a store has are its opening day, and the day it closes." This too-large, too-intimidating store never did attract the White Plains customer.

Lesson Learned

- When asked a question by a professional, answer as tactfully as possible. But give your professional opinion, not what you think he or she would like to hear.

Bergdorf Goodman failed in White Plains because the store was over-spaced for the lines of merchandise to be carried. Departments that were relatively small in New York had to have larger spaces in the branch. Over the years, retailers based allocating space not only to appeal to customers, but on sales productivity per square foot. Bergdorf Goodman did not utilize this concept or the calculations. On Fifth Avenue, an outstanding location and a prestigious fashion reputation may have helped them get away with that, but the store was still relatively underproductive from a sales requirement. Unfortunately, the deficiencies of the New York store were simply built into the White Plains store. You could say it was like the merchant who sent a sample of a cup and saucer to Japan to have a thousand duplicates made. When he received them, the merchant complained that all thousand had a crack in them. The Japanese potter explained the sample had a crack, and he was duplicating the original.

Stepping back to the source of the over-spacing problem: The people who designed Neiman Marcus stores also designed the Bergdorf Goodman branch. As a result, the store seemed more like a Neiman Marcus clone than a recreation of the Bergdorf Goodman classic look. Neiman Marcus had many well-developed departments that required larger space such as men's, decorative home, linens, and gifts. Bergdorf Goodman had no major position in any of these classifications. Hence, the White Plains store looked empty for want of these departments.

About six months after the opening of the Bergdorf Goodman White Plains store, Leonard Lauder asked me to lunch. We discussed the progress of B. Altman's new cosmetic department, and other points of mutual interest. He then surprised me: "Are you happy at B. Altman?"

I was taken aback. "Yes," I said. I hesitated, "Why, am I not supposed to be?"

He went on to say that Phil Hawley would like to talk to me. Would I be interested in a meeting with Phil and Ed Carter? My answer was yes. One of the main reasons I was willing to meet with them was that I was concerned that B. Altman & Co. could soon be sold to a larger retailer. Jack Burke had mentioned conversations with Marshall Field and John Wanamaker, and others interested in a merger which seemed around the corner. I didn't want to be back in the same position that I was in at G. Fox.

An equally compelling, if not more important, reason was my comment to Phil Hawley the night of the branch opening of Bergdorf Goodman. In the dim recesses of my mind, I think I recalled him asking, "Could you make this work?" The thought of running Bergdorf Goodman would bring my retail dream full circle.

I believe not many people felt Bergdorf Goodman on Fifth Avenue had a great sales and profit potential. Harold Krensky, former chairman of Federated, once told me that his company had looked at Bergdorf Goodman and rejected it. My positive feeling about the store rested on my growing up at Bonwit Teller on Fifth Avenue. I knew the location and reputation of Bergdorf Goodman, and the wealth of the world either living in or visiting New York. The store could be a gold mine. With all of this in mind, I arranged an appointment to meet first with Ed Carter, who was living in the Waldorf Towers. They were looking for a merchant for the Broadway Stores in California, for Neiman Marcus in Dallas, and for Bergdorf Goodman on Fifth Avenue.

He explained the growing sales and profitability of both the Broadway and Neiman Marcus. He noted the problems with Bergdorf Goodman White Plains. Bergdorf Goodman Fifth Avenue, he felt, had tremendous unrealized potential. Which of the above would be of interest to me if I were to leave B. Altman? "Bergdorf Goodman," I replied. "And yes, I am interested in pursuing the conversation with Phil Hawley."

He said he would set up an appointment with Phil as soon as possible.

The Wrong and Right of Bergdorf Goodman

17

1975

I met with Phil Hawley at the Plaza Hotel about a week later. He had lots of problems—but not with me. Clearly, he viewed me as a source of turnaround ideas for the nearly empty White Plains store and sluggish Bergdorf Goodman on Fifth Avenue. Another great concern was the lawsuit involving Leonard Hankin, Bergdorf Goodman's executive vice president.

The lawsuit included Bergdorf Goodman, Saks Fifth Avenue, and Bonwit Teller. As reported in *WWD*, in October 1974, a federal grand Jury indicted Hankin, along with executives from Saks Fifth Avenue and Bonwit Teller, for conspiring to fix the prices of women's apparel in the New York City area. In addition, there were class action suits filed against the three stores. In August 1975, Hankin was fined $25,000. The legal actions were a demoralizing blow to Carter Hawley Hale and the Bergdorf Goodman management, not to mention the fact that they feared the loss of customer loyalty and long-term erosion of their reputation as merchants.

On behalf of himself and Ed Carter, Phil asked me to be the President and CEO of Bergdorf Goodman. Andrew Goodman would be the Chairman. We discussed the contract and financials that would make the move from B. Altman attractive.

One thing stopped me from jumping at the opportunity immediately. I told Phil that, before I accepted the position, I thought it imperative to have a discussion with Andrew

140

Goodman. I wanted to be certain I knew how he felt about my heading up Bergdorf Goodman since I would be the first non-family member to run the store in two generations.

Knowing of B.F.A.'s trauma in handing over her family's store, I presumed it would also be difficult for Andrew Goodman to have me take his place. He had been president of Bergdorf Goodman since his father had asked him to run the store in the mid-1950s. We agreed I would meet Andrew Goodman at his home in Rye that weekend.

I think Andrew knew of me only as the executive vice president and general merchandise manager of B. Altman. In the back of his mind, I'm sure he wondered, "How can he relate to the merchandising of Bergdorf Goodman?" Visiting with Andrew, I told him how intense my interest was in serving as the chief executive. I went back to my being brought up by Bill Holmes at Bonwit Teller. How I always related to better apparel. Andrew knew Bill Holmes, and greatly respected him. He also felt reassured that I had a solid fashion background.

In conclusion, he vowed to support me in taking over his position. The deal was done.

I cringed at telling Jack Burke and Randy Stambaugh of my decision to leave them. Jackie helped me through this. She recalled the time when I was associated with G. Fox, then under May Co. management, and felt so uncertain about my future. We had been staying at the Sherry Netherland Hotel on a trip. She recalled looking across the street at the splendid Bergdorf Goodman, never dreaming that, one day, I would be the CEO.

The day after I met with Phil Hawley, I called Jack and Randy and asked if I could meet with them together. A rare request of that type signaled a problem. Sitting with the two of them, I explained that I would be the new President and CEO of Bergdorf Goodman. Jack Burke was angry, and rightly so.

I volunteered to stay as long as they would like me to, and to help locate a successor. No, that wasn't necessary, they said. I could leave the company as soon as I finished my existing assignments in

Andrew Goodman, Leonard Hankin, Neal Fox and Ira Neimark

about two weeks. I understood their unhappiness, and left the meeting knowing that I had disappointed two men whom I held in the highest regard. Randy later told me that I had made the right decision, since it wasn't many years later that B. Altman & Co had to close.

Press releases came next. *WWD* and the *New York Times* were invited to the announcement of my appointment to Bergdorf Goodman in Andrew Goodman's office.

This caused a stir in the retail and wholesale community. Rumors swirled about what it would mean for the store, for fashion merchandising, and so on. Unfortunately, B. Altman had no replacement for me and decided to try to hire a key merchant from Carter Hawley Hale. That attempt failed, and a search continued for a very long time, which conveyed a sense of floundering. Meanwhile, since Andrew Goodman was to be on vacation during February of 1975, I felt it would be best for me not to report for work at Bergdorf Goodman while he was away. I officially joined Bergdorf Goodman after his return on March 3rd. By coincidence—and are there any coincidences, really?—March 3rd was the day I left for the Army Air Corps in 1943 to go to war and the day I returned in 1946 to Bonwit Teller. Being a bit superstitious, I felt this was my lucky day and a good omen. It was.

The pinball once again bounced in the right direction.

Lessons Learned

- As uplifting a feeling as it is to join a company as CEO that you have long admired, it is most important that the previous management of that company and you have a <u>clear</u> understanding of the <u>specific</u>—and clearly written—job responsibilities of all the executives involved.

- As difficult as it is to leave a company that you feel has been helpful in your career, particularly in being close to the senior executives, it is most important to leave on the best terms possible. Your paths will undoubtedly cross many times.

Upon my arrival at Bergdorf Goodman, Andrew had arranged a cocktail party for me to meet all the executives. A changing of the guard can seem strained in any company, but when a family dynasty hands a business over to a non-family member, questions arise in everyone's mind. Having experienced this situation at G. Fox., I imagined that Andrew Goodman was wondering. "How much does this man, whom I don't really know, want to change the family business that I have run for so many years?" Top management were also concerned. Would their jobs be secure? Merchandise management and buyers also wondered how the change would affect them. Below this level, people probably felt that, if they went about their own business, life would go on.

So what would I change? Who would feel shaken up?
Bergdorf Goodman had to determine where it stood in the
context of modern retailing. A critical factor was that Bergdorf
Goodman's customers were not only from New York, but also
from all over America and Europe. This determination did not
require demographic studies and expensive consultants. The
picture was very clear to me as to which retailers were the fashion leaders in New York.

Bloomindales, under Marvin Traub's aggressive management
and that of his fashion director, Katherine Murphy, had put
together all of the important fashion names. They had
cultivated the best of New York, Milan, and Paris. Yves Saint
Laurent Rive Gauche, Valentino, Ise Miyake, Missoni and many
more—Bloomingdales had it all. Young customers gathered
there and bought the young, contemporary lines, like Calvin
Klein. Fashion conscious customers found the most up-to-date
designer lines. The store advertised only the young and
designer lines to create a young "with it" store image, but more
conservative customers also felt at home. The men's division
adopted the same strategy: young fashion lines, as well as more
traditional designer lines. The successful combination of both
men's and women's made Bloomingdales *the* place to meet and
to shop. Ralph Lauren had been exclusive with Bloomingdales
up until the time, as my offer to take him over Manhattan in a
helicopter illustrated, that Bloomingdales was not the only store
in New York.

The other great success story was Henri Bendel, which
Geraldine "Jerry" Stutz had transformed into the hottest store on
or near Fifth Avenue in the 1960s. Recognizing Henri Bendel
held a great location on 57th Street across from Bergdorf
Goodman, but being limited in space, she devised a merchandising
concept every store in America was to copy at one time or another. First, Henri Bendel targeted the small-size fashion customer.
The best European and American designer lines available were
bought in sizes 2 to 6. Secondly, the Street of Shops for fashion

accessories was the envy of all retailers, and copied in various formats around the country. It seemed that every small-size fashion-conscious customer flocked to Henri Bendel for its merchandise assortments and cachet.

Saks Fifth Avenue was the third competitor to watch. Under the management of Robert Suslow, the store shifted from primarily carrying and advertising the Saks Fifth Avenue label. Instead, Saks added and promoted fashion labels at competitive pricelines, in addition to those already carried. This approach allowed Saks to carry an array of quality merchandise and store sales increased dramatically. There may have been a diminishing of the Saks exclusivity treasured by previous management, but the dramatic sales increases overcame that concern. Marvin Traub, Geraldine Stutz and Bob Suslow were consummate professionals.

My mission: to devise a strategy to overcome their dominance. My feeling from the very beginning was that fashion conscious women preferred to shop in a classic store like Bergdorf Goodman if we would carry broad and deep fashion assortments presented with drama and class. Good as it was, Henri Bendel was limited by space as to how many fashion lines it could carry. Bloomingdales had it all in terms of fashions and pricelines, but its abundance did not lure wealthy woman, who preferred a more intimate atmosphere. Saks, a formidable competitor, was growing very rapidly by promoting moderate prices as well as fashions. Our strategy then was to concentrate on luring the best European and American designer collections, be exclusive whenever possible, and present them with elegance.

Bergdorf Goodman had a fine reputation as a prestigious fashion store, but at this point, the important fashion lines at Bergdorf Goodman were limited to Halston, Givenchy, Hanai Mori, Pauline Trigere, Scherrer, and certain sportswear exclusives, such as Tiktiner. Recognizing the lack of the new labels at Bergdorf Goodman, I had to devise a strategy to convince the preeminent fashion designers that there was an important fourth player in the game who planned to be first.

I could see the potential in sales and profits, but the changes that would produce them could bother the previous management. Since the sales base of approximately $38 million—the Delman shoe lease contributed approximately $8 million to the total—was so low for a store with such an outstanding reputation at one of the best locations in the country, I felt the time to move forward aggressively was now. In all fairness, a family business not affiliated with other retailers lives in corporate isolation. Store planning, sales per square foot requirements, fashion lines, and all of the other ingredients necessary to stimulate profit and remain competitive in the future don't necessarily sit high on the list of priorities. Fortunately, with the fashion background I absorbed from Bonwit Teller, merchandise planning from Gladdings, storekeeping learned at G. Fox, and space allocation planning at B. Altman and Co., I felt qualified to move ahead.

Lesson Learned

- Whenever you take on a new responsibility, it is imperative to study the previous administration's strategies, as well as its strengths and weaknesses. The same study applies to your competition.

Shortly after my arrival, I asked the treasurer, Richard Silva, for a detailed financial history of the store. The information confirmed my original thinking: This was an opportunity equivalent to striking oil on Fifth Avenue. The analysis concentrated on need to reduce expenses and increase the gross profit. The need to increase sales was treated as secondary, something that would be helpful. This was surely putting the cart before the horse. It concerned me that even Andrew Goodman, as the owner and proprietor, had executives who should have pointed out to him their poor market share. I also confirmed my thinking that the merchants in the store were living in the comfort and security of a name and reputation, and not neccessarily utilizing their full abilities. I kept this report in my top desk drawer throughout my career at Bergdorf Goodman to remind me of how far we had come along. It was tempting, if I were ever to receive criticism from the previous management, to bring a reminder of this financial history to their attention. I showed restraint, and never did.

Lesson Learned

- Businesses and executives who are insulated and live in a vacuum tend not to see growth opportunities. It is important to measure your performance against your peers. One of the first measurements is productivity, that is, sales per square foot. The second is gross profit per square foot. The comparisons are easily available if you look for them. The next important step is to act on the information.

Out With the Old

18

1975

Bergdorf had room for younger customers, but they weren't there. I saw that as an opportunity, but one that could only be realized by cleaning house. The main floor of the store was the one most desperately in need of changes, some of which could be made quickly at little expense and some of which involved long-term headaches. Quick changes involved the cosmetic department, which had a terrible location, and art needlework, a destination department that had a prime traffic location. The Delman women's shoe department, on the other hand, not only took up a majority of the best space on the main floor, but it also was a potential source of a long-term headache.

The cosmetic department sat in an off-traffic location at the rear of the 58th Street entrance. It was too small to carry the assortment of cosmetic lines necessary to bring customers to that area. Over a weekend, the cosmetics department switched places with the handbag department at the front of the Fifth Avenue entrance. We also began the process of integrating new lines and dropping unpopular ones.

The handbag department moved to the back until the merchandising direction could be restructured. I had noticed over the years, whenever I was on a market trip to New York, I would stop off at different stores to see the newest merchandise presentations. Whenever I walked through Bergdorf Goodman's handbag department, I noticed a plastic tray at the end of the counter with a handwritten clearance sign for Walborg handbags. My puzzlement over that ended when I arrived at Bergdorf Goodman and found that, in most cases, the buyer of the department made the merchandise decisions.

Neither Andrew Goodman nor his executive vice president, Leonard Hankin, were merchandise managers, nor were they supposed to be. Andrew Goodman focused on the store's reputation as well as overseeing all major decisions of Bergdorf Goodman. As general manager, Leonard Hankin handled all day-to-day operations. He had great expertise regarding the fur department, and customers often solicited his advice, but there really was no general merchandise manager to give the buyers direction, or to develop an overall merchandising fashion point of view. Hence, the buyers went their own individual ways.

This was dramatically proven to me a few weeks after I arrived. The costume jewelry buyer and glove/hosiery buyer were departing for Europe. As was my habit whenever buyers were going into the market, particularly Europe, I would meet with them to review their buying plans, to clarify merchandise objectives, vendors to be visited, and budgets. In this case, both buyers were vague. Giving them the benefit of the doubt, I figured I was too new to judge their strategy. Upon their return ten days later, I met them for my customary debriefing. The costume jewelry buyer saw nothing new that appealed to her and filled in her stock as she had done in the past. The glove/hosiery buyer had done the same. A few months later, I was in Europe and met with the European office's accessory buyer, Franca Bini. I asked her to explain why the two buyers who had just returned found nothing exciting to buy. A real professional, Franca explained the Bergdorf Goodman accessory buyers were always looking for non-fashion merchandise to avoid markdowns. This confirmed my feeling that our buyers, for the most part, made individual merchandise decisions and that meant "playing it safe." Over the years I learned that buyers who had neither the conviction nor taste to find the newest and most exiting merchandise should not be in the fashion business. But we obviously had them in some key departments. I asked Franca Bini to take me to the best, and most expensive handbag and costume jewelry resources. Many had never seen a Bergdorf Goodman accessory buyer before, and welcomed me enthusiastically.

Other problems arose that required a complete revision of customer policy. I asked the costume jewelry buyer why she had "no returns after six days" on the price tags of merchandise. She explained that some customers would wear the merchandise to a party or wherever and then return the jewelry for credit. "Is that the policy of the jewelry departments in the local competition," I asked? She didn't know. The knit dress buyer set her own policy on returns as well. No more would buyers make a policy like that. I eliminated this problem immediately.

To finish my review of the main floor, the Delman shoe department had been there front and center for many years. When Andrew's father, Edwin Goodman—famous for his custom-made clothes—was building the store, he wasn't sure what to put on the main floor. He decided that women's shoes would fill that space and leased it to Delman Shoes, an English company. The lease was long term, and the rent was the lowest I had ever seen. In most retail companies, the leased shoe departments paid rent somewhere around 15 percent and up. Delman was paying Bergdorf Goodman 11 percent. So we had a high volume, low-rent shoe department occupying approximately four thousand square feet of the best space in the store. And since it was a leased department, their management decided what shoe lines to carry. With high sales and low markdowns the order of the day, they settled on Bruno Magli and Ferragamo, two good lines, at the exclusion of others. It took years for the lease to run its course, to give us the ability to move the shoe department to the second floor, and to add the necessary fashion lines. When we did, we replaced the shoe area on the main floor with high-margin jewelry, Barry Kieselstein-Cord and Angela Cummings shops, and many other top, precious jewelry collections.

After this department-by-department and floor-by-floor analysis, I allowed myself to dream. It was time to build a stronger fashion and buying organization to do justice to this fine store. That included hiring a fashion director, as well as taking a closer look at what the store had done right in terms of fashion.

First, I had to overcome a small administrative barrier. When I became CEO, Carter Hawley Hale recommended having a young fashion merchant from Neiman Marcus, Neal Fox, move to Bergdorf Goodman as executive vice president and general merchandise manager. I did not think this was a good idea. At this point, Bergdorf Goodman was still a small store and I intended to develop its growth personally based on my merchandising experience. To have two people developing merchandising concepts would be self-defeating, and I made my strong feelings known. CHH, however, had made the firm decision, and asked me to do it. "But," I said, "The monkey is on your back." This made it difficult for Neal Fox, who understood fashion, but he didn't feel it was necessary to have a fashion director. Or if we did have a fashion director, he thought, that person should report to him as the general merchandise manager of the store. This idea undermined my whole concept of the fashion director, as it had worked so successfully at B. Altman. Neal Fox left the store a year later, but went on to become a successful retailer as president of Sulka.

Lesson Learned

- Business principles and standards must be set and maintained. Principles as to what you stand for should not be compromised, and standards should never be lowered.

Bergdorf Goodman had, of course, cultivated strengths over the years that helped it rise above competitors.

In the nineteen fifties, Bergdorf Goodman had launched an effort to bring younger customers to the store. They built new departments and offered moderate prices specifically for these new customers. The shops were called Miss Bergdorf, catering to the daughters of their regulars. For the teens, there was Bigi. On many trips to New York from New England, I visited the impressive Miss Bergdorf shops. Other retailers and I recognized the strategy, and in various ways adapted the idea and used some of the same fashion resources.

Decades later, the shops were still there and hadn't changed a bit. Fashion retailing doesn't stand still, so most other retailers had taken steps to develop a moderate-priced apparel business with a contemporary feel. Harrod's "Way In Shop" in London and Bloomingdales young departments in New York were two successful examples.

In contrast, Miss Bergdorf departments were developed when the dress business dominated sales in ready-to-wear. Miss Bergdorf was strong there, with lines like Jerry Silverman. However, the misses sportswear business had grown tremendously in most retail stores, whereas it hadn't at Bergdorf Goodman.

Miss Bergdorf had to get into the sportswear business, at least in proportion to its dress business. Here, too, I saw the buyer's mentality that had kept down the accessories departments. When I asked the Miss Bergdorf sportswear buyer, who had a small Calvin Klein business, "Why will a customer buy from your small selection instead of Bloomingdale's large assortments four blocks away?" Her response was that she had a better selection. Needless to say, one of the first and easiest projects to accomplish was to build the sportswear business with larger space, larger assortments, and an experienced fashion buying staff who did not delude themselves that the competition was asleep on their feet. We moved Calvin Klein to a larger location on the third floor and brought in Barbara Lamonica from B. Altman, who built one of the strongest Calvin Klein businesses in New York City.

Not all of my early ideas worked well, by the way. In an effort to have younger and more fashionable looking women shopping in the store, I contacted some modeling agencies and offered the models a 50 percent discount on purchases made at Bergdorf Goodman. The response was negative for two important reasons.

One, the models already received discounts on lines they modeled. Two, Bergdorf did not have the fashion assortments to interest the models. I am pleased to add that when Bergdorf Goodman regained its rightful fashion position, the models shopped in the store without discounts.

It was at this time I decided that every employee in the store should have a clear definition of what I felt the store stood for, and who the customer was that we wanted to cater to. I didn't need demographic studies or consultants, since I had grown up across Fifth Avenue at Bonwit Teller, and for many years, observed the customers there very carefully. I was confidant I knew the customer Bergdorf Goodman should target. She was:

• The woman who went to the best restaurants

• The woman who stayed at the best hotels

• The woman who belonged to the best clubs

• The woman who went to the best resorts

This woman should have a store that treats her as she expects to be treated at all of the above. And because the contemporary fashion woman considered Bergdorf Goodman:

• Old, dull, expensive, and intimidating.

It was our goal to make the store:

• Young, exciting, expensive and intimidating.

A number of years later at the Hotel Ritz in Paris, I told the president of the hotel, Mr. Klein, when I return to Bergdorf Goodman, I ask my people, "Why can't we run our store like they run the Hotel Ritz?" His reply was, "That's funny, when I return from New York, I ask my people, 'Why can't we run the hotel like Bergdorf Goodman runs their store?'"

An example of maintaining our standards is an experience we had with Halston. Halston had developed a strong reputation as a millinery designer at Bergdorf Goodman years earlier. During the early 1970's, he had his own design house and great success, especially using a new fabric called Ultrasuede. His shop on the second floor of Bergdorf Goodman attracted good publicity, but only a small clientele. One night, in passing the Museum of Natural History, I saw a large flag flying that announced a party for Halston selling a complete collection of women's inexpensive apparel to JC Penney. Halston's owners had made the licensing arrangement without discussing the implications with us. We immediately dropped the line. A fashion reporter called me from an out of town newspaper asking, "Why?" I explained, "If you had bought a Halston evening dress for $1,000 at Bergdorf Goodman, and then saw a JC Penney ad for a Halston evening dress for $100, would you feel pleased with your purchase?" She replied, "Enough said." This experience was long before the fashion designers began making different divisions in order to cover from the lowest price customer to the highest, nevertheless, they still have to differentiate what each line stands for and to be cautious regarding what type of store will represent them.

Lessons Learned

- When taking over an underperforming business it is important to analyze the strengths as well as the weaknesses of the business. The strengths should be developed and the weaknesses eliminated. This applies to merchandise as well as people.

- It is important that all levels of personnel be made aware of what the goals and ambitions for the business are. They, in turn, in carrying out their responsibilities must reflect the chief executive's visions for the company.

First on Fifth

19

---- **1976–1978** ----

R ichard Hoffman, a legend in the men's business, represented
Christian Dior neckties, sold to high quality retailers on a
semi exclusive basis. Dick Hoffman, with whom I developed a relationship when I was at B. Altman, was the last of a breed of sales
representatives. He was on a first-name basis with the head of every
store that he sold to and to many that he didn't.

Less than six months after coming to Bergdorf Goodman, Dick
asked me to lunch with Bill Arnold, then the CEO of Associated Dry
Goods, and Joseph Pivirotto, the president. Lord & Taylor was their
flagship store in New York, and I knew them from various social
events such as The Good Guys Club. Bill's question took me by
complete surprise: Would I consider moving to Lord and Taylor as
president? Flattered as I was, I didn't see how I could ethically or
morally justify such a move so soon after joining Bergdorf Goodman.

They chose Joseph Brooks who was an excellent merchant. Joe
Brooks successfully took Lord & Taylor on an aggressive expansion program that increased the sales, and broadened the customer
base considerably.

I never regretted my decision to stay at Bergdorf Goodman, and
you will soon see why.

Lesson Learned

- In considering opportunities of any nature, business ethics
  should be at the top of the list of not only retailers, but all

155

business people. Fine reputations can be destroyed by lapses in good and honest judgment.

I wanted to do everything to succeed at Bergdorf Goodman, of course, so I once again recruited Dawn Mello to head the fashion office. We'd had a good run together at B. Altman, and in joining Bergdorf, I quickly set her on the task of recommending new apparel and accessories lines. An early idea she had was to bring a few young magazine fashion editors to be buyers; she felt they would have the proven instincts with a natural feeling for fashion. We also had to evaluate the lines we already carried and determine their position in the store's future. I described Dawn's job as a three-legged stool. One leg was to be sure that she and her staff shopped every new and important fashion line. The second, make sure the merchandise division bought the fashion lines her office recommended. The third, promote those lines with Fifth Avenue windows and by having them featured in ads. This promotional support obviously encouraged the merchandise division to follow the recommendations of the fashion office. In order to be truly creative, I also believed that the fashion director needed to report directly to senior management, unlike the view that many others held. To use another analogy, like the Supreme Court, the fashion office should be independent of the legislature, if you will.

At that time, Pauline Trigere was the largest designer line in the store. Her line had such importance for Bergdorf Goodman, and *vice versa*, that she was the only designer who had permission to work in the windows with the display department. The problem, however, was the Trigere merchandise suited only the mature customer's tastes. We needed younger designers, domestic and foreign. I told Ms. Trigere that we intended to add another designer buyer to our staff, someone who would buy Geoffrey Beene, Bill Blass, Oscar de la Renta. Fearing the loss of her position as the major fashion collection for the store, she got upset.

Her concern captured the kind of conflicted perceptions about our fashion direction for the store that made a transition difficult. As I told Pauline Trigere, we felt responsible to our mature customers, and did not want to see an erosion of that business. But we needed to add the younger fashion conscious customer as well. It would not be to Bergdorf Goodman's benefit to swap one customer for the other. The net gain would be zero.

Our goal to achieve and then to maintain Bergdorf Goodman's dominant fashion position required the judgment as to which "luxury" fashion designers would grow for the future, and further, would be able to maintain their fashion leadership for the years ahead. There were many designers, but relatively few who would fit those criteria. In France, luxury collections were from Yves Saint Laurent, Karl Lagerfeld for Chanel and Jean Claude Gaultier. In Italy, Giorgio Armani, Gianfranco Ferre and Valentino. In America, Geoffrey Beene, Bill Blass, Oscar de la Renta and Calvin Klein's couture for Bergdorf Goodman, would also qualify, as would, Ralph Lauren.

There were also many younger designers emerging who would hit their stride in the years to come. But luxury designers would always be an important part of the mix, in contrast to those designers who would change their fashion direction based on their interpretation of the latest trends. (The "grunge look" is one example of a bad idea gone wrong that some designers use.)

Geoffrey Beene maintained his outstanding reputation with his couture status as a creative innovator, limiting his distribution to relatively few stores. Bill Blass was a leader in luxury fashion and also distributed his licensed lines, such as BlassPort to selected retail outlets. Oscar de la Renta combined the aura of couture with his early association with Balenciaga, later with Lanvin, and much later as couture designer for Balmain in Paris, in addition to his own designer business in New York.

So Dawn and I set about to do two things with the fashion market: convey our intentions, and understand their thinking about

Bergdorf Goodman's position compared to the competition. To that end, Dawn and I had a series of lunches with designers.

Two lunches stand out in my memory. Bill Blass bluntly stated that we should take down the Bergdorf Goodman name and put up Neiman Marcus. We assured him that we had every intention to build Bergdorf Goodman's name as the leading fashion store in New York and America as well. We invited him to help us accomplish that goal. He responded graciously, and a few years later even acknowledged that his callous remark was out of order. He also made a point of saying that we were well on our way to accomplishing our goal.

Molly Parnis was just as blunt, but came at us from a completely different direction. The ladies room, she noted, did not meet her standards of cleanliness. And by the way, neither did other areas of the store. She, too, eventually became a friend and a fan—of the cleaner store.

Lessons Learned

- In attempting to imbue a store with personality, to make it clear what it stands for, and to determine who your customer is, you need exquisite and defining judgment. A top-flight fashion director can best do the balancing to keep the older customer and attract the younger customer. Over the years I have noticed some retailers asked their wives for advice. Not recommended.

- Asking professionals, as well as customers their opinion regarding your efforts, will give you some candid thoughts you may not have been aware of.

The breakthrough came while I was attending the couture fashion shows in Paris in 1976, which gave me a thrilling idea to jump-start the recognition of Bergdorf Goodman in the fashion world. I had been at the store for a year by that time, and was anxious for a way to take its reputation for fashion to the top. The idea took shape after seeing the Yves Saint-Laurent peasant costume show, which featured the most exciting merchandise that I had ever seen. I knew that this was the type of merchandise that would bring the attention of the fashion press as well as the fashion customers necessary to reinvigorate Bergdorf Goodman.

For many years, Bergdorf Goodman was famous as one of the few retailers in New York to make custom clothes, and as a major importer of Paris originals. Bergdorf Goodman moved into the ready-to-wear business a bit later than the competition, but still maintained a high profile reputation in made-to-order. Eventually, as American ready-to-wear became more important, the store gave up the custom-made business except for the millinery and the fur departments. Recalling the couture background of Bergdorf Goodman, and seeing the beautiful clothes of the 1976 Paris shows, I felt this was the time once again for the store to import the couture and reclaim its place in the world of fashion.

The Paris Couture experience also helped Dawn Mello confirm her fashion strategy as to which designer lines we had to carry to catch up to the three leading fashion stores, Bloomingdales, Henri Bendel and Saks Fifth Avenue. She stressed two collections in this strategy. First, if we were to have the French designers sell to us, Yves Saint Laurent's Rive Gauche, the top fashion ready-to-wear line out of Paris, had to be convinced to come to Bergdorf Goodman. We knew that the others would follow.

The City of Lights itself played an important role in our success. Over breakfast meetings at the Hotel Ritz, lunches at La Voltaire, dinner at Le Grand Vefour, Taillevant and L'Orangcrie and many others, we solidified our business relationships at the same time we enjoyed some of the best restaurants in the world. Their fine ambiance and cuisine combined with our conversation produced the results we wanted.

The Hotel Ritz at Place Vendome was my headquarters. The breakfast meetings in the main dining room could have as many as three meetings going on at the same time, and I moved from table to table to be sure everything was going in the right direction. One table could have the executives from Yes Saint Laurent, another Dennis Colban of Charvet and the third could be the Grandes, from our buying office.

The Hotel Ritz was and is one of the great hotels of the world, and always added class to the many successful business arrangements completed there. A humorous aside: Andrew Goodman told me on one of his visits to the Hotel Ritz, he and Nena Goodman were having drinks in the Hemingway Bar and saw Halston, the Bergdorf Goodman millinery designer, with a friend having champagne and caviar. Andrew said he wasn't sure he appreciated having Halston living so high on the hog on Bergdorf's expense account.

One particular dinner meeting at Le Grand Vefour has stayed in my mind. Early on, we knew it was imperative to have Yves Saint Laurent's Rive Gauche collection at Bergdorf Goodman, and had many meetings with their executives, to no avail as we didn't get a definitive answer. We finally figured that Didier Grumbach who was a principal in the YSL company, could make it happen. I invited him to dinner at Le Grand Vefour, described in promotional materials as "tucked away in the Palaise-Royal Gardens, Le Grand Vefour—one of the gems of the 18th century decorative art—[and a] temple of Parisian gastronomy for politicians, artists and writers for over 200 years."

We were seated at a banquet, Diddier inside, and I sat next to him. During the wonderful dinner, I did my best to convince him of the wisdom to sell the Rive Gauche collection to Bergdorf Goodman. When we finished dinner with no commitment forthcoming I told Didier, that I wasn't going to move in order to let him out of his seat until he agreed to my request, even if we had to stay there all night.

As I recall, he commented, "Let me see what I can do." Knowing Didier, that was a big step forward. We left the restaurant with my feeling that this restaurant that had hosted Napoleon, Danton, Hugo, Colette, and Cocteau was a great place to have won the collection.

Part of luring Rive Gauche meant eliminating the bad feelings that the management carried from a past rejection. Bergdorf Goodman had, I'd heard, been one of the original stores Rive Gauche had approached to carry the line, and turned it down. We worked out a plan with Pierre Berge of Yves Saint Laurent, Hubert Givenchy, and Jacques Rouet of Dior that laid the foundation for more serious efforts later. They agreed to sell Bergdorf Goodman fifteen styles each to be presented at special French couture fashion shows at Bergdorf Goodman. The format they all insisted on was that each designer would show the same number of couture models—fifteen each; no more, no less. At one show, due to a Givenchy two-piece ensemble, an extra model was shown in error. Mr. Rouet immediately complained. We calmed him down, but this highlights how carefully they watched each other, and now Bergdorf Goodman. Elieth Roux, in charge of the couture production, had a superior group of customers who bought at the shows. Nancy Reagan and Betsy Bloomingdale were among them.

Nancy Reagan and Friend

The second part of Dawn's strategy, and possibly more important, was attracting the Italians. Dawn was convinced that the Italian designers were in the ascendancy, and not really developed as much as they could be by the New York retailers. If we

Diana Vreeland and Two Models

could attract Fendi, who had become the "must have" handbag and fur coat designer line, to Bergdorf Goodman, then we felt the other Italian designers would follow. The hurdles to overcome were that Bloomingdales carried the Fendi leather goods, and Henri Bendel carried the Fendi furs.

Our respective roles in implementing the two-part strategy were as follows: Dawn Mello identified the fashion houses we were to carry. I crafted the tactical plan to convince the targeted fashion houses that, if you weren't in Bergdorf Goodman, you were missing the opportunity to be presented in the highest profile fashion store in America.

My financial colleagues at Bergdorf confronted me about the wisdom of this grand scheme: How can we afford to buy the couture models at their high prices, sell them at cost, or less, and not lose a fortune? I explained that we took markdowns each season on hundreds of thousands of dollars of merchandise that no one cared about. For the publicity alone, it would be invaluable to

From the Ira Neimark Collection

Dennis Colban of Charvet

enable our customers to buy couture at a price comparable to Paris. Fortunately, the French couture fashion show project, which ran for two years, got overwhelming attention from the press, the market, and most importantly, the customers.

One immediate effect came directly from the press coverage. Dennis Colban, the owner of the Charvet shop on the Place Vendome in Paris, told me when he saw the French couture once again being shown at Bergdorf Goodman, he knew something important was beginning. He was one of the first of many famous European shops and designers to sell to Bergdorf Goodman, many of them exclusively.

Throughout this time, through different intermediaries—from Richard Salomon, the head of Charles of the Ritz and a principal of Rive Gauche, to John Fairchild, the head of *WWD*—I worked to bring the Rive Gauche line to Bergdorf Goodman. After two years of negotiating, the line finally came to Bergdorf Goodman and met everyone's expectations, including those of my financial colleagues.

An interesting aside: When we were finally told we could write the Yves Saint Laurent, Rive Gauche line in 1978, there was a caveat. The manufacturer for Rive Gauche also manufactured Chanel. At the time, Phillipe Guibourge designed Chanel, which was not very successful. We were required to purchase a certain amount of Chanel in order to buy Rive Gauche. This situation reminded me that during World War II in order to buy a bottle of scotch, you had to buy a bottle of rum. The caveat led to a good outcome, however. Alain Wertheimer, the owner of Chanel, made two wise decisions and eventually hired Karl Lagerfeld to design Chanel, and brought in Arie Kopelman, the vice-chairman and general manager of Doyle Dane Bernbach, as president of Chanel U.S.A.

As our influence grew steadily, I was in a good position to speak directly to the designers about what Bergdorf Goodman wanted. For example, when Yves Saint Laurent launched their new fragrance, Opium. In what I saw as a peculiar move, the distributor selected Bloomingdales and Bendels as the retailers in New York to introduce the perfume. I was disturbed, and called Pierre Berge to tell him so. After all, Bergdorf Goodman represented Yves Saint Laurent, and not being included in this important introduction seemed untoward. Being a gentleman and good businessman, he sent dozens of bottles of Opium at no cost to be given as a gift to our Yves Saint Laurent customers. This stimulated good press, and shortly after, Bergdorf Goodman also carried Opium.

Lessons Learned

- A good idea, whether old or new, is a good idea. Going back to the couture to jump-start Bergdorf Goodman's fashion image worked beyond our fondest dreams. Fashion-conscious customers are always interested when the fashion press recognizes exciting ideas.

- Tobé's comment many years ago, "Front page news is front page fashion" applied appropriately to the reintroduction of couture to Bergdorf Goodman.

- Whatever ingredients are required to complete the successful product mix of a company, identifying the right ingredient is first, and determination and tenacity to procure the merchandise is next.

As plans rolled into realities, I would occasionally remember walks through the store in my early days at Bergdorf with people like Alain Wertheimer and Claude Arpels of Van Cleef and Arpels. A small Van Cleef boutique opened into Bergdorf Goodman and I wanted to assure Claude that Van Cleef and Arpels would be in good company then, and going into the future. Both men seemed to think I was dreaming as I described the coming grandeur. I was.

The Italian Strategy **20**

---------------------------- **1976–1978** ----------------------------

Dawn Mello's two-part fashion strategy looked like a promising way for Bergdorf Goodman to reclaim its luxury cachet. The store had spent the credibility it had earned over the years and was now drawing on its principal. As her "Italian Strategy" took shape, we saw a clear path to returning the store to the forefront of fashion retailing. Step one: Bring Fendi into Bergdorf Goodman.

Though at that time the Fendi name had not yet reached the heights of popularity it enjoys today, it was clear that things were headed in that direction. For instance, a side trip to Rome had become essential for store buyers and fashion editors on their way to Milan for the Prêt-a Porter, for only in Rome could they buy what was quickly becoming a "must-have" item: the Fendi handbag. In addition to leather goods, the Fendi furs, under the cultivation of Karl Lagerfeld, were beginning to develop the most novel, unconventional, and relaxed silhouettes, attracting attention across the high-end fur market.

Despite their growing popularity, we felt that Fendi was missing an opportunity to establish a real presence in the New York market. Their products were split between Henri Bendel and Bloomingdale's—Henri Bendel sold Fendi's furs while Bloomingdale's carried their leather goods. What we intended to propose to Fendi was an exclusive arrangement with Bergdorf Goodman that would guarantee prime locations within the store, plus aggressive marketing for Fendi merchandise through Fifth Avenue windows, advertising and fashion shows, and so forth.

Convincing Fendi, which was still a family-run company, to bring their leather goods and furs into Bergdorf Goodman was an adventure. It began with a request placed through Count Franco Savorelli di Lauriano, the grand advisor to Fendi, for an introduction to Carla Fendi, the head of the firm. Carla was one of the five sisters who were all involved in running the company. Through Count Savorelli, Dawn Mello, my wife Jackie, and I made plans to meet Carla Fendi at the Plaza Athenée in Paris for lunch, right after the Givenchy fashion show. Of course, as luck would have it, the show ran late. Knowing that people are not generally flattered by tardiness, and also aware that we had a choice between offending Givenchy or Carla Fendi, we decided to take our chances with the French and rush off to meet the Italian. Carla was very polite, considering how late we were. We explained our proposal over lunch, and were either convincing enough or entertaining enough to be invited to Rome to meet with the other four Fendi sisters. As we exchanged farewells, Carla said that she would also appreciate it if we would be discreet about our visit to Rome.

At the end of the Paris Prêt-a Porter shows, most of the buyers and principals of the other U.S. stores were heading back to New York, while Jackie, Dawn and I were surreptitiously flying to Rome. Acutely aware of Carla Fendi's directive, I had to use every trick Ian Fleming had ever taught me in order to slip unseen into Charles De Gaulle Airport. Everything felt distinctly cloak-and-dagger. Not only were there merchants that needed to be avoided, but we knew that John Fairchild, the head of *WWD*, was somewhere in the terminal. If he saw us boarding a flight to Rome instead of New York, he would have been the one most likely to put the pieces together. A story in *WWD* would not only have blown our cover, it would have seriously jeopardized our strategy to be the dominant Fendi store in Manhattan. So while we waited for the New York flight to depart, each of us huddled in a separate telephone booth, conversing very intently with the France Telecom dial tone. James Bond could have done better, but at least it worked.

Once in Rome, our meeting with the Fendi sisters took place in Count Rudi Crespi, the public relations representative for Fendi USA, and his wife, Consuelo's magnificent 16th-century apartment. The five sisters were seated around a large oval dining room table. As Dawn and I presented our case to this forum of five powerful women, I couldn't shake the feeling that we were arranging a marriage contract of some sort. Later, as they were discussing the proposal among themselves in Italian, one of the sisters, Anna, directed a question at us in English. She had a daughter, Maria Theresa; when Maria comes to the States, would we take care of her? Jackie, mother that she is, said she would be delighted to look after Maria Theresa. Now, whether this seemingly innocent question was a calculated litmus test of some sort I can't say, but all of a sudden it was "Cara mia," and smiles all around. Later, Dawn and I told Jackie that if we got the Fendi line, it would be thanks to her.

Later that day, we were told that the Fendi sisters' final decision would be made only after Count Savorelli (I was never able to discover whether hiring Italian aristocracy was a Fendi company practice, or they simply enjoyed having royalty on staff) visited Bergdorf Goodman to appraise the possible locations for the Fendi products. Savorelli was from one of the oldest royal families in Milan. A charming gentleman, he was so proud of his city that one night he took us on a long tour to prove that it was just as beautiful and important as Rome. After an impassioned tour that included La Scala, the Duomo Cathedral, and the Santa Maria della Grazia (with Leonardo da Vinci's "Last Supper"), I was convinced that except for the Vatican and Forum ruins, Milan was everything Count Savorelli claimed.

When Savorelli visited the store a week later, we showed him the large area at the front of the main Fifth Avenue floor where we anticipated placing the handbag and leather goods shop. After working out some display details, we had our first disagreement—where to put the furs. We finally agreed to keep the furs in the fur department, and one night, less than a week later, I received a long distance phone call from Rome. It was Count Crespi. I still recall his words: "Ira," he said, with his wonderful Italian accent, "the Fendi's have made their decision. Bergdorf Goodman is the store of their choice." I was so excited, I think I might have gotten a bit emotional.

Lesson Learned

- When building a business, you have to know both who your present customer is, and who you want your new customer to be. After that, the objective is deciding what type of merchandise or service will satisfy them both.

While there was little doubt that the Fendi bags and leather goods would be a success, not everyone was enthusiastic about the furs. Andrew Goodman, like his father, Edwin, before him, took a great interest in the Bergdorf Goodman fur department. The store's furs, under the supervision of the legendary Murry Singer, were at one time considered to be the best in the country. Andrew Goodman was a traditionalist and he told me that "those unconventional Fendi furs should not be carried in the store." It was too late. The furs had been bought; and a few days later they were on the floor.

I wasn't pleased that the chairman was unhappy with part of our new strategy. For the first few days after the furs went on sale, I kept finding reasons to drop by the fur department to check on sales. I remember one incident in particular that happened just a few days after the furs arrived. Stanley Marcus had stopped by to see the new Fendi furs. Before leaving, he asked us to call him at his hotel and let him know how many furs we had sold that day. By the time he left the store we had sold four. By the time we called him that evening, we had sold eight.

Printed with permission of *Women's Wear Daily*

Fendi Fur Fashion Show

Part of our success was due to an aggressive young salesman named Jack Cohen. Jack related to the Fendi furs. He understood Karl Lagerfeld's unconstructed furs, for example, making novelty furs like squirrel look like mink.

Just before Christmas of that year, Yoko Ono called and asked for an assortment of furs to be brought to the Dakota for her and John Lennon. Jack and his assistant took over about 40 furs. When they arrived, Yoko selected one fur jacket. John approved, and then they asked Jack and his assistant to leave the room. Jack was downcast to think that he had only been able to sell one fur. When they asked him back into the room, John and Yoko said they would buy all 40 furs as Christmas presents for friends.

Our arrangement with Fendi gave them a shop in Bergdorf Goodman that opened onto Fifth Avenue, and with that came a very high profile and strong sales volume. We presented their merchandise in our Fifth Avenue windows, ran ads in *The New York Times*, *Vogue* and *Harpers Bazaar*, and also held major fashion shows to help build excitement about both Fendi and Bergdorf Goodman. In fact, the fashion shows became the place where many of our customers went to see and be seen. But much as Fendi benefited from Bergdorf Goodman, Bergdorf Goodman profited hugely from the Fendi relationship. Our exclusive deal with them gave us a unique cachet, as well as the ability to stage the trendsetting fashion shows that helped redefine the public image of the store. Thanks to Fendi, and soon thereafter, Aldo Pinto and Mariuccia Mandelli of Krizia, and other Italian designers became eager to enter into similar arrangements with us. Before long Bergdorf Goodman was becoming the fashion store of the Eighties.

This mutually beneficial relationship with Fendi continued for a number of years, until the Fendis decided that it would be to their best interest to broaden their distribution. Because our strategy had always been to build the Bergdorf Goodman reputation through exclusive or semi-exclusive arrangements with top designers, Fendi's new distribution strategy did not fit into our game plan. Therefore, it was my bittersweet responsibility to visit Carla and her sister Paola, who was in charge of the furs, and tell them of my decision to discontinue our business relationship. Happily, there was no rancor. We did well for each other, and we both knew it. Thanks to Fendi, and later, Armani, Yves Saint's Rive Gauche, Chanel, Krizia, Valentino, and Ungaro, as well as many other important designer lines, Bergdorf Goodman had established itself as the place where fashion-conscious customers came to shop.

Lesson Learned

- When trying to revitalize a business, there is almost always something—a trend, product line, or expert—that has enough recognition in your industry to redefine your company's meaning in the eyes of customers. As soon as you discover this critical element, it's imperative that you pull out all the stops to align your company with this new direction.

Friends and Enemies Within

21

All the while we developed new merchandise concepts, problems in the back office had the potential to derail our progress. The financial management of Bergdorf Goodman was unlike their counterparts that I'd worked with at Bonwit Teller and G. Fox. They were defensive, instead of facing the realities of the new world of retailing.

As I mentioned, early on in my days at Bergdorf I had come across a McKinsey & Company report, written a few years before I arrived, that recommended expense reduction as the path to Bergdorf Goodman's profitability. It didn't occur to the financial or merchandise divisions that the great financial potential for Bergdorf Goodman was to build sales on the newest fashion collections that Bloomingdales and Bendel had developed so successfully. They saw Bendel across the street and Bloomingdales only four blocks away as competition to be ignored.

Other basic facts had escaped them. For example, bills to our customers were going out late, and our receivables were slow coming in. The legal implications of late billing were serious; that was another problem we didn't need. I asked Phil Hawley to send us one of Carter Hawley Hale's professional financial executives to help straighten out receivables and payables functions, while I concentrated on the merchandise areas. Phil sent us Ardern Batchelder, the retired president of The Emporium, San Francisco.

173

After plowing through the billing problems, he and I discussed the need for a capable chief financial officer. Mutual contacts introduced us to Stephen Elkin, the financial head of Hahnes, New Jersey, a department store owned by Associated Dry Goods. He had sterling references, one of which described him as "being too smart." This concerned a few of our executives, but I had a self-made motto, "pros hire pros, and dummies hire dummies." Steve was a pro who belonged with us.

After convincing Steve Elkin that, even though his present company did $50 million annually in sales, the same as Bergdorf, their $50 million was different from ours. He accepted my logic and agreed to join us as chief financial officer. He also wanted the responsibility of chief operating officer. First things first, I told him. Straighten out the financial division, and then add on operations responsibilities. My rationale was, if operations reported to him they would be camping at his door, asking what to do. That, in my opinion would have inhibited his financial responsibilities.

Steve began by disallowing some of the financial entries, thereby correcting our notion that we had actually made a small profit. He did help us move toward real profitability, however, by recognizing the merits of the weeks-of-supply/unit open-to-buy procedure. He embraced it, developed it, and eventually had it programmed on our computers. Because of Steve's keen business judgment, his ability to control inventories and manage expenses with our growth in sales, eventually helped to make Bergdorf Goodman become a highly profitable retailer. Later, Steve went on to become the Chairman and CEO of Bergdorf Goodman.

Lesson Learned

To be successful in the fashion business, as in other businesses, there are three basic elements required for success.

One. Is the concept correct for the business? As a corollary, what does the business stand for?

Two. Is the financing appropriate?

Three. Is the organization professional?

All three are required; otherwise the business will collapse like a house of cards.

With Steve and Dawn Mello on board, I had partners to help me smooth the road ahead. Dawn had the taste and talent to select the right designers, and promote the merchandise in order to attain the "Bergdorf Goodman Point of View." Steve added his skill to plan the sales and to monitor the expenses, both necessary to give the service required for the Bergdorf Goodman customer—while operating profitably.

Two other critical merchandising techniques were used to generate the sales, and to maintain the proper inventory in relationship to sales for a respectable gross profit.

One was the unit weeks-of-supply program in which buyers, with the supervision of their divisional merchandise manager, entered the number of units they planned to sell by classification each week for the planned season. This was based on the number of units sold last year, as a guide. If a fashion collection looked strong, the buyer could increase the plan. If the collection was not strong, the buyer would reduce the unit sales plan. After the units were filled in, a weeks-of-supply number was agreed to, and the inventory computed accordingly. This program allowed designers who were growing, such as Calvin Klein or Donna Karan, to have as much inventory as was required, as long as the buyer could plan realistic sales figures after viewing the shows.

In effect, the dollar open-to-buy was the result of the unit plan, not the other way around. In most stores the buyer is given a set dollar amount of open-to-buy based on many variables, usually decided by the financial department. They are locked in with little flexibility. The unit weeks-of-supply plan allowed the open-to-buy to increase or decrease depending on the weekly trend of each department. This approach was one of the major factors that contributed to Bergdorf Goodman's rapid sales and profit growth.

The second technique was the vendor program. To use another Bill Holmes maxim, "If the manufacturers are with you, half the battle is won." I included Beatrice Auerbach's "term books" listing the sales and discounts with each vendor. Both concepts were combined for the Bergdorf Goodman vendor program marketing plan. After vendors were selected to be in the store, or selected to remain in the store, I introduced them to this program.

When we selected a manufacturer for the vendor program, the merchandise manager and the buyer knew that they were part of a consensus agreement with the fashion office that the vendor was a candidate for inclusion. I and the vendor's CEO determined the planned potential sales growth, and gross profit requirements in order to determine the sales promotion programs required to build the line over at least a three year period. The buyer and the divisional had input, but it was management of Bergdorf Goodman and the principal representing the vendor who agreed to the strategic plan. I found that all vendor principals desired a long range plan, whereas buyers and vendor sales managers were more interested in the tactical program, as they should be.

We recorded our agreements on a page, not a contract requiring signatures, but a page of goals. We mutually agreed to the amount of sales we felt that could be developed in the first year and beyond for the next three to five years. I had never met a principal of a wholesale business who was not interested in growing his business for five years when talking to the retailer he was interested in doing business with. We also mutually agreed to a target for gross margin. We committed when Bergdorf Goodman would feature the designer in major ads, windows, and fashion shows. We listed provisions for special purchases, cash discounts, and return privileges, if any. The vendor program had to be beneficial to both parties.

Example
Vendor Program

Division: Sportswear
Department: Designer
Vendor: Designer X

	Actual 1992	Actual 1993	Plan 1994	Plan 1995	Plan 1996	Plan 1997	1998
Sales	$926	1,421	2,000,000	2,500,000	3,000,000	3,500,000	4,000,000
Gross Margin	46.9	47.1	47.5	48.0	49.0	49.5	50.0
Sales Per Square Feet	1140	1464	2,000				
Sell Through %	85	80	80	80			
Distribution	Bloomingdales, Saks						
Exclusivity	Semi						
Markdowns	To be negotiated						
RTV's	Yes						
Advertising	1/2						
Discounts	Yes						
Other	First Trunk shows						

The big benefit in the program: The agreed to designer had a commitment from Bergdorf Goodman to achieve sales in an amount agreed to by the principals, not the buyer.

When buyers were told of the vendor programs selected for their departments, they always asked the question, "What about other resources we want to buy from?" If you have open-to-buy after you have met the vendor program obligations, I told them, that's fine. The objective, of course, was to have the buyers concentrate on the important lines and have as little open-to-buy left over for those lines the fashion office felt were not as important.

I often explained that management, like generals, had the responsibility to decide the strategy, not the soldiers in the foxhole or the individual buyers, whose vision and skills were trained on immediate tasks. *WWD* interviewed one of the merchandise managers who left us and he complained that management made the decisions. He could only carry them out. I was asked for a comment and replied, "He is damn right."

There were three instances related to the vendor program that still amuse me. When Bill Blass was introduced to it, he said he was a designer, not a vendor. Then he came on board. Pauline Trigere came right out and said she wasn't writing a check to help achieve her gross margin goal. I asked her if she sold her over-cuts and cancellations to Loehmann's. She said she did. If she would sell them to me near the end of the season at the same price, I suggested, this would cover any markdowns we would have to take on her merchandise. She thought that was a pretty smart idea and agreed to do so. And when Massimo Ferragamo took over the American operation, he visited with me. I opened the vendor program book to his page. When I finished reviewing the performance of his company, he said I knew more about Ferragamo USA than he did. All three, and many more, did very well in Bergdorf Goodman as part of the vendor program. These were among the more than one hundred vendors included in the "preferred list." And I am pleased to say, both Bergdorf Goodman and most of the vendors on that list went on to great success.

The caveat: Unless top management takes direct responsibility for planning the initial goals with a vendor, and has quarterly or semi-annual reviews to determine that the arrangement benefits both parties, some merchandise managers and buyers will use the vendor program to their advantage. Their trick is to force the vendor to supply more mark down funds than the program calls for by threatening to remove them from the program.

Lesson Learned

- Successful business relationships are best developed when both parties understand and agree to their mutual objectives. Writing down these objectives as in any contract will help to eliminate any misunderstanding.

When I first joined Bergdorf Goodman, I tried to include Andrew Goodman in the kind of merchandise decisions I've just described. As a matter of fact, one of the first meetings to decide how large a markdown we needed to take to clean up the inventories of old and slow-moving merchandise was held in his office at my suggestion. We were looking at big numbers and I thought that justified involvement of the principals. Andrew was marginally interested, but left these decisions to the financial department.

After a week or two I showed Andrew Goodman a new advertising format we were considering. He said it looked fine to him, but the next day, decided he didn't like it. I moved ahead. Later on I recommended moving the fur department to another part of the second floor in order to have all the designer apparel departments together. Again he said he had no problem with the decision. The next day, once again, he declared he didn't like the idea Again, we moved ahead with the changes. Both times, and many others like this, left me puzzled.

Andrew Goodman was a gentleman of the first order, polite and considerate as any person I have ever known. He came to his office every morning perfectly dressed. He would receive the daily sales reports, and offer opinions from time to time as to why sales in some departments were up or down. He and Nena Goodman had lunch nearly everyday upstairs in their apartment. Periodically, I would be invited to join them, to give them an update on the steps that we were taking to bring the store back into the mainstream of a top fashion retailer.

There is no doubt in my mind that retail pioneers like Beatrice Fox Auerbach and Andrew Goodman wondered why the new owner who had wanted them so badly would want to change so many features that the stores were known for. I was more successful in explaining to B.F.A. what it was that the May Co. was doing than I was explaining what CHH was doing to Bergdorf Goodman. In the case of G. Fox, the new owners had a select number of stores similar to it and had a right to ask for sales and profit performances from G. Fox to equal these stores. In contrast, CHH-owned stores such as Neiman Marcus, and Holt Renfrew in Canada in addition to Bergdorf Goodman. Andrew Goodman was no fan of Neiman Marcus, and Holt Renfrew seemed to be stumbling around trying to find its way. These were not comparable stores, so I had a challenge explaining to Andrew how Bergdorf Goodman fit and why we were justified in taking certain actions to overtake the competition.

One of my many concerns was not to give our employees the impression that two people were running the store. If the employees got mixed signals everyone, and the business, would suffer. Looking back, I am sure I could have done a lot better in the transition than I did. However we were moving fast in restructuring the store floor by floor, moving and installing new designer departments. To ask Andrew his opinion, and in some cases, his approval since he still owned the physical building, seemed to me a handicap, but it had to be done.

On one of Ed Carter and Phil Hawley's visits to the store, they explained that Andrew Goodman was unhappy with how I was not involving him in many of the major store decisions. They wanted that to change. They explained that when they attempted to acquire a store, the owners would call Andrew Goodman and Stanley Marcus for their references.

The fact that I understood their problem and pledged to try to comply with their wishes did not negate the fact that they had given me other, somewhat conflicting, marching orders. They wanted me to continue building the store to its true potential. I couldn't do that very well if I had to review all of my decisions with Andrew Goodman. In truth, all his good intentions did not equip him to relate to the current retail market. If he'd been in touch, Bendel and Bloomingdales would not have achieved the great success they enjoyed while Bergdorf Goodman had stood frozen in time. Furthermore, if he thought I was difficult, another CEO worth his salt would be even tougher to deal with.

After we discussed these issues over lunch, we walked from the Plaza Hotel and faced Bergdorf Goodman. Ed Carter asked if I could get Bergdorf Goodman's sales to $75 million. If we do this right, I said, the sales will be more than triple that. I made it clear that I required their support to achieve that objective, not their complaints.

In the long run, Andrew stood with me. Of course, that wasn't necessarily obvious in the short run. In 1989, when I was the honoree at The Good Guys Lunch, Andrew Goodman gave a testimonial in which he said something to the effect of, "Ira is doing a great job at Bergdorf Goodman." Jaws dropped on most of the retailers present. They knew it was very difficult for Andrew Goodman to turn the store over to a stranger, and possibly equally as difficult to admit its success. But as I've always said, Andrew Goodman was the prefect gentleman, and he continued to prove it. As a footnote, Tubby Burnham, a long time Bergdorf Goodman board member, said to me years later, "Ira, you made Andrew a very rich man."

Lessons Learned

- If you believe what you are doing is right stick to your guns. Successful results will overcome nearly all adversity.

- Whenever taking on a responsibility that requires the previous executive to be involved, a clear understanding between both parties is imperative as to each executive's responsibilities. It must be understood that in most cases the previous executive will be reluctant to turn over responsibilities in areas that he or she feels they have a superior background.

- It is important to be successful in the initial changes in order to convince everyone involved that you are on the right track. The more people telling the previous management that they made the right decision to bring you on board, the easier the transition.

It is hard to miss that a number of stories and lessons in this book mention "lunch" as the occasion for some important decisions and events. This is because "lunch" was often an integral part of a strategy, rather than just a time to eat.

When I lived and worked in New England, I would travel to the New York wholesale market at least one day a week. This habit allowed me to spend time with buyers and divisional merchandise managers to ensure we were all on the same page. Periodically there would be time, not only to meet with our suppliers, but also to have lunch with them to discuss the degree of our progress, or lack of it, in reaching our mutual goals.

Moving to B. Altman in New York gave me the opportunities to not only spend more time in the markets, but also to host luncheon meetings with manufacturers and designers on a more frequent basis. My feeling has always been to have direct dialogue whenever possible, with our manufacturers, designers and the principals of their businesses, as well as the merchandise, fashion and financial press.

Moving the lunch meeting uptown to the Bergdorf Goodman neighborhood brought this strategy to a near art form. With most of the fashion stores located uptown, the ability to have a good restaurant conveniently located near Bergdorf Goodman that other retailers also visited was a plus. Orsini's on East 56th Street served this purpose. Two or three times a week, I would invite to lunch either Dawn Mello a divisional merchandise manager and a manufacturer we did business with to review our mutual performance, or I would have lunch with Michael Coady of *WWD* or some writers from the *New York Times* or the fashion magazine press. The luxury of having our own table added to the convenience of not ever waiting to be seated. And, we could be back to the store within an hour.

Many of the other retailers used Orsini's for the same purpose. It was not unusual to see Geraldine Stutz having lunch with fashion editors a table or two away, or some of the people from Saks Fifth Avenue going through the same drill.

Georgio Armani initially preferred "21," but later on, he, the Fendis, and most of the Italian fashion people always wanted to dine at the new trendier restaurants south of 14th Street, "where the action was."

The importance of these luncheon meetings to advance the cause of Bergdorf Goodman became apparent to me when Ed Carter, then the chairman of Carter Hawley Hale, invited me to lunch. That same day I had previously arranged a lunch with Leon Talley, who was then associated with *WWD*, Dawn Mello, and Susie Butterfield, Bergdorf Goodman's publicity director. I declined Ed Carter's lunch invitation, explaining to him my previous commitments. As far as I was concerned, the interview for *WWD* would do more for Bergdorf Goodman than my having lunch with the chairman. Ed Carter never invited me to lunch again. But Bergdorf Goodman continued to grow due to our efforts with the press and meetings with the principals of the companies we did business with.

Years later, Orsini lost his lease and the retailers and fashion press scattered to other restaurants in the neighborhood, until Arrigo Cipriani came along to fill the bill.

In 1984, while on a buying trip to Italy and visiting Venice, Beppe Modenese, one of the heads of the fashion organization in Milan, invited Jackie, me, and some others to have dinner at Harry's Bar. The restaurant, service, food, presentation—every aspect of their establishment impressed me, especially Arrigo Cipriani, the owner. Since we were in the process of remodeling the seventh floor for a gift department, I felt it would be a coup if we could have a Harry's Bar of Venice restaurant on that floor.

When I presented my proposal to Arrigo Ciprani, he courteously said he was not interested in moving to New York. Within a year, he changed his mind. He decided he would open his restaurant across the street from Bergdorf Goodman in the Sherry Netherland hotel. It worked out well for both of us. Arrigo named the restaurant Cipriani. In Arrigo's words, "When in 1985, we opened Cipriani's we created a sensation." The retail crowd, fashion press, designers and young society from Europe and America made it their luncheon headquarters.

Bergdorf Goodman had the best of both worlds. The gift department on the seventh floor turned out to be a rousing success and needed every inch of space available on the floor. The Cipriani restaurant across the street served as the perfect location for ladies to have lunch and cross the street to shop at Bergdorf's.

And the Bergdorf Goodman business luncheon moved to Cipriani; we picked up where we had left off with Orsini's.

There was an important lesson to be learned from Arrigo Cipriani's marketing strategies that would apply to retailers as well. Many years before Cipriani opened at the Sherry Netherland, there was a small bar at that location. Dull, but convenient. When I worked at Bonwit Teller I would stop in and have a drink with a friend or two on my way home. Like Bergdorf Goodman across the street, a great location, but not developed to its potential.

Arrigo's planning and marketing savoir-faire made the restaurant a sensation. For the first months of the opening, he brought from Venice some of his best people, including the highly identifiable bartender, his best captain, and some waiters. When a customer asked the bartender if he remembered him, with a great flourish, he would greet him like a lost friend, as would the captain. Not only was the customer pleased, his wife or girlfriend was very impressed. I mentioned this to Arrigo a year or two later, asking if he and his people remember all the customers from Venice. He looked at me, puzzled, smiled and then said, "Of course, only the steadies."

I bring this up because, a few years later, there was a lease dispute with Trusthouse Forte, and Cipriani closed on Fifth Avenue. The owners of the lease put an Italian restaurant in the Cipriani location. The new restaurant never got off the ground. Most of the time the restaurant was nearly empty.

Whatever Arrigo did with the owners of the lease or they with him, I don't know. However, a few years later, he reopened Cipriani at the Sherry Netherland and his personal involvement again created a sensation. That is marketing excellence.

Lessons Learned

- Constant communication with your market principals and your own executives minimizes any signals or direction confusion that may occur from time to time.

- When the Chairman asks you to lunch, and you have a very important lunch arranged, invite him or her along.

- A store or a restaurant, like a person, must have a personality. The personality must be geared to the customer you are trying to attract. Consistency, recognition, service, and or good food are necessary, but not the only key elements.

Signs of the Times

22

—————— **Landscape changes in the 1970's** ——————

Following in his father's footsteps, Andrew Goodman had operated Bergdorf Goodman conservatively, although he made a number of decisions that had long-term benefits to the Goodman family and, ultimately, to the store. In 1972, he made the decision to sell Bergdorf Goodman to the then Broadway Stores for $11 million in stock plus a minimum $1,100,000 in annual rentals. (The rent was shrewdly based on sales, not on profit.) (Source: *WWD*, 5/8/84.) He did so with conditions embedded to ensure that the new owners maintained the fine reputation his father had built and that he sustained.

Among the provisions that I heard about from Andrew Goodman and Phil Hawley, Bergdorf Goodman was to stay as it was, at 754 Fifth Avenue, with a long-term lease. The name was to remain Bergdorf Goodman. A competing Neiman Marcus store was not to exist in New York City; this eliminated the concern of the name ever being changed from Bergdorf Goodman to Neiman Marcus. There were other conditions that I was not privy to, but these had the primary goal of realizing Andrew Goodman's objective to perpetuate what his father and he had built. (The "Bergdorf" name came from Herman Bergdorf who was a Frenchman from Alsace. He lived over his dress shop on Fifth Avenue and Nineteenth Street. Edwin Goodman came to Bergdorf in 1899 when he was 23-years-old. He wanted to learn tailoring, as the older Bergdorf was a master. With money borrowed from his uncles, Goodman bought a partnership in the company, and it became Bergdorf Goodman).★

★ Bouton Herndon, *"Bergdorf's On The Plaza"* (New York: Alfred A. Knopf, 1956) 23, 25.

Amid criticism from the financial markets, including some directors, Phil Hawley was the champion of Bergdorf Goodman. He had an innate sense of the potential of a store on Fifth Avenue, bounded by 57th and 58th Streets. After the initial start, he advocated steps to maximize the sales productivity. From the very beginning, for example, he said the store could not reach it's potential without escalators. One of the first major physical moves was to relocate the executive offices off the fifth floor to the eighth floor, to make room for new apparel departments. The large alteration department that occupied a prime location overlooking Central Park, on the eighth floor, was moved to the 57th Street side of the building.

The display warehouse, which had occupied half of the seventh floor, was moved to the basement. A skylight was installed in the other half, which had been an open roof. This created an extra floor for selling and ultimately became a highly specialized gift department. Dawn Mello had a vision to follow the format of The British Trading Company, a highly successful gift store in London. This idea adapted to Bergdorf Goodman had excellent success.

Despite Phil's appreciation for Bergdorf Goodman New York, Carter Hawley Hale's initial strategy for Bergdorf Goodman was to expand its sales volume through branch stores. The first venture, that cavernous store in White Plains, was a notable failure. It was not only because of White Plains, however, that I recommended not investing capital on proposed branch stores in Paramus, Short Hills, and Manhasset. I believed that investing the capital budget on Fifth Avenue and 58th Street was a better decision as it would further develop Bergdorf's position as a highly profitable, successful fashion retailer.

Lesson Learned

- Some executives tend to view a business from the expense reduction opportunities. Merchants view a business from its growth opportunities. Both are right. However, it becomes a matter of not putting the cart before the horse. A merchant's responsibility is to build sales profitably. Financial people should manage expenses in order to grow the profit of the business. But without sales growth there will be no additional expenses to manage.

My early exposure to uptown Fifth Avenue at a young age left me with the impression that Fifth Avenue and 58th Street was "the tip of the iceberg." The apartments and upscale hotels lining Fifth Avenue, Park Avenue, as well as Central Park West stretched from 58th Street all the way to the nineties. Thousands of the highest income apartments in the country were literally and figuratively at our front door.

The women living on these avenues needed a complete specialty store to shop in. Just as in the story of the three bears, Bloomingdales was too large to create a feeling of intimacy, Henri Bendel was too small to be able to carry larger and more design-er oriented collections, and Bergdorf Goodman was just the right size.

Carter Hawley Hale accepted my recommendation of not pursuing branch stores around New York. Plans for a capital budget to upgrade Bergdorf Goodman on Fifth Avenue developed to not only take advantage of the prime location, but also the overabun-dant amount of non-selling space. This would be converted into designer shops, and could feature lines of merchandise not previously carried, such as a decorative home floor. I would frequently be asked the question, "Should Bergdorf Goodman have stores in Chicago or Beverly Hills?" My answer was always: "The Bergdorf Goodman customer in either of those cities would always compare their Bergdorf Goodman stores to New York. They would never be happy, since New York cannot be duplicated to everyone's satisfaction. I visualize customers walking into a Bergdorf Goodman branch and instantly complaining, 'this isn't like Bergdorf's in New

York.'" Retailing is tough enough without trying to make it tougher by inviting comparisons of one's own stores.

A Chicago branch had been planned at one point at the recommendation of Leonard Hankin, Bergdorf Goodman's executive vice president and Cresap McCormick & Paget. "Edwin Goodman, Andrew's son, who was slated to operate the store, declined, and the concept never materialized," according to Sam Feinberg in a May 8, 1984 article for *WWD*. This was fortunate because the New York store was not a high profit operation. For a Bergdorf Goodman branch store to mean anything to Chicago, it would have required heavy financing. For a privately owned company this is a risk that could have endangered the total business.

From "Andrew Goodman: 'It's A Different Ball Game'" (*Women's Wear Daily*, May 8, 1984) by Sam Feinberg, here quoting Andrew Goodman:

> "Cresap told us we were preoccupied with fashion shows, advertising and windows, that nobody was watching the bottom line on a formal basis. We were advised it was not gauche to think of making a profit. Our reaction was: Taxes were such that there wasn't that much incentive to accumulate a lot of money. Just as was true of Father, I enjoyed the business and the people who worked for us, and I wasn't trying to be the richest man in the cemetery.
>
> Cresap later made another survey for us—this one on possible branch expansion—noting that Chicago was not overstored. I didn't want a Chicago store—expansion was Hankin's idea. But I went along with the idea to keep Eddie (his son, Edwin Andrew) interested in carrying on the business. We were set to go into the John Hancock Building on North Michigan Avenue, where we had signed a letter of intent for 110,000 square feet on three floors.
>
> But, in April 1967 Eddie sent me a five-page type-written letter telling me he wanted to leave us after 4½ years. I was disappointed but accepted his decision and backed out of the Chicago deal."

...In 1972, Goodman sold the company, then doing $36 million, to CHH for $11 million in stock plus a minimum of

$1,100,000 in annual rentals. CHH pays the Goodman family rent on a net lease until the year 2050. The rent is based on volume, not on profit. The parent corporation also pays the taxes…

Before the sale was consummated, the Federal Trade Commission frowned upon the deal. In testimony before the FTC, Goodman said the store lost money on 1970 volume of $32 million and said the sale was "the only way to guarantee the store would continue." He threatened to close the store and sell the real estate unless the FTC approved the merger. The FTC withdrew its objection.

It is interesting to note that Neiman Marcus's flagship store in Dallas was not visited by nearly the same quantities of customers as visited Bergdorf Goodman's iconic flagship store on Fifth Avenue. Therefore, it was unnecessary for Neiman Marcus to be concerned with customer's reactions comparing their Neiman Marcus branches to the fabled store in Dallas.

So Carter Hawley Hale and Bergdorf Goodman made the logical decision: Close Bergdorf Goodman, White Plains and turn it into a Neiman Marcus branch. My concerns were finding jobs for those employees who were interested in coming to New York City and the backlash from the publicity of the store closing. Could it have a negative affect on the anticipated growth of Bergdorf Fifth Avenue? From a business point of view it was the right decision. Bergdorf Goodman was not in the branch store business and Neiman Marcus was, but public perception of the store was very important to me. In their search for stories, the newspapers could hurt as much as help. When the reporter Barbara Ettore called from the *New York Times*, and asked to interview the Bergdorf White Plains employees the night of the store closing, I feared a negative impression.

I arranged to meet the reporter and take her to White Plains at about 5:00 PM. Unfortunately the driver arrived late, so by the time we got to the store the employees were gone due to the anticipated closing of the store. She was disappointed, but I made it up to her by giving her an exclusive story on the expansion plans of Bergdorf Goodman New York. A better story, to be sure.

Lesson Learned

- When a strategic decision is made by a company, it is most important that all concerned, executives, employees, suppliers, customers and the press be given the positive reasons for the decision, otherwise negative thinking can snowball. Sometimes selling the positive is more like pushing water uphill. But the positive must prevail.

The mergers and acquisitions, the physical expansions and contractions of stores—these were signs of a tectonic shift in retail during this period that also involved an astonishing number of chief executives. In fact, one of the largest turnovers in the history of New York City retail management took place in 1975 and 1976. Isadore Barmash wrote in the *New York Times* in June 1976: "In all, nine of the city's twelve largest retail companies have changed either their chairman or president—or both." The nine were Edward Finkelstein at Macy's, Matt Kallman at Gimbels, Robert Suslow at Saks Fifth Avenue, Sanford Zimmerman at Abraham and Straus, John Schumacher at Bonwit Teller, Herbert Solomon at Orbach's, John Christian at B. Altman, Joseph Brooks at Lord and Taylor and Ira Neimark at Bergdorf Goodman." This group of retailers, including Marvin Traub of Bloomingdales and Geraldine Stutz of Henri Bendel, was a lineup of heavy hitters. To be equal to or come out ahead of this group was the objective.

The reasons for so many changes in retail management at this time were twofold. One was ownership changes at Saks and Bergdorf. (My moving from B. Altman, for example, led to a change in leadership there.) The reason for the others: "The difficulties of the national economy and of New York in particular

MONEY SUPPLY STEADY

Interest Levels Up Further, Fed Reports—Prime-Rate Increase May Be Next

By TERRY ROBARDS

Business loans at leading New York City banks climbed $439 million in the week ended Wednesday in their largest increase in more than 17 months, the Federal Reserve Bank of New York reported yesterday.

The increase was the second in a row, following a long string of declines, and it indicated a firming of demand for credit by corporate borrowers. Over the last year, business loans have declined a total of $4.7 billion in the aftermath of the national recession.

The Fed also confirmed the continued upward trend in interest rates, and it reported that the nation's money supply had remained virtually unchanged in the latest reporting week. The rise in interest rates indicated that major commercial banks would consider another increase in their prime lending rate.

The prime rate, which banks charge on loans to their biggest and most creditworthy corporate borrowers, moved up to 7 percent from 6¾ percent a

Credit markets regained their footing as bond prices rose yesterday and new issues sold well. Page D9.

week ago in response to the upward trend in money market rates.

Market analysts suggested that Citibank, which often sets the trend in prime-rate changes could justify a quarter-point increase in its base lending rate today, based on an increase in its prime-rate formula, which involves a three-week moving average of commercial-paper rates.

However, Citibank, which is New York's largest commercial lending institution, has raised its prime rate by a quarter-point in each of the last two weeks and might be reluctant to announce a third consecutive rate increase in such a short time span, analysts said.

The Cost of Money

The prime rate has moved independently of the demand for business loans for more than a year and has reflected mainly the cost of money. However, the increase in these loans could become a factor in base-rate pricing if it is sustained. The $439 million increase in business loans in the latest week brought the total outstanding at major New York banks to $34.04 billion.

The upsurge followed a revised increase of $129 million the previous week and supplied

Continued on Page D9

44 Wall Street. The Center of

---

the sales results for the month of May indicate the possibility of further changes. Last month, seven of the city's largest department stores had a sales decline of 7.6 percent, the biggest monthly sales drop in more than a decade.

Early this week, the latest change in top

Sanford J. Zimmerman

Robert J. Suslow

Matt Kallman

Joseph E. Brooks

Ira Neimark

John W. Christian Jr.

Herbert Solomon

The New York Times/Women's Wear Daily
Nine of New York City's largest retailers have made changes in top management during the last two years.

& Straus, will be Ohrbach's fourth president in seven years.

In another recent change, Saks Fifth Avenue appointed Robert J. Suslow as its third president in three and a half years.

In all, nine of the city's 12 largest retail companies have changed either their chairman or president—or both. The nine retailers are Macy's, Gimbels, Abraham & Straus, Bergdorf Goodman, Saks Fifth Avenue, Bonwit Teller, Ohrbach's, B. Altman and Lord & Taylor.

This wave of top management changes in the New York retailing field has raised questions in many corporate suites. Why the unusually large number of changes in one field and in one geographical area? Is the volatile retail business more hazardous for executives than other fields? And why the unusually large compensation offers to lure new talent?

"The difficulties of the national economy and of New York in particular have led to some of the top executive changes in stores," observed Herbert T. Mines, president of Business Careers Inc., a management recruiter specializing in retailing. "And when things turn tough in the economy, it is natural to question whether those at the top are right for the job."

But Mr. Mines said that some of the

Edward S. Finkelstein

John Schumacher

recent top shifts would have occurred because of ownership changes regardless of "qualitative reasons." As often as not, be explained, new owners tend to seek a redirection of a business they acquire and prefer to have new people implement it.

But why the big cash offers that have suddenly raised recruitment salary levels for top retailers? Retail industry observers point out that huge salaries were not necessary in the past. So why now? What lured executives to new retailing jobs in the past but doesn't seem to do the trick nowadays unless the financial package is sweetened?

Most observers say that the swinging door has been pushed by bottom-line problems and by the continuing trend of lower retail sales in the city and metropolitan area than in the country. The city's economic difficulties, merchants assert, have caused retail business in New York to rise less than inflation and have caused the number of sales transactions to fall.

Also, because most big New York stores are flagships whose operational patterns are usually reflected directly at branch stores elsewhere, the city stores' erratic

Continued on Page D15

have led to some of the top executive changes in stores. And when things turn tough in the economy, it is natural to question whether those at the top are right for the job," according to Herbert T. Mines, president of Business Careers Inc., as quoted in the Barmash's *New York Times* article.

During my career at Bergdorf Goodman, further attrition took place, not only with more executive changes, but due to the closing and merging of some of the stores referred to in the article.

Federated Department stores went through a most difficult period under new Canadian ownership that brought Bloomingdales and Federated to a near disaster. Macy's went into chapter 11 and was eventually merged into Federated Department stores. Abraham and Straus merged into Macy's. Bonwit Teller went through more management and ownership changes, and eventually closed, as did Gimbels, Orbach's and B. Altman. After Robert Suslow moved up to senior management in British American Tobacco, Saks Fifth Avenue also went through an ownership change and a number of management changes.

At Henri Bendel, Maxie Jarman sold the store to Leslie Wexner, who had visions of expanding the store to a national chain. Geraldine Stutz left shortly after. With the disappointment in the first few stores, that project was halted. Henri Bendel now has one store, moved to Fifth Avenue. Later on Associated Dry Goods who owned Lord & Taylor was "merged" into The May Co. Joseph Brooks, Lord & Taylor's CEO, left and was replaced by a May Co. executive, Marshall Hillsberg.

Of the original nine executives, I was "the last man standing."

The ownership change from the Goodman family to the Broadway Stores, and then the name change to Carter Hawley Hale, and finally the sale to General Cinema (changed to Harcourt General) insured the continuation of Bergdorf Goodman as a viable fashion store for the foreseeable future.

Dawn Mello, Steve Elkin and I, first with the help from Phil Hawley and later with the support and encouragement from

Richard Smith, chairman, and Robert Tarr, president of the General Cinema, continued our strategy of building the best collection of fashion designer names from Europe and the U.S. The goal was to continue to create what I called the "critical mass": complete assortments of fashion collections with points of view that would satisfy the needs of the fashion conscious customer.

It was equally important to have the right exciting atmosphere for the designer shops within the store for each designer, as well as a superior selling team, and an alteration staff to match. The visual displays inside Bergdorf Goodman had to be as creative as the Fifth Avenue windows. We accomplished this by having an extremely talented person, Angela Patterson, whom Steve Elkin, interestingly enough, had recruited. Since the financial head usually is not qualified to recommend a creative display person, I felt before my interview with her that she would be the same type of personality that I envisioned in our accounting department. I was wrong again. This lady was both attractive and very talented.

In recruiting the head of personnel, Marita O'Dea, I felt she had the good judgment, sensitivity and understanding of what it was we were attempting to build in Bergdorf Goodman. My pride in building careers was rewarded many times over. Angela Patterson went on to become the head designer for Calvin Klein stores around the world. Marita O'Dea was appointed Senior Vice President, Human Resources for the Neiman Marcus Group which included Bergdorf Goodman. And our assistant to Susie Butterfield, our PR director who is mentioned many times here in conjunction with the precedent-setting fashion events we staged, was Mallory Andrews, who became head of PR at Barneys and then a few years later returned as head of PR for Bergdorf Goodman. There are too many career successes to mention here, but I often think with pride and satisfaction of the many hundreds of jobs created and the successful careers that were launched because of the success of Bergdorf Goodman.

Lesson Learned

- Being the last man standing confirmed my philosophy that tenacity, hard work, and a lot of good luck is a combination tough to beat.

Donald Trump has a special role for me in the stories of store closings because of his unique relationship to Bonwit Teller. He asked me, as Bergdorf's CEO, to attend a meeting of the New York City Council. He wanted me to give the Council my opinion on how Bergdorf Goodman felt about his possible building of Trump Tower on the site of the now closed Bonwit Teller. My answer was to give my enthusiastic support since I felt it would be to Bergdorf Goodman's advantage to have a prestige building in our neighborhood, instead of further downtown. When Bonwit Teller was to be demolished, I asked Donald if I could have the doorknob from the 56th Street door, to remind me of one of my first jobs in retailing. He was very generous, and gave me not only the doorknob, but also the 721 address that was positioned over the Fifth Avenue entrance. I wish I had also asked for the Art Deco Façade. The doorknob has been on every one of my desks over the years. It always reminded me that no matter how far I had advanced in my career, it all started with a humble beginning.

Perhaps because I was the "the last man standing," Columbia Business School and The Fashion Institute of Technology thought I might know something that could prepare their students for the realities of retailing. One of my proudest moments came when Columbia invited me to serve as Adjunct Professor of a retailing course for MBA candidates. Unfortunately for the students, this was in the early 1980s, when nearly all budding MBAs wanted to score on Wall Street—a fixation captured a few years later in the Michael Douglas movie, *Wall Street*. I'm afraid I didn't attract many to retailing with my engaging presentations of how the business worked, as well as insights into its past, present, and future. My surprise exam at the end of the course didn't earn much enthusiasm, either. I even invited the 36 students from the class to meet the principals of any store they desired. No one took me up on my offer.

Like it or not, the one thing they most certainly did take away from my class was an improved sense of decorum. I required all students to be in the room at the required time. If they were late, they had to knock to be admitted. I did not allow them to bring coffee to the class, and if they wanted to talk during my presentation, they were welcome to take over the podium. Needless to say, they resented my approach until I explained that within a year most of them would be working in or near an executive suite. The basic manners I required from them—common courtesies I thought they should have learned at their mother's knee—would be expected from them by their superiors.

This experience was not too different from my retailing lectures to an FIT class soon to graduate. I required young men to wear a tie and jacket, and young women to wear "proper" sportswear or a dress. When a hundred or so walked into the auditorium, they glowered at me. Who is this guy telling us how to dress? I explained that since they were coming from FIT the business world would expect them to have some sense of style.

I offered all of the FIT students in that lecture hall a selling position at Bergdorf Goodman after graduation. I explained that no matter where they wound up, selling would always be an integral part of their career. Very few applied, but the group as a whole eventually warmed up to me as they began to understand that I was giving them the facts of life. School had obviously not covered these.

I believe that my exposure to top executives in the retail world at a very early age provided me with role models to study and emulate. In practical ways, most of those students I taught entered their work force years with a serious deficit: They waited until they graduated before they met any business executives who brought to life the principles of success that they had merely studied. I know my interaction with mentors and role models helped to mold me and guide my career. I wanted these students to also be aware of the importance of these relationships.

Lesson Learned

- Selecting an ideal role model at an early age is important and requires mature judgment. Those who do, go on to success. Those who do not have a much more difficult row to hoe.

Europe in New York 23

Admiration from national and international press regarding Bergdorf Goodman's reintroduction of the Paris couture in 1977 stirred further interest from our present customers, and caught the attention of those who felt that Bergdorf Goodman had fallen behind the times. The excitement created by featuring Christian Dior, Yves Saint Laurent and Givenchy at the special couture shows convinced us that the upgrading of Bergdorf Goodman would start on the second floor. We reconfigured it as a floor for "European Collections." It held a number of designer shops, among them, discrete sections for Fendi Furs, Geoffrey Beene (he showed his collection in Milan so we felt he qualified), Yves Saint Laurent, Chanel, and Givenchy. Elieth Roux, our couture specialist, selected the couture collections.

Each shop carried each designer's fifteen couture models as well as their ready-to-wear collections. The shops were an immediate triumph. *WWD* devoted over a page to the new floor: "Bergdorf Goodman's new second floor brings together an impressive collection of European designers, all presented in elegant contemporary settings. The store feels its new statement is a distinctive reflection of each designer." Eugenia Sheppard in her *New York Post* column, "Around The Town," also very generously described the new floor: "Many of Seventh Avenue's top designers attended the opening party along with Nancy Zeckendorf, Nan Kempner, Sam and Judy Peabody and Robert Joffrey, himself."

The party launching the floor, planned by architect Norwood Oliver and decorated by Larry Laslo, occurred in early April 1978. Larry Laslo, Bergdorf Goodman's display decorator, was very creative. I believe he was the first display director to remove printed signs designating designers in the display windows, and print the name of the designer on the window itself.

Lesson Learned

- "Build a better mousetrap," or "build a great baseball team, and they will come," are not empty phrases. If the management of the business stresses service and uniqueness, as well as complete and broad assortments of whatever is to be sold, it will be a success.

The publicity for the new European floor and couture fashion shows brought us attention that included notice from American and other European designers. Dawn Mello began to receive requests from designers who wanted to be represented in Bergdorf Goodman. Most importantly, the ready-to-wear was selling very well. We continued the couture shows for one more year knowing that the couture had served its purpose—Bergdorf Goodman had been noticed.

The press wrote many positive articles about Bergdorf Goodman starting about two years after my joining the store as CEO. The reviews were very supportive of the steps Bergdorf Goodman was taking to become more relevant as a top fashion store, and the reviewers, a bit more critical of the other four competing stores. My thinking at the time, based on past experiences at Bonwit Teller many years before and my more recent experience at B. Altman, was to make the press a partner. An interesting example of this relationship took place at the couture shows in Paris in 1976. Knowing that the reporters of *WWD* would be writing their stories of the shows they saw that day, I knew they wouldn't be able to have dinner until very late that evening. Since I was staying at the Hotel Ritz located across the street from *WWD*'s office on the Rue Cambon, I arranged with the concierge to have a waiter carry sandwiches and a chilled bottle of champagne across the street to the reporters. They were surprised and pleased, and so was I to see their reaction.

With many factors coming together, including our publicity strategy, we had achieved one of the first objectives in our plan: Let the important designers, domestic and foreign be aware that Bergdorf Goodman was the fashion store of the future! Not to be in Bergdorf Goodman was something a designer had to think about twice.

Of course, you can't please everyone, and we didn't please Hubert Givenchy. When I arrived at Bergdorf Goodman, the Givenchy shop was over spaced, and in my opinion poorly merchandised. The new floor had a smaller Givenchy shop, well positioned, and re-merchandised. Even though it was successful, I don't think he ever forgave me for reducing his space.

On the other hand when Karl Lagerfeld saw the floor for the first time he said, "It is to die for." I always liked Karl. Along with his brilliance as a fashion designer, he was a sound businessman. When I explained my strategy for Bergdorf Goodman, he sent me a small, framed, hand-written letter that I kept in my office. It read: "If you start to regret change, you're lost. It's better to be part of the change than to stand still and have regrets."

Shortly after the floor opened, Jacqueline Kennady-Onassis came into the store. I invited her for a tour of the floor saying, "The floor was designed for you." She thanked me for the compliment and the tour and from then on, we always had a pleasant greeting whenever we saw each other in the store.

In addition to being a good customer, who often relied on assistance from Elieth Roux., Jackie Onassis was also very gracious and generous. One day by mistake, a sensomatic security tag was left on a purchase that she was carrying through the 58th street entrance.

Givenchy and Gerald Van Der Kemp

Doing his duty, the security guard stopped her. Fortunately, Pat Salvaggionne, Bergdorf Goodman's legendary doorman, saw the problem and escorted her through the door as though nothing was out of order. In fact he joked with her about it, saying if they didn't remove the tag, garage doors she passed on her way home would automatically open. She liked Pat so much that when Pat was in the hospital, Mrs. Onassis sent him flowers with a get well card.

Aside from helping us reinforce relationships with notable customers like Mrs. Onassis, our approach to launching the European Collections held another major benefit. Bergdorf Goodman dedicated the shows to high profile charities, which drew the interest of leading society women. In July 1978, Gerald Van Der Kemp, the curator at Versailles, and his wife Florence gave a dinner party at Versailles for Bergdorf Goodman and 40 guests who were in Paris for the couture showings. Bernadine Morris quoted Mrs. Van de Kemp in the *New York Times* as follows, "Ira Neimark is giving a fashion show to benefit Giverny on Sept. 27, so we're giving a dinner party for him tonight." Our effort was to support

Venet, Kempner and Wyatt

the restoration in Giverny, to help return it to the grandeur that Claude Monet saw when he painted his wonderful water lilies. Mr. Gerald Van Der Kemp was in charge of the restoration as he had been for Versailles. The article continued, "Mr. Neimark happens to be the biggest supporter of the French couture among stores in the United States. The show at Bergdorf Goodman Sept. 27 will be the one that will introduce the styles he is now purchasing."

Printed with permission of photographer *Jean Luce-Hure, Paris*

Jackie Neimark at the palace of Versailles

Those attending the dinner included Nan Kempner—famous for the saying "The best part of a party is getting dressed to go"— Lynn Wyatt, Jacques and Louise Rouet, Estée and Joseph Lauder, Jackie Neimark, plus Marc Bohan, of Dior and Hubert Givenchy. It was an affair to remember. Dinner at Versailles, and the guests, all who made it into the international press coverage, further raising the profile of Bergdorf Goodman to the position it deserved.

Lessons Learned

- Retailing requires showmanship. No matter what the type of store, customers and the press relate to drama and presentation. Fashion interested customers do not need "new clothes," but they do need clothes that bring about an exciting feeling and conversation.

- The press has always been and will always be helpful to those merchants who show creative merchandising, and business ability. On the other hand, the press can do much harm to a retailer who appears not to be holding on to and not building its share of market.

- When deciding a marketing strategy it is imperative to know who your customer was, is and will be. Equally as important is to know what type of environment this customer feels comfortable in? (This applies to high fashion stores as well as department and discount stores.) Who the future customer will be, is most important, since the future is now.

- The new "European" second floor, realizing a rapid growth of sales and profit, was a high profile reason that Carter Hawley Hale could claim that the capital budget invested in Bergdorf Goodman on Fifth Avenue was possibly one of the best retail investments ever made.

Designers as Stars

24

In October 1982, *Women's Wear Daily* owner John Fairchild was quoted in the *International Herald Tribune* saying, "You know, designers have a following. Like movie stars they have become the new stars of our age." (*International Herald Tribune* October 1982.)

As movie stars received career boosts from favorable reviews by the movie critics, fashion designers found that the retail stores' fashion directors could quickly lift them from obscurity. Bernard Ozer of Federated Department Stores, Katherine Murphy of Bloomingdales (later Kal Ruttenstein), and Bergdorf Goodman's Dawn Mello were the "star makers." In addition to the fashion directors, a few store presidents, such as Geraldine Stutz of Henri Bendel, Mildred Custin and Dorothy Shaver, also had their talent. My daughter, Janie, played a small part in this movement, too, when she worked in the fashion office at *Vogue*. When she first saw Perry Ellis's new line, she brought it to the attention of her boss, who in turn made it known to Grace Mirabella, *Vogue*'s editor-in-chief. Grace always new a good thing when she saw it and helped make Perry Ellis a star. Compliments came back to Janie.

Not meaning to minimize the fashion director's talent, I equate it with a horse racing tout: "You sure can pick a winner." Dawn Mello had the ability to identify not only which established fashion houses should be in Bergdorf Goodman, she also discovered the emerging fashion designers with remarkable growth potential. Dawn often said there was a "fashion underground" that you had to be smart enough to tap into.

Geoffrey Beene and Ira Neimark

Dawn and her staff diligently covered the fashion markets to identify the fashion lines we should have in the store—whatever would help us develop a "fashion point of view." Dawn's fashion office was like one that belonged to the editor of a newspaper. Often Dawn said, "It isn't what you carry in the store, it's what you don't carry that makes us right."

Both inside and outside Bergdorf Goodman, I

Dawn Mello and Gianfranco Ferre

explained the function of the fashion office many times, using as an example, the *New York Times* and the *New York Daily News*. Both have news editors, I'd say, but where the *Daily News* editors may play up a fire in Brooklyn for their readers, the *Times* more often than not will put the fire story in the back section, and feature in the front a national event for their readers. The fashion editors at Bergdorf Goodman directed the buyers to the fashion stories that had a point of view for our audience.

Gianfranco Ferre was among Dawn's "discoveries." A relatively little known Italian fashion designer, he had just started his business in the late 1970s. Of her first meetings with him, Dawn said, "I spent months talking to him in sign language, thinking he didn't speak English. He did, but he just listened so he could learn more" (*Women's Wear Daily*, November 10, 1982).

In 1981, when Dawn convinced Gianfanco to sell exclusively to Bergdorf Goodman, she introduced me to him in Milan. I explained that we had planned a Ferre shop, Fifth Avenue windows, advertising, and a fashion show. I will never forget the tears of joy rolling down his face.

Most of the time Dawn would introduce me to the fashion designers she wanted me to meet, however since we always couldn't both be in the same place at the same time, I would sometimes introduce myself. This brought a few surprises. In Paris, around 1981, Dawn was very excited about a woman's shoe designer, Maud Frizon. Dawn gave me the address and arranged an appointment for me. Arriving at the

Maud Frizon

building, I rang the bell to the flat. When the door opened, I expected to meet a typical shoe designer (if there is such a thing), and was greeted by a very attractive young woman whom I thought was the shoe model. Maude indeed had been a shoe model, and had gone into designing, manufacturing and retailing her shoes with her husband, Gigi. Their small shop on the Left Bank was so successful; customers who couldn't fit into the shop to try the shoes on would try them on in the street outside the shop. After a number of meetings, we made an exclusive arrangement and brought Maud's shoes into Bergdorf Goodman. The Bergdorf customers didn't have to try the shoes on in the street; they were standing in the aisles.

After Dawn targeted the stars and those to be, my role in these scenarios was to convince them to sell to Bergdorf Goodman on an exclusive basis. In some cases where they were already selling another major account, we would offer a semi-exclusive arrangement, promising them a reasonable sales objective, and featuring them in their own shop in the store, with the appropriate sales promotion. This approach in most cases accomplished our objective.

We did have to customize our tactics for some situations, though. When building an expensive shop in a unique Fifth Avenue location for a designer, we determined the line had to be exclusive with Bergdorf Goodman. This happened with Issey Miyake, the important Japanese designer whose reputation was flourishing in the early 1980s. We told him that we would build his shop on the main floor using his architect if he would make an exclusive arrangement in New York with Bergdorf Goodman. His small problem was that he was already selling to Bloomingdales, and didn't know how to go about not selling to them. We suggested he tell Bloomingdales that his company's new marketing strategy was to only sell to specialty stores, not department stores. He did. Marvin Traub turned right around and told him that Bloomingdales was a specialty store. (Nice try.)

Nevertheless, in order to have this great location on Bergdorf Goodman's main floor and the high profile it would give him, Issey Miyake decided to be exclusive with Bergdorf.

When we felt the time was right to make a major effort with Valentino, a similar situation developed. Once again we explained that, in order for us to build an appropriate shop, we felt department store distribution was not in keeping with our specialty store approach. They, too, made the decision to come to Bergdorf Goodman, so I went to Rome to finalize our arrangement with Valentino's partner, Giancarlo Giammetti. Rome had just had a blizzard, which doesn't happen very often. The city was unprepared and made little effort to clear the streets. Magnificent statues topped with snow gave the city an even more poetic image than usual, but the going was slippery and dangerous. After I successfully concluded my business with Giancarlo, I slid and slipped down the Spanish Steps on my way to the Fendi office on via Borgognona. It was freezing cold and Carla Fendi offered me a glass of whiskey to get myself back among the living.

Step by step, no pun intended, we were building a strong luxury designer base that would put Bergdorf Goodman at the forefront of the fashion retailers. And the Italians were playing a key role.

Lessons Learned

- Fashion like any other business has its stars. It is important to have the ability to identify the present leaders, but it is even more important to find the new talent before the competition does.

- There is a tremendous competitive advantage if you can arrange to have the best merchandise lines exclusive to your store or business. Today the designer's distribution strategy makes this approach almost impossible. However, it can still be done if you structure exclusive arrangements that will benefit the designer as well.

Bergdorf's Ira Neimark in his Giorgio Armani gray flannel suit with the Armani clan, Adriano Gianelli, Sergio Galeotti and Cesare Giorgino.

Armani Show

About the time Fendi and Krizia came to Bergdorf Goodman, Dawn also identified Giorgio Armani as a leading, if not the top, designer of Italian men's and women's ready-to-wear. Dawn mentioned meeting Armani in Milan, at which time he was already selling Barneys. Fred Pressman, one of the most knowledgeable men's merchants, was the first to carry the Armani men's line. When we brought the woman's line into Bergdorf Goodman, there was a relatively limited distribution uptown at Bloomingdales and a small collection at Henri Bendel. We installed Bergdorf Goodman's first Armani boutique in the sportswear department on the third floor. It was later moved to a large shop on that floor. Eventually, it grew to an even larger shop on the second floor, home of the European Collections.

In the early days Armani had a small staff. He headed up the company with his business partner, Sergio Galeotti, and his sales manager, Adriano Gianelli. On our side, we had Dawn Mello, Barbara Lamonica as the divisional merchandise manager, and Mary Filbin, our Armani buyer. From the beginning, we always had fun working with the Armani people. They had a great sense of humor and enjoyed their association with Bergdorf Goodman. Before I knew it, I was wearing Armani suits and became a big Armani fan. In 1990, when Bergdorf Goodman moved the men's business to the new men's store across Fifth Avenue, the small Armani business grew to be the single largest men's line in the store.

On one of our buying trips to Milan, I picked up Dawn Mello; Susie Butterfield, Bergdorf's publicity and special events director; Barbera LaMonica; and Mary Filbin for an appointment with Georgio Armani. To my surprise, and to theirs, they all were wearing the same Armani blouse. Some wore the blouse with a skirt, and some with pants. When we arrived at Armani's Palazzo—he had shown in a mere hotel room when Dawn first met him—he stood aghast at the top of the staircase. He called for a photographer, being so impressed that four very attractive women from Bergdorf Goodman were wearing his, and their, favorite Armani blouse.

The Armani woman's business at Bergdorf Goodman grew very rapidly due in part to a number of dramatic fashion shows. The first year we did an Armani show at Studio 54; in 1980, the ice skating rink at Rockefeller Center. The drama of the Rockefeller Center show was so spectacular that we achieved our goal of throwing the best fashion party of that year. It was at night, with the runway at the statue of Prometheus lit up for the models to parade by. Best of all, it was right in front of Saks Fifth Avenue. And Saks didn't have the Armani line. Since that time, Giorgio Armani has grown his distribution to every major department store worldwide. His many own freestanding stores are also in every major city. His early promotions at Bergdorf Goodman helped propel both him and Bergdorf Goodman to the forefront of the fashion world.

The relationship with Armani did not always remain as blissful as it began. It was my routine every Monday morning to review the *New York Times* fashion section with our advertising and publicity people, in order to see whether Bergdorf Goodman received the proper credit line for the styles photographed of our major collections. One Sunday, the Armani credit read "Barneys." I instructed the display department to remove the Armani sign over the entrance to the Armani shop. I told the Armani people if they gave the credit to Barneys, let Barneys put up the Armani sign in their store. Unfortunately, Georgio Armani was in town, and came to the store with Gabriella Forte, his new business manager, and Lee Radzwill in tow. He was very unhappy with my removing his name from the shop, and insisted it be put back. It became apparent, although not from that experience alone, that the designers were now in charge of their destiny—an outcome that had taken shape over decades. Of course we put the sign back after making our not so subtle point.

Department and specialty stores began promoting designer names slowly in the 1950's and the trend accelerated rapidly thereafter. Initially, better apparel was bought by specialty store retailers from fine tailors such as Ben Gershal, Maurice Rentner, Montesano and Pruzan, Davidow Bros., Philip Mangone and later from designers like Pauline Trigere, Harvey Berin, Larry Aldrich, Adele Simpson, Jerry Silverman, and Molly Parnis, to name a few. However, the retailers who carried these lines of merchandise normally featured their own labels on the garment, and carried the manufacturer's label as well. In women's accessories, some of the important handbag labels were Koret, Pichel, Coblentz and Rosenstein. Fashion costume jewelry had names, such as Trifari, and Coro. David Evans and Ferragamo were among the better priced major shoe designers. There were also many women's sportswear lines of that era that also had customer recognition, such as Villager, John Meyer of Norwich, David Crystal. Creative sportswear designers such as Claire McCardle, and Bonnie Cashin, were just beginning to be known by the general public. In some cases, the retailer's label in the so-called better lines predominated the designers name.

In the late 1950's and early '60's, a dramatic change occurred. The development of designer recognition began to accelerate. Geoffrey Beene, Bill Blass, and Oscar de la Renta started their companies under their own names. Also about this time, couture designers in France began to develop secondary lines of ready-to-wear at lower prices than their couture, such as Yves Laurent's Rive Gauche and Chanel. The initial development of name fashion designers was also beginning in Italy, and soon would dominate the fashion scene with Giorgio Armani, Fendi, Krizia, Valentino, and many more to come. In America, Ralph Lauren, Perry Ellis, Liz Claiborne, Ann Klein (soon to be followed by Donna Karan), and Calvin Klein were also beginning to take center stage.

During these years up until the middle 1980's, the American retailers who bought these American, French, and Italian fashions made the decisions as to the size, and where the designer's shop would be located in their stores. They also negotiated individually with the designers in most cases, the degree of exclusivity, or semi exclusivity the lines could have among the competition. I believe the next phase of the development of the fashion designers could be called "Retailers hoisted on their own petard." The advertising and sales promotion of the designer lines became intense as retailers realized the tremendous news and interest the new and important designer names had for their present and future customers.

The fashion designers gradually realized the importance of the fashion excitement and prestige that they brought to stores such as Henri Bendel, Bloomingdales, Saks Fifth Avenue, Barneys, and later Bergdorf Goodman, as well as other premiere stores around the country. The designers then decided their fashion reputations and labels, in many cases were as strong if not stronger than some of the stores themselves. The validation the fashion designers received from the retailers in effect, put the designers in business for themselves.

Thus began the negotiations of the designers, not only to what stores they would sell, but also where they wanted to be located in these stores, as well as the size of the shops that they would require. In addition, the designers recognized they were now strong enough to have their own freestanding stores in many prestigious locations, in the shadow of those stores who built them to their current importance. The final result for the fashion designers is that with very few exceptions their merchandise in one form or another, is carried in nearly every retail store (department or specialty), as well as in their own shops around this country and the world.

Today on Fifth Avenue, many of the department and specialty stores that once dominated the neighborhood are gone. In their place the designers have built large stores featuring their various collections of designer clothes and accessories. The role of the retailer has been reversed by the fashion designers. Perhaps this is how it should be, since in many cases the retailers were not quick enough to recognize the changes that were taking place, and the designers were smart to capitalize on the situation. They were the stars, and they took the spotlight. As Ralph Lauren said at his company's sixth annual meeting as a public company in August of

**Jackie Neimark and Geoffrey Beene at the Ideacomo Ball,
May 27th, 1978**

2003, "The reason I'm excited about retailing today is that it is in our hands. We are in control of our destiny." Enough said.

Lessons Learned

- Nothing is forever; marketing is always in a state of change. Customer acceptance and loyalty is only maintained when the retailer or the designer create the merchandise, the image and the environment that stimulates the customer in order to satisfy his or her desire.

- Short range planning will help to keep you in business a short time. Long range planning will keep you there much longer.

The Value of a Good Party 25

“The gala evening is a sign of the marriage of society and fashion that was noted in the 1960s, which was nurtured by Diana Vreeland in the 1970s and looks as if it will go on forever,” wrote Bernadine Morris of the *New York Times* in December 1979. American retailers and the fashion designers recognized that designer fashion show parties, whether in the Metropolitan Museum, their stores, or other high profile locations presented prime opportunities for great publicity. Newspapers, magazines and television all recognized the enormous number of fashion events taking place with newsworthy celebrities. Fashion editors from the *Times*, *WWD*, *New York Post*, and *International Herald Tribune*, to name a few, competed to keep their readers up to date as to the goings on in the "Fashion World."

Seeing the great interest of the international press, the fashion houses began inviting movie stars and other celebrities to their fashion shows. The front and center seating formerly assigned to the heads of the stores and their buyers were now assigned to the stars of the moment. In the 1940s and early 1950s designer fashion shows relied on a sedate, businesslike atmosphere in the designer's show room. Attended by fifty or sixty merchants per show, low music and the designer's assistant announcing the style number each model was wearing were the usual background elements.

The audience today is usually composed of three groups, aside from the celebrities. Group one: Store principals their merchandise managers, buyers, publicity and display people. Group two: the worldwide media. Group three: favorite private clients and social friends of the designer. Today, a leading designer's fashion show could easily have anywhere from five hundred to a thousand people in attendance.

Lesson Learned

- The store's fashion directors know before the buyers, the designers who are or will be the new successes. It is the function of the buyers to make the designer selected by the fashion office a merchandising success. It is not the job of the fashion office to enhance the prestige of a buyer's selection for a "safe designer's line."

As Bergdorf Goodman was assuming its position at the top of fashion retailing, the events turned from sedate to spectacular and the audiences began to grow. Yves Saint Laurent launched his new perfume, Opium, in September 1978 on the Tall ship, the Peking. To quote *WWD*: "It was a successful media event to sell perfume, but as a social party it never set sail ... And it wasn't only YSL who was

Printed with permission of Women's Wear Daily

YSL and Alva Chinn

selling perfume: Halston (with Cher), Calvin Klein, Oscar de la Renta, Bill Blass, Mary McFadden, all...held mini press conferences with NBC, CBS, ABC and Channel 5 in hot pursuit; While Marion Javits, Nan Kempner and Diana Vreeland—Who don't even have perfumes to peddle— jumped into their TV lights ... Struggling to make those longed for Drop Dead entrances, some 900 guests

YSL and Diana Vreeland

Lena Kansbod, Giorgio Armani and Gene Pressman

swarmed through the canopied path and tripped down the gangplank;   St. Laurent meanwhile, tried to evade the TV crews."

The value of the party for me was that I had the opportunity to thank Pierre Berge personally for his sending Opium perfume for our YSL couture customers. Also, for his directing the distributor to have Bergdorf Goodman included in the list of stores carrying the perfume in the U.S.

It was at one of these designer shows that I realized how intense the interest still was in the retailers themselves. In the spring of 1977 the Italian Trade Commission staged a dinner and fashion show, called Modapronto, for the press and American retailers in New York at the Hotel Pierre. Most of the important Italian fashion designers were involved; each was represented in the fashion show with selections from their Fall collections. I recall I had just taken what at that time would have been considered a rather large markdown to clear slow moving and old inventory. At the dinner, Aldo Pinto, the president of

Anna Fendi

Krizia indicated, he was well aware of the markdown. "Ira," he asked, "are you going to be alright?" This was one of the first indications I had that both the European and American designers were watching carefully, as to what was going on with the new management at Bergdorf Goodman.

The American designers had their promotions as well, not the least of which was the American Fashion Designers Award dinner. This event was always held in high-profile locations like The Temple of Dendur in the Metropolitan Museum of Art and The New York Public Library.

Cheray Duchin, Gov. Carey, Anne Ford Uzielli

Gov. Carey and Mayor Koch

Jimmy and Rosalynn Carter

Jackie and Ira Neimark

**Claude Montana
makes his entrance**

Once in a rare while politicians would be convinced fashion, manufacturing and retailing deserved their attention. The New York Fashion Council represented "Seventh Avenue" and was made up of most of the best known American designers. In August of 1978, Mayor Ed Koch hosted one Council event at Gracie Mansion that drew President Jimmy Carter and his wife Rosalynn and Governor Hugh Carey.

Not to be outdone, retailers had their own fashion events. As the fashion designers were emerging, the stores were vying for their customer's attention as well as for the customers of their competition. Each season, Spring and Fall, Bergdorf Goodman staged a major show, featuring the collection from a top

Aldo Pinto and Ira Neimark

Perry Ellis

designer. I would be remiss not to describe some other unusual and newsworthy fashion events that we created. In February 1981, for example, Bergdorf Goodman hosted a fashion show for Krizia in the Elephant Room of the American Museum of Natural History. The animal theme was tied in with the novel big game looks on the highly identifiable Krizia sweaters. The show marked a monumental gain—in publicity, sales, and credibility—in our efforts to overtake the retailers we had been merely trying to catch up to only a few years earlier. Claude Montana's show in September of the same year was held in the Seventh Regiment Armory. The show, featuring thirty-five models, duplicated his Paris fashion show and earned this remark from John Duka in the *New York Times*: "Bergdorf Goodman kicked off the Fall fashion season Wednesday night with a suitable lavish mega-fashion production for Claude Montana at the Seventh Regiment Armory on Lexington Avenue—a flamboyant tribute to one of the most explosive young fashion

Jackie Onassis

Bill Blass and "OK" Gloria Vanderbilt

talents around. It all started at 8 o'clock when 1,700 of New York's more heavily costumed citizens walked through a tunnel of aluminum and parachute fabric into the cavernous armory." (*New York Times*, September 11, 1981)

I am a bit embarrassed to say, the cost of some of these shows, with what was called vendor participation and other contributing sponsors, in some cases exceeded the cost of the designer merchandise that we bought for the event. However, the objective was to generate interest in the designer's merchandise which in turn over the long run more than made up for the expense.

In addition to the major fashion shows, high profile "charity parties" centered on fashion gathered momentum. The desire to create an event important enough to be hosted by a prestigious charity able to attract the "right group" continues to this day.

I particularly recall a gala organized by Diana Vreeland in December of 1979 when the Metropolitan Museum of Art presented an exhibition of the "Fashions of the Hapsburg Era: Austria-Hungary." Again, quoting

Michaele Vollbracht, Francoise and Oscar de la Renta

Pauline Trigere, Bill Blass

Bernadine Morris: "Some 630 people in present day versions of court regalia sipped aperitifs in the museum's Medieval Sculpture Court, dined in its fountain restaurant and danced in the Great Hall. These exhibits started in 1974 based on the grand days of Hollywood clothes. The Russian show of 1976, drew close to a million visitors." (*New York Times*, December 4, 1979)

Thus, fashion has helped raise large sums of money for worthy causes, in no small part because fashion draws celebrities of all kinds. The Metropolitan Museum's Hapsburg Splendor event had in attendance such notables as Martha Graham on the arm of Halston, Ali MacGraw, Margot Hemingway, Nan Kempner, Marc Bohan, Jacqueline de Ribes, Calvin Klein, Bill Blass, Estée Lauder, Gloria Vanderbilt, and Jacqueline Onassis escorted by Hugh Fraser, head of the House of Fraser department store chain in Great Britain.

Lesson Learned

- Good press will speed a talented designer on to success. Bad press will speed a mediocre designer to his or her demise.

————H 8. Expansion at Bergdorf Goodman 1983————

After transferring the Bergdorf Goodman's White Plains store to Neiman Marcus in 1979, we concentrated our total effort on Fifth Avenue. Our sales and profits were beginning to grow at a rapid rate

Printed with permission of *Women's Wear Daily*

Jackie and Ira Neimark

and more space was required for the many new designers coming on board. There also was a great need to expand underspaced departments, as well as relocating certain department for better adjacencies. Our long-term goal was to increase the selling space throughout the store. This process would enable us to increase the sales, and achieve our goal of becoming a very profitable fashion apparel business. There was no question in my mind that once we demonstrated the feasibility of our successful growth strategy on Fifth Avenue to the principals of

Nancy and Henry Kissinger

Carter Hawley Hale, the additional capital required for future renovations to be invested in Bergdorf Goodman, New York, would be made available.

Two of our major projects were escalators from the main floor to the seventh and the second project, the new seventh floor addition, that would house the grand decorative home gift department. The escalators were designed to relieve the pressure of three small elegant elevators on 58th street and the elevator bank on 57th street. The plan was not to eliminate either elevator bank, but to have an escalator well placed through the center of the store in order for the escalator to deliver the customer to the center of each floor. "The escalator was encased in vertical wells of aqua with frosted white Art Deco sconces on the walls, the escalators look as if they had been in place since the store opened at its present site in 1928."★

The overall plan was to increase the selling space from approximately slightly over one hundred and twenty six thousand square feet to eventually one hundred and eighty thousand, and possibly additional room after that. What intrigued me was that with Bergdorf Goodman being located in such prime real-estate, every extra foot of space, properly merchandised, and devoted to selling could yield an additional one thousand dollars of sales.

Finally, being able to move the Delman shoe department off the main floor allowed me to realize one of my major goals since I first arrived at Bergdorf Goodman. This move was a priority of

Pierre Berge

mine, since here was a leased business that had a merchandising strategy that was different than where we wanted to take Bergdorf Goodman. But the shoe department also occupied the most valuable four thousand square feet of space in the store. Delman was paying a rent that, even if their fashion concept matched Bergdorf Goodman's, the rent was set at too low a percentage. It was based on the early days when Andrew's father Edwin, was looking to just have the space occupied.

Moving the employee's cafeteria from the fourth floor to a new location overlooking the park on the eighth floor made room for the Delman shoe department to move to that location. Finally, the main floor had a space that was developed into a highly successful jewelry area. Although many people were concerned with the move of Delman off the main floor, their customers continued to support us. It took a number of years before the Delman lease ran out. Meanwhile it was difficult to have Delman develop into a fashion shoe department, since a leased department strategy is to make a location pay off, not to be a fashion innovator. A few years later, after the Delman lease finally ran out, the new shoe department under Bergdorf Goodman management moved to it's present location on the second floor.

Jackie Neimark, Leonard Lauder

More significant design changes were also to be made on the fourth floor where Domestic and foreign designers were to be featured. These included shops for Valentino, Galanos, Bill Blass, Oscar de la Renta, Ungaro and a Plaza Boutique.

The big excitement was the launching of Bergdorf Goodman's new escalators. Over four hundred guests were invited to celebrate, and to make it known to the world that Bergdorf Goodman was a growing and a successful business. The guests of honor were Carla Fendi and Aldo Pinto. They were the first two

Printed with permission of *Women's Wear Daily*

Ira Neimark, Carla Fendi and Aldo Pinto

European designers to commit themselves to us when many others doubted the future of Bergdorf Goodman's growth to be the leading fashion store in New York.★★

Stanley Marcus said, "I think it's going to be the single most important thing Bergdorf's has done in years. It's a miracle this store has done what it has with inadequate elevator service."

---

* N.Y. Times 8/25/1983
** WWD 8/25/83

Lesson Learned

- In retailing as in other businesses, productivity is the key to success. High sales and gross margin productivity will bring a good merchant great success. Low productivity will always eventually bring failure.

Royal and Political British Hospitality **26**

1985–1987

Each season the British Fashion Council would have a gala reception in London to greet the American retailers and fashion press. Sir Edward Rayne, president of the Fashion Counsel, arranged our first meeting with Princess Diana at a very small reception. The princess was the hostess at Lancaster House on the occasion of London Fashion Week. I called Ken Williams, the head of Turnbull and Asser, to ask whether a white button down shirt and a blue and red regimental tie would suit the occasion. He responded with, "no, no, no, that will never do." He recommended his creating a white on white shirt for me, with a teal blue tie featuring red dots, the teal blue being the princesses favorite color for a tie she had recently bought one for her husband.

He would have the shirt and tie ready the next day in time for the reception, with the admonition not to tell anyone how fast the delivery was since a special order of that type would normally take in excess of two weeks.

Jackie and I arrived at the reception just as the ladies in waiting entered the room. I tried to see which of the women was Princess Diana. In a moment following the ladies in waiting, a rather tall very attractive, movie star quality young woman, holding a bouquet of violets entered the room. Since most of the photographs that I had seen of the princess showed the prince

Princess Diana

standing taller than the princess, I thought she would be shorter. (The prince, I learned, was usually standing on a step in order to look taller). We were first on line to greet Diana. Since I was sure most people meeting her would be quite formal, I tried a different approach, and said, "Your Royal Highness, I am delighted to meet you. In your honor I had Ken Williams create this special tie." She smiled and responded with, "The tie matches your eyes." I was awed and happy with her response. I then introduced the princess to Jackie. She asked Jackie what she did while I was busy all day? Jackie responded by saying she had been shopping for a Jaguar at Jack Barclay since I had "promised to buy her a Jaguar." The Princess replied, "I have a Jaguar as well."

While that event was a highlight of all of our experiences in England, it was followed up the next year with another reception featuring the princess. I decided to wear the same tie. After saying hello, the princess said to me, "You are wearing our tie." And to Jackie, "Did your husband ever buy you your Jaguar?"

Shortly after, in October 1986, Jackie and I attended another English event called the British Fashion Week Banquet given by the British Fashion Council with the Princess of Wales as the guest of honor. The two hundred guests in the grand Fishmongers Hall consisted of international retailers, fashion press, British designers, and fashion personalities.

At the dinner I was seated to the right of Princess Diana. The Princess was, to quote Hebe Dorsey of the *International Herald Tribune*, "radiant in a Bruce Oldfield off-the shoulder, royal purple velvet dress."

After recovering from my good fortune to be selected as the Princess' dinner partner, I had to think of what conversation would be appropriate and best hold her interest. I asked her, other than Bruce Oldfield, who were her favorite designers? Over the years I found no other subject holds a fashionable woman's attention more than that question. The Princess didn't let me down. She had a long and good list, starting with Giorgio Armani, and including the British designer of the year, Jasper Conran.

The princess was a most entertaining dinner partner. The conversation was going quite well, even as she was suggesting that I should eat the chocolate truffles during dinner. I was a bit puzzled since having chocolate during dinner was never encouraged when I was growing up. However, when the princess began cracking walnuts after dinner, and said, "walnuts are a good aphrodisiac." I, for the first time that I can remember, was at a loss for words. I am sure I said something less-than-clever like, "Really?"

Later on after the dinner, when Jackie and I were back at our hotel, I met a friend and described what the princess had said to me about walnuts. He thought it was amusing. I woke up in the middle of the night in a sweat, remembering that my friend was also a friend of Hebe Dorsey's. I realized that if he told the story to Hebe Dorsey, and if it appeared in the *International Herald Tribune*, I would be run out of England the first thing the next morning. Fortunately, he either forgot, or neglected to pass on this gossip tidbit. In any case, much to my relief, nothing appeared. I was then able to continue about my business in the U.K. with a very pleasant memory of an outstanding evening.

Prime Minister Thatcher alternated with Princess Diana in hosting the London Designer Week. That is how Jackie and I arrived at 10 Downing Street the following year.

Initially, Jackie and I felt it would be just another commercial designer event at a hotel and I came close to not accepting the invitation. When we learned that the prime minister would host the reception at 10 Downing, you can imagine how fast we changed our minds. The event, I soon learned, was for executives only—no spouses. I called Eddie Rayne and told him I would be unable to attend if Jackie, who was in London, was not invited with me. Shortly after, a new invitation arrived for Mr. and Mrs. Ira Neimark, inviting us to the prime minister's reception. Eddie Rayne, always the perfect diplomat, made things happen.

Going through the famous 10 Downing Street black door was an experience in itself. Walking up the spiral staircase, the wall covered with the pictures of all the Prime Ministers in English

Ira Neimark golfing at Windsor Castle

history was also a thrill. Being greeted by the prime minister was the crowning touch.

After the introductions in the reception area, I noticed three or four women being taken on a tour of the various rooms by the prime minister. Jackie was among them. The next time I looked, Jackie and the prime minister were alone, walking around like two housewives, examining the paintings and furniture. Margaret Thatcher explained to Jackie that one of the smallest desks was used by William Pitt; she didn't say whether it was the elder or the younger Pitt. Jackie told me she asked, "How could he run the British Empire on such a small desk?" Mrs. Thatcher explained that Pitt had a full staff upstairs.

As they talked about the new decorations in the planning stages—wall colors, paintings, furniture to be added and replaced—Jackie thought, if her mother and father could only see her now. As many Americans did during World War II, Jackie's family had huddled around their radios, listening to

Prime Minister Winston Churchill from 10 Downing Street, encouraging Britain to carry on, and win the war. That memory made this an even more special visit.

It always seemed strange to me how the governments of England, France and Italy found the time and made the effort to have highly placed government officials and members of royalty host affairs honoring their fashion industry. In the USA, except for a selected few fashion designers being invited to the White House, the fashion industry has to self promote itself with events such as The Fashion Designers Awards. Aside from Jackie Kennedy, America's lack of effort in this area gives the impression that we are lacking in style and class compared to Europe when it comes to recognizing the outstanding fashion designers of America.

We did return to Britain in the years that followed for more memorable events, and two other occasions related to Princess Diana stand out the most. On one trip to Europe, I brought my golf clubs hoping to be able to play golf in Milan, Paris and London over the weekends. The game in Milan worked out fine, with Aldo Pinto as it did in Paris with Count Hubert d'Ornano. I was looking forward to playing in London over the following weekend at Sunningdale. Eddie Rayne called to tell me that unfortunately our game had to be cancelled due to a tournament being held at that time.

The next day I was having lunch with Ken Williams of Turnbull and Asser and Michael Fawcett, Prince Charles's equerry, when I mentioned my frustration of bringing my clubs to London and not being able to play. Fawcett said, since I was meeting the princess at reception that evening, why not ask her if I could play golf at Windsor Castle? As the princess greeted me that evening, I said "Michael Fawcett suggested that I should ask you, would it be possible since I brought my clubs to London to play at Windsor Castle?" She responded not by saying yes or no. Instead she said, with a big smile, "You boys are always looking for trouble."

The next day I had a message from the Royal Household Golf Club to be available early the next morning to be picked up at my hotel to be taken to Windsor. The next morning I wore a very proper blazer, shirt and tie, and carried my golf clothes in a bag. Instead of going to the palace to change, I was taken to a small caddy shack on the grounds that also served as a locker. It wasn't very grand, but it was practical.

The golf course had interesting features: nine holes, with two tees at each hole in order to play eighteen holes. I noticed a great number of untended divots. My partners from the Royal Household explained they were from Prince Charles's horses. They were allowed to gallop on the golf course and surrounding grounds. I was also told not to mind the sand traps being "messed up a bit." When the royal children were in residence, they were allowed to play in the sand with their pails and shovels.

I heard later that when any member of the royal family was in residence, the golf course was closed to guests. There were, as I was told, family at Windsor when I was there. When brought to the princesses attention she said, "tend to it." And so I played at the smallest golf course with Windsor Castle in the background, the largest and grandest clubhouse in the world.

When I left, I was presented with a maroon sweater and tie embossed with the emblem Royal Household Golf Club. I was pleased, but a bit puzzled. The sweater felt like wool but was 100 percent Acrylic made in England. With the wool industry so important to England, I would have thought the Royal Household would have capitalized on that.

To express my appreciation to the Princess, I wanted her to have a gift from America that was new, different, and exciting. Since the Estée Lauder Company had just introduced their newest product, Origins, at Bergdorf Goodman, I felt a gift of Origins would be appropriate. I called William Lauder, who was then heading that division, and requested a large gift basket of all the Origins products to be sent to the Princess. Word came backed to me that Princess Diana received the package when she was traveling and opened the basket in the car like a child opening a birthday present.

A number of years later when Princess Diana was going through a very difficult time in her life involving her divorce from Prince

Charles, Jackie and I wrote to her expressing our sympathy for her problems. We explained that no matter how upsetting the present situation was, she would go down in history as one of the outstanding women of her generation. Whereas in the past we had correspondence from her various ladies in waiting, this time we received a hand written letter from the Princess herself saying, yes indeed she remembered us, and thanked us for our words of comfort.

KENSINGTON PALACE

February: 9ᵗʰ
1996.

Dear Mr Neimark,

    I was enormously touched by your lovely letter & I wanted to thank you & your wife so much for thinking of me during this difficult time.

    I recall very well as two meetings with fond memories,

but you forgot to include (!)
the discussion we had
about a British designer, Bruce
Oldfield who we thought
might have brought his
talent to Bergdorf Goodman;
no lapse of memory from this
lady I fear!

Thank you, more than I
can, possibly say for sharing
such kindness in writing to
me — Your words brought a
great deal of comfort ....

With my love to you both,
from, Diana.

After the Princess' untimely passing, Jackie and I wrote the following letter to her older son.

November 14, 1997

H.R.H. Prince William
c/o The Prince of Wales Office
St. James Palace
London SW1A 2BS

Your Royal Highness,

Recently, I was reviewing some correspondence I had with your late mother nearly two years ago. I was thanking her for her many kindness' to me and Mrs. Neimark on our visits to London when we attended the receptions for the American fashion press and retailers hosted by the British Trade Board.

In addition to thanking her I also reminisced about what a wonderful memory she had remembering us at each of the receptions, even to the detail that I was wearing her favorite Turnbull & Asser tie, and did I ever buy Mrs. Neimark the Jaguar that I had promised her?

Possibly you may remember about ten years ago your mother had you stand at her side at one of these receptions at Kensington Palace. As she introduced us to you, she explained, "I want Prince William to see what it is that I do." We were impressed.

Inviting me to play golf at Windsor was of course one of the highlights of my long golfing career, and being her dinner partner at Fishmonger's Hall was another unforgettable highlight.

I wrote to Her Royal Highness at a time that I felt was difficult for her, and Mrs. Neimark and I wanted her to know that we and her friends in America felt that your mother was and would be considered one of the most outstanding women of her generation.

To our pleasant surprise, Her Royal Highness replied in person, writing, indeed she did remember us and also recalled my being her dinner partner and how we discussed the famous fashion designers she preferred.

Sadly this is over. Mrs Neimark and I wanted you to know that her Royal Highness had a special place in our hearts and in our lives, and we share your sorrow with you and your family at this difficult time.

Respectfully,

Ira and Jacqueline Neimark

Leaders and Followers 27

As I entered the retail business, I noticed that successful merchants had a common element: They knew that professional merchandising, financial, and operating people had to have professional "fashion people" as partners. As my career matured, I also noticed that many stores focused on well-structured financial, merchandising, and operating divisions and allowed their fashion area to remain nebulous and undefined.

Role models for retailers include Dorothy Shaver, the president of Lord & Taylor in the 1950s, blessed with a great fashion eye, and one of the first to promote American designers. She had the ability to identify the new talent, such as Bonnie Cashin, Claire McCardle, and John Weitz. Later Mildred Custin, the president of Bonwit Teller, discovered Calvin Klein and Henri Bendel's president, Geraldine Stutz, also had the talent to select and promote the new fashion talent. Their combination of fashion and business gifts are rare today.

Other merchants, such as Beatrice Fox Auerbach, are role models because they had the keen judgment to know they needed the input of professional fashion people. Tobé, one of this country's early fashion consultants, visited G. Fox once a month to keep the store on the right fashion track. Her role was to tour the store with B.F.A. and to give her opinion as to how up to date G. Fox looked compared to the major New York stores, particularly, Lord & Taylor and Bloomingdales.

The weekly Tobé report showed the latest style trends, and the new best sellers, it was a "must read" for all the ready-to-wear buyers. B.F.A. insisted that the buyers send a report weekly to her office regarding their position with the best sellers listed in the report. I have found buyers have a natural tendency to resist supervision of what they feel is their prerogative, even from a highly respected professional.

By the time I became the general merchandise manager of G. Fox, Tobé had retired, and two competent women ran the company, Joan Harwood and Marjorie Dean. Since my instincts were to always be ahead of the competition, I made them a proposal. Would it be possible for me to attend the Tobé weekly editorial meetings in order to have an advanced preview of the newest trends they were recommending, as well as the latest best sellers? They politely declined in order to keep faith with their other subscribers, but my curiosity kept turning in that direction.

It was about this time that G. Fox joined the May Co., and I met Dawn Mello. Since Tobé Associates was not in a position to give me advanced information, I decided to give that responsibility to Dawn. She and her fashion staff at May Co. were knowledgeable about trends in women's ready-to-wear and fashion accessories markets, and gave the G. Fox buyers early indications as to where the fashion action would be. And since many of the May Co. stores did not take full advantage of this in house talent, G. Fox had the advantage of a fashion office always available to provide advanced fashion information.

Dawn's assisting me in the transformation of B. Altman—like moving the Egyptian Pyramids one inch—convinced me that she was in the same class as legendary leaders such as Dorothy Shaver, Mildred Custin and Geraldine Stutz. But it was at Bergdorf Goodman that Dawn Mello's talent had the opportunity to reach her potential. Her ability was a major contribution that brought the store to its leading fashion position in the retail world of today.

Dawn Mello's "Italian Strategy" broke the ice for Bergdorf Goodman, in not only the European fashion markets, but also in the United States. If Dawn felt that a line of merchandise should be in Bergdorf Goodman, she would invite me to view the line and arrange a meeting with the principal of the company. Hellen

Galland, then president of Bonwit Teller and my friend for many years, said, "When you and Dawn come into a showroom together, we know the line is going to Bergdorf Goodman."

By 1983, Dawn's success at Bergdorf Goodman was so obvious that she was getting a lot of phone calls. I was told that Dave Farrell, Chairman an CEO of May Co., Bob Suslow, the head of Saks Fifth Avenue, and Howard Goldfedder, Chairman of Federated Department Stores, all of whom at one time worked with Dawn, were talking to her. For the benefit of all concerned, primarily all of us at Bergdorf Goodman, we decided to promote her from Executive Vice President and Director of Fashion Merchandising, to President and Director of Merchandising. In addition to Dawn Mello's being pleased with her promotion, the reaction in the fashion market was very positive. Having a woman with Dawn Mello's talent as president of Bergdorf Goodman gave us an even higher profile.

Lessons Learned

- In the fashion business, it is just as important to have the best talent possible available for fashion guidance, as it is for financial, operational, and merchandising guidance.

- It is also important to have the merchandise divisions recognize that the head of the company often makes the key decision for the fashion executives. It is not for the people in those divisions to decide that they don't require guidance and that they can do just as well on their own. Those who feel they can do as well on their own should be let go to do just that.

Publicity directors with a sense of style can support the fashion leadership of a store well by knowing how to feature the fashions in appropriate advertising and displays. Sara Pennoyer, Bonwit Teller's sales promotion director, and other Bonwit talent such as Tom Lee and Gene Moore, later to gain fame at Tiffany, were in this elite group. I was fortunate to have been exposed to these people on a daily basis, and I was grateful to be able to absorb some of their good taste and wisdom.

When I first joined Bergdorf Goodman, most of the advertising consisted of small, 300-line sketched "item ads." Items were selected from throughout the store and advertised in the *New York Times* on a weekly basis. Store sales were small, and the advertising budget comparably small, so ads never created much of an impact, nor did they reflect imagination or design sense. The largest ads ran around Christmas time and would consist of possibly nine to twelve of these small ads grouped together on a single page in the *Times*. In considering a change, I recalled George Neustadt, the advertising analyst, saying, "Good advertising will speed a good merchant on to great success. Good advertising will also speed a bad merchant to his demise." My feeling at that time was that we should first prove we were good merchants and then develop a more aggressive advertising program to compete with our peers.

When taking over the responsibility of merchandising a store, many new presidents want to change the advertising format as one of their first priorities. It seems they want to broadcast to the public: A change has occurred; this is my personality. When I joined Bergdorf Goodman, Stanley Marcus, in addition to being Chairman Emeritus of Neiman Marcus, was also a consultant to Carter Hawley Hale. He was undoubtedly one of the best sales promotion people in the business, and offered me his advice as how to put a successful advertising campaign together. We gave up the small ads that gave the impression of a small store, in favor of larger ads that ran less frequently and created a fashion look. My focus was on putting together a merchandise strategy for carrying the major fashion collections, however, and concluded that big advertising campaigns would come later.

The least expensive approach with the most amount of impact would be a strong public relations effort. *WWD*, the *Times* and *Post* helped to realize this plan.

After we secured the fashion collections and felt we had a "critical fashion mass" to promote, we then retained the artist George Stravinos. His artwork of a different designer was featured each Sunday in a full-page advertisement in the *Times*. We coordinated the Fifth Avenue windows with the ad for impact and our floor displays also picked up the ads' themes. The approach built on the premise "repetition is reputation." I believed if you repeated a fashion statement often enough, a fashion reputation would arise.

In the early 1980s, I was very impressed with a fashion writer, the late John Duka, who wrote a fashion column every Tuesday for the *Times*. His column covered what was new and exciting in fashion, primarily in New York.

I felt that running the one important full page ad each Sunday, featuring one important fashion designer, did not allow us to get the complete story across about the other excitement in the store. I invited John Duka to write a fashion column for us, similar to his column in the *Times*. His objective would be to capture important store events as he had captured fashion events in the *Times*—an innovative way for us to tell a thorough "what is going on throughout Bergdorf Goodman" story each week, in addition to our major full page designer ad.

John accepted the challenge, and his first column ran Sunday February 10th, 1985. It carried the title "BG" and was fabulous. The feature of the full page was the opening of Bergdorf Goodman's Angela Cummings shop. The BG's one column, adjacent to the seven-column Angela Cummings ad, gave us a full-page impact. John's BG column appeared in the same typeface as that used by the *Times* and each week he wrote about the events and new merchandise in the store with a great sense of humor. As an example, one paragraph poked fun at the competition: "Did everyone in the world go to Bergdorf's last week? Not quite, those who wanted to get doused with perfume went elsewhere. Those who wanted a little chic and sanity came here."

The *New York Times* was gracious about losing John to Bergdorf Goodman. They had but one request, though: Run the column if you will, but kindly do not use the *Times* typeface in your BG column. We changed the type, and kept everyone happy.

Lesson Learned

- As war is an extension of politics, advertising is an extension of merchandising. No advertising campaign is worth its salt unless it reflects a sound merchandising strategy, policy and concept.

With our ads, spectacular shows, displays and other publicity, we as a retailer reinforced the names of designers in the minds of thousands of customers, and millions of potential customers. We had few or no options other than to promote the fashion designers since that is where the fashion news and excitement was coming from. We followed this strategy to build our designer labels to unprecedented heights. In the process, in addition to acquiring prime locations in retail stores all over the world and also opening their own boutiques, a financial bonanza for the fashion designers came from licensing their now-famous names. The licensing in most cases developed into lower price line apparel, using the designer's name. In cases such as Pierre Cardin, product licensing arose in addition to apparel, in the form of anything from toothbrushes to eyeglasses. Eyeglasses in turn became one of the most distributed licensing classifications for nearly every designer.

Extreme examples of this business strategy are Christian Dior, built by a variety of owners into an international fashion empire, and Perry Ellis, a lucrative license "designer name" available to whoever owns the name at any given time.

One designer at Bergdorf Goodman brought this trend home to me early on. We selected Krizia, along with other Italian designers, to be featured with a major shop on the sportswear floor. The exclusivity of the Krizia shop, promoted with fashion shows, advertising, and Fifth Avenue windows was an immediate success for both Bergdorf and Krizia.

Mariuccia Mandelli and her husband Aldo Pinto, the owners of Krizia, had shops in major cities in Europe. They were (and still are) a very successful partnership. Both professional, smart, and a joy to work with. Aldo asked my opinion regarding licensing. I said the licensing concept was gaining momentum quickly, and if and when he did licensing for Krizia, his life would never be the same. I didn't realize how right I was. Soon after, Aldo made an arrangement with the Limited to license a lower price line under the Krizia label. (A smart move on the Limited's part.) Krizia merchandise was one of the leaders of Italian fashion, and very popular with Bergdorf Goodman's customers. Since we felt that most of our customers knew that the designer's name for Krizia was Mariuccia Mandelli, we opted to continue selling the collection, but only under the Mariuccia Mandelli label and to drop the Krizia name. Aldo and Mariuccia were upset with me and the reason was obvious. The success of the Krizia collection being featured at Bergdorf Goodman gave the Krizia name a high profile, which made the name desirable for lucrative licensing arrangements around the world. Bergdorf Goodman continued to feature the Mariuccia Mandelli collections, and Krizia continued to license their name, particularly in Japan.

Lessons Learned

- The fashion customer is <u>always</u> interested in something new. Designer names were and are news and exciting for this customer.

- Retailers should not only have promoted the new designer lines, they should have financially invested in the designers so they could monitor their products and also benefit from their licensing revenues.

Unexpected Advances   **28**

1986

In 1986, Carter Hawley Hale was the target of a hostile takeover by Leslie Wexner, head of the Limited stores. In order for Carter Hawley Hale to avoid the takeover, they devised a strategy that involved spinning off Neiman Marcus, Holt Renfrew, and Bergdorf Goodman from Carter Hawley Hale to General Cinema.

General Cinema had movie theaters, a soft drink bottler, and very shrewd investors with no retail store experience. I had enjoyed and appreciated working with Phil Hawley for twelve years and expected that General Cinema would offer a sharply contrasting world of management.

Their approach to inventory management confirmed this early on. All through this memoir, from Bonwit Teller to Bergdorf Goodman, I have stressed the importance of proper inventory management as the key to having new and exciting merchandise, and as a result, an increase sales and profits.

In most cases, department store chains' management monitors markdowns—how much, when, and when not to be taken—always protecting the gross profit. A case of profit before expenses. As an example, when G. Fox was merged with May Department Stores, I would receive a weekly call from headquarters in St. Louis. Their question: "What did I estimate the markdowns would be for that week, and the balance of the month?" As politely as I could, I told them not to call me about this subject. If I needed help, I would call them. In general, many retailers would fudge their numbers by not taking timely markdowns,

which brought about untold quantities of old stock that customers were less and less interested in as time elapsed.

Carrying these old suspicions and doubts forward, I wondered
what strategies awaited Bergdorf Goodman under the new owners.
I was in for a surprise.

When General Cinema took over, Richard Smith, the new
Chairman and CEO of the Neiman Marcus Group, being a smart
financial executive, outlined his strategy regarding the value of
inventory. If we had an inventory on the books for one million
dollars of his money, he wanted that inventory to represent one
million dollars of current inventory. His instructions were to take
the markdowns necessary to keep the inventory current. What
he didn't say, but implied, is that if markdowns are continually
excessive to keep the inventory current, someone else will have
the responsibility for that decision. This valuation of inventory is
the way retailers who owned their stores used to operate. Not
necessarily so, once these stores went public.

At this point in time, Bergdorf Goodman was increasing its sales
by about fifteen percent annually, with a substantial profit. So
much so, that Richard Smith recommended we have a cocktail
party and dinner in the store for the directors and their wives, to
include Nena and Andrew Goodman, and our senior executives.
He also asked me to say a few words as to our progress and how
I saw the future of Bergdorf Goodman.

I announced proudly to the guests, seated at a lovely dinner on the
fourth floor overlooking Central Park, that when I joined Bergdorf
Goodman in 1975, the store was losing money. Now, our sales had
passed the $100 million dollar mark—up from $38 million in 1975—
and that we were on our way to a new sales and profit record for 1987.

The next morning Andrew Goodman called me, quite upset, to
tell me the store hadn't been losing money if you didn't include
White Plains. I said nothing, but remembered the joke about the
prizefighter. As his opponent bloodied him, his ring manager
yelled, "Get in there; he isn't laying a glove on us!" "Maybe not on
you," the battered fighter replied, "but I'm getting killed."

Andrew was not concerned with my early days at Bergdorf Goodman, trying to increase sales, implementing new systems, working my way though markdowns, expenses, and trying to get us out of the red. Andrew was doing fine, and I was getting killed.

The president of General Cinema, Robert J. Tarr, had no retail store experience but had been the president of PepsiCo Bottling. When he told me he would ride the Pepsi trucks to see the positioning of his bottles compared to those of his competition, I knew I had found a kindred spirit.

Bob Tarr was impressed with Bergdorf Goodman's sales and profit growth compared to Neiman Marcus. So in 1987, in addition to being chairman and chief executive of Bergdorf Goodman, he appointed me vice president of the Neiman Marcus Group. My main function was to give direction to Neiman Marcus's merchandising people.

After Stanley Marcus retired as CEO, the management of Neiman Marcus had endured many changes under Carter Hawley Hale. As I saw it, a major problem they faced was, again, inventory management. Merchandise arrived late, and was also late in being marked down at the end of the season. A difference of two or three weeks late in receiving merchandise, and two to three weeks late in marking it down can put a fashion store at a tremendous disadvantage. Among the divisional merchandise managers at Neiman Marcus was Ron Frasch. He was told by Bob Tarr: "Sit in Neimark's office at Bergdorf Goodman and see how he operates." Ron Frasch went on to be the chairman and CEO of Bergdorf Goodman.

Ron didn't just sit in my office. In 1987, on a fact finding trip to Neiman Marcus, I visited their Houston store. Knowing that Calvin Klein was not included in their assortments, I asked the manager of the designer section of the store, "Why not?" The line was a difficult fit, she told me. This is a perfect example of the soldier in the foxhole making decisions on how to run the war. Soon after, Ron Frasch and I visited Calvin Klein and met with Barry Schwartz to present him with our merchandising program for Neiman Marcus. Today, I believe Neiman Marcus is Calvin Klein's largest account.

Lessons Learned

- Sometimes a change in ownership can be a negative to a career, as was my experience when G. Fox was acquired by May Co. Other times, it can be a positive, such as Bergdorf Goodman to General Cinema. So remember the ball bouncing in the pinball machine. It can bounce good or sometimes bad.

- When there is little control over the situation, a lot of luck helps.

- When a business isn't doing well, and has weak management, consultants are helpful, but that is never a substitute for professional management—professional management being defined as "<u>proven</u> professionals."

Within a year or two, General Cinema management asked me about Allen Questrom. Grab him as soon as you can, I suggested. Allen had recently resigned from Federated Department Stores, and was on a sabbatical. He had a wonderful reputation, not only as a merchant, but that of a top executive as well. General Cinema hired Allen as CEO of Neiman Marcus and that was the beginning of the reemergence of Neiman Marcus as the now successful dominant fashion retailer in America.

That success almost didn't happen. Previous to my recommending Allen, the Neiman Marcus Group came very close to making one of the very few mistakes that I'd experienced during my association with them.

Being quite busy bringing Bergdorf Goodman to its full potential, I was not involved in the initial search for the Neiman Marcus CEO. By the time I learned that The Neiman Marcus Group had arrived at a candidate, they were ready to meet his wife. This usually meant the process was far along, and they would soon make an offer to the candidate.

Prior to the appointment, Bob Tarr asked me to evaluate the candidate's store, which was somewhat comparable to Neiman Marcus, in order to finally determine whether he was qualified to run Neiman Marcus. I agreed to make the visit the next day.

The store had a reputation of being a fine specialty store with a few branches. (I prefer not to mention the name to save the store embarrassment.) I parked the car a block away, and to avoid being recognized, I wore sun glasses. The windows came first. A store's window display, in my opinion, gives as accurate a picture of what a store stands for as a person's dress conveys the individual's personality. The windows were the poorest looking display that I had seen in a long time. This usually gives a tip off as to what the interior of the store will look like. True to form, the interior displays and the lines of merchandise came nowhere near to what I deemed comparable to Neiman Marcus. I flew home the same day, submitted my negative report to Bob Tarr, and soon after Allen Questrom became CEO of Neiman Marcus. Whew!

—————————The Changing Retail Scene—————————

Allen Questrom, when arriving at Neiman Marcus, brought along his protégé, Terry Lundgren, as the general merchandise manager. Lundgren then became CEO of Neiman Marcus when Allen Questrom left to eventually become the CEO of Federated Department Stores, where he did the remarkable job of bringing Federated back from the brink of disaster. A few years later, Terry Lundgren left Neiman Marcus to again join Allen Questrom, this time at Federated, to be in charge of merchandising. When Allen Questrom left Federated, William Zimmerman became the CEO. Zimmerman retired in 2004 and Terry Lundgren then became CEO of Federated Department Stores. Since then Terry spearheaded the drive at Federated to buy the May Department Stores.

The following is a good example of how the pinball bounced in the right direction.

When I was CEO of Bergdorf Goodman and also appointed as vice president of The Neiman Marcus Group in 1987, Bob Tarr, the president of The Neiman Marcus Group, asked my opinion regarding a candidate that The Neiman Marcus Group was considering for the position of CEO of Neiman Marcus. As mentioned, my being negative about their candidate, instead helped to convince them that Allen Questrom was the executive they needed. This decision bounced the pinball of fate in the right direction that possibly changed the course of retailing in the U.S.

This is because, when Terry Lundgren left Neiman Marcus to join Allen Questrom at Federated, again I was asked by Bob Tarr, who I thought would be a good replacement for Terry Lundgren at Neiman Marcus? I suggested that he move my successor, Burt Tansky, from Bergdorf Goodman to become the CEO of Neiman Marcus, which they did.

The recommendation of recruiting Allen Questrom (When Allen's name came up, I said, grab him) for Neiman Marcus and Questrom then selecting Terry Lundgren to succeed him, and then bringing Lundgren to Federated, led General Cinema to appoint Burt Tansky to take Terry Lundgren's place. These management changes started a chain reaction for Neiman Marcus, Bergdorf Goodman and Federated Department Stores, to become the top retailers in America. The pinball once again bounced in the right direction.

Federated Department Stores is set to rename more than 400 stores in 11 regional chains as Macy's.
(NY Times, August 26, 2006)

Lundgren's strategy of converting the venerable names of the former May Department Stores to Macy's has many caveats. As outlined earlier in this book, I wrote about the May Company and other major chains, imposing their merchandise and operating philosophies on the regional department stores they acquired. In time the regional department stores lost their identity and ceased to exist.

The key to the success or failure of Federated's approach, name change or not, as I have repeatedly stated, will come down to "merchandise, content and presentation." No matter what name the store has, Bonwit Teller or John Wanamaker were two examples of great names, but both lost their way by not being consistent and not being able to recognize who their customer was and equally as important, who their future customer will be.

The challenge and opportunity for Federated Department Stores to capitalize on its acquisition of the May Department stores (and the others) by using the Macy's name, will be a function of Federated's ability to properly and aggressively cater to the middle income customer, as it has successfully accomplished in the past. This will work over time, whatever the name of the store, if executed properly. That is the caveat.

The more difficult task will be to attract the upscale customer who does not relate to the Macy's of years past, with the long history of strong price promotions and presentations of moderately priced merchandise.

Terry Lundgren is a merchant with a long and successful career at all merchandise price levels, from specialty stores to department stores. Using sound merchandising principals with a strong organization, his strategy will work as long as each of the so called, venerable May Department Stores, reflect the best of Macy's, with outstanding assortments of merchandise, great presentations and most important of all, service to the customer, that seems to be a lost art in department stores today.

Lesson Learned

- When searching for a key executive in an organization, it is critical to define clearly to all those making the decision, that they agree on what the highest standards and objectives are for that position. In addition, every resource available must be employed, from personal contacts to a professional executive recruiter familiar with all aspects of that industry's inner workings. Unimpeachable references are also a requirement.

Only in New York or Istanbul

29

O n one of my early trips to the Paris couture, Calvin Klein and I encountered each other in the Concorde Lounge at Kennedy Airport. We talked about the importance of Bergdorf Goodman reintroducing the couture. I was always impressed with Calvin as a person as well as a fashion designer, and told him how great it would be if he would do some couture models for us one day. He thanked me and I thought that was the end of it.

Fast forward to 1986: After Bergdorf Goodman successfully launched our "Italian strategy" and had built a strong base of European and American designers, we looked for another way to differentiate ourselves from the competition. Dawn and I had conversations with Calvin and his business partner Barry Schwartz, and suggested adding a location to their Bergdorf Goodman shop for an exclusive line of a Calvin Klein made-to-order. They liked the idea and the implementation was quite innovative. Bergdorf Goodman would select twenty styles to be shown at their fashion show for both their department and specialty store customers. These styles would be withdrawn from the line, and six to eight pieces per style would be hand-made in their workroom to be exclusively for Bergdorf Goodman.

At the end of the fashion show, Calvin Klein announced his exclusive couture arrangement with Bergdorf Goodman. At this point, it is the custom for the heads of the stores and their key

Calvin with his models after the show

fashion executives to compliment the designer on the collection. Marvin Traub, the Chairman and CEO of Bloomingdales, and Burt Tansky, the President and general merchandise manager of Saks Fifth Avenue, approached Calvin and Barry, visibly upset that Bergdorf Goodman had this arrangement and that they were not included. Calvin and Barry's response to them was brilliant. They explained that Bergdorf Goodman had been promoting and selling couture exclusively in the USA, and they wanted to be included. Neither Saks Fifth Avenue, nor Bloomingdales were in that business. That ended any further discussion.

As I noted before, Spring and Fall of each year, Bergdorf Goodman staged a major fashion show featuring the collection from a top fashion designer. With the Calvin Klein couture shop scheduled to open in Bergdorf Goodman September 18, the day after the show, Susie Butterfield felt this was the "perfect show" in terms of timing and appeal. We selected the Pulitzer fountain again, as we did for our Fendi show, but this time we decided to cover

Nancy Kissinger and Steve Rubell

the whole area with a tent. Bergdorf Goodman, Calvin Klein, Mrs. Henry Kissinger, and the women's committee of the Central Park Conservancy were sponsors of the show. The fashion show was scheduled for Wednesday, September 17.

Barry Schwartz and I had to approach Henry Stern, the Park Commissioner, for his approval. The meeting was short. "If you want a party, fix the fountain."

Leonard Lauder, Ira Millstein and I, were already in the embryonic stages of developing a campaign for the restoration of the Pulitzer Fountain and the Grand Army Plaza. The fountain that I looked at daily from my office window, as did Leonard Lauder, had fallen into great disrepair. Instead of being enjoyed by sightseers, it was an eyesore.

The fashion show proved to be a good beginning for the restoration of the Pulitzer Fountain by raising over $100,000 toward the goal of $3 million. The group led by Leonard Lauder developed a "window tax." That is, he asked owners of buildings facing the Grand Army Plaza to contribute toward the restoration according to the number of windows their building had facing the Plaza. We raised the money and the goddess Pomona was removed from the top of the fountain on October 28, 1988, and repair completed the latter part of 1989.

Bergdorf Goodman opened the new Calvin Klein couture shop, designed by Angela Patterson, our store designer, the day after the party and fashion show. The show, dinner party and new shop reflected a successful collaboration of Bergdorf Goodman, Calvin Klein, New York City, and Leonard Lauder's Pulitzer Fountain committee.

Lessons Learned

- Never be satisfied with your progress. There is always another idea, different from that of your competition. Competition must always be looked at as a threat to your business's success. It should be studied carefully, and fought aggressively.

Following closely on the heels of doing my civic duty to fix the Pulitzer Foundation, I had another occasion to serve the great city of New York.

Ever since I started working on Fifth Avenue, I always felt this was the best of America's grand boulevards. A retail location on Fifth Avenue was the mark of distinction and success. The street peddlers apparently agreed. About the mid-1980s, a proliferation of them occurred up and down Fifth Avenue from below 34th Street to 59th Street. The situation deteriorated to the point that the Fifth Avenue merchants held a news conference at the St. Regis Hotel on December 18, 1986.

"New York City has become a disaster area as far as this topic is concerned," Donald Trump said at the session. He further said, "Sidewalk peddlers; many of them illegal immigrants from West Africa, have multiplied along the Avenue and constitute the biggest department store in the world" (*New York Times*, December 19, 1986).

I had always felt that Mayor Ed Koch was an admirable man, faced with the nearly impossible task of managing New York City. His initial position regarding the street peddlers, however, went against everything that I felt Fifth Avenue and Bergdorf Goodman stood for. Multitudes of illegal street peddlers scurried in front of prestige stores and set up stands cluttered with

Donald J. Trump, Anthony Conti, Ira Neimark and Harry Huberth

cheap watches, windup toys, bad costume jewelry, tee shirts, and other junk.

To have peddlers standing in front of Bergdorf Goodman on Fifth Avenue and blocking the display windows on 58th and 57th streets upset me—and that's putting it mildly. After spending a great deal of time and money to create a fashion impression, to have customers walk past street peddlers to get into the store was also frustrating.

The rhetoric got out of hand when the Mayor said that his grandfather was a peddler: "Peddling is a noble profession."

I countered with, "In those days, peddlers would not be allowed on Fifth Avenue." Unfortunately, I added, "Fifth Avenue is a disaster that looks like Istanbul on a Sunday."

The mayor of Istanbul wrote to me asking for an apology, saying Istanbul was cleaner than New York City any day of the week. Some Turkish customers also cancelled their charge accounts. I wrote to Istanbul's mayor and the customers to apologize, and told them I was referring to the Souk and I hoped they understood. The customers eventually returned.

Mayor Koch finally got the message and did the necessary job of clearing most of the street peddlers from Fifth Avenue. They still exist, but to a much lesser degree and I still consider them a blot on what used to be called, "maintaining high standards."

The Mayor and I have long ago forgiven each other. He invited Jackie and me to Gracie Mansion and we have invited him to dinner. Coincidentally, Ed koch and I share the same birth date.

Lesson Learned

- To be a good businessman also means being a good citizen. As high standards are required in a successful business, so they are required in the society that surrounds us. To cater to the lowest common denominator will eventually bring you there.

The Price and Rewards of Exclusivity

30

New York, Paris and Milan—by 1986 Bergdorf Goodman had secured exclusive arrangements for important fashion collections from the United States and Europe. James Galanos was a rare holdout due to his exclusive arrangements with Martha on

James Galanos

Park Avenue and Palm Beach. When I tried to lure Galanos, I first had to convince him that his luxurious fur line licensed to furrier Peter Dione should be exclusively in Bergdorf Goodman. After a couple of store tours and chats, Peter concluded that Bergdorf Goodman would best represent their new fur collection.

After the Galanos furs were launched in 1986, Peter Dione invited me to attend the 1987 summer fur auction in Leningrad with him. The biggest American sable buyer to attend the Leningrad auctions, Peter had been a regular there for twenty years, and knew intimately the do's and don'ts of the Soviet methods and systems. I became aware of this a number of

262

times when he stayed calm and I was in shock. The first was when our Swiss Air flight from Helsinki to then Leningrad banked steeply. Peter explained that international airlines had to fly a very tight flight pattern to stay within Soviet security zones.

When we landed and went through the passport control, I handed my passport to the uniformed officer and put my reading glasses on. He brusquely demanded, "Take your glasses off."

As the words, "Who the devil do you think you are, talking to me like that?" shot into my head, Peter grabbed my arm before they shot out of my mouth. He said, "Don't say a word or they will put you on the next plane out." The next stop was luggage inspection. Peter opened his bag and revealed dozens of Galanos perfume samples that he used as gifts and tips where necessary during his visit. The customs inspector put his hand in Peter's luggage, grabbed half a dozen, and shoved them in his pocket. Once again, outrage had nearly made it out of my mouth when I felt Peter's hand on my arm. Just another normal procedure at a Soviet airport.

On the way to the hotel Pribaltiyskaya, Peter explained that all the floors of the hotel would be lighted except for the third floor. That dark floor was for the KGB. He added that whenever he said, "Black Cat," that would mean he'd spotted a KGB officer. Whenever that happened I should be careful of what I was saying. (Who could miss the irony of spies being so obvious?)

When we checked in, I learned it would take about a half hour to place a call home to tell Jackie I had arrived safely. When I finally got through to Jackie, she asked how did I like my visit to the Soviet Union? Knowing the KGB was listening, I answered, "They aren't ready for you."

A little old lady sat all day doing nothing in the middle of the hall on the way to my room. She seemed to ignore me, but after a few days she knew who I was, and when I came in and went out. Other features of the place made it even less inviting. The sheets on the bed looked as though they hadn't been changed since the last guest, and the water coming out of the pipes in the bath and shower was too dark to bathe with.

The next day we went to view the furs on display previous to the auction. I had never seen so many furs in one place. It seemed as though the warehouses went on for hundreds of yards with thousands of skins from sable to squirrels and every animal in between. To me, it served as a visible reminder of the vastness of the Soviet Union.

A man in what appeared to be a military uniform conducted the fur auction. Fast and efficient, he appeared to favor bidders of his preference. With the aid of an interpreter—one of the few (if not the only) attractive women at the auction—Peter purchased the top sables for Bergdorf Goodman and the Neiman Marcus catalogue. Our interpreter dressed well, spoke English beautifully and had majored in Spanish art of the 17th and 18th century. I mention her since she was so helpful at the auction as well at a tour of the Hermitage, where Neiman Marcus was having furs photographed for their catalog. I asked her for her home address in order to send her a gift from Bergdorf Goodman. She gave it to me with no hesitation, but Peter got quite upset with me. If the KGB knew I was corresponding with her, he said, she would be in big trouble. Peter certainly knew how to fuel my paranoia. Back at the hotel I tore up and flushed the address down the toilet, hoping an agent wasn't at the other end with a strainer to catch her name and address.

Even in this environment, Peter's concern seemed excessive—but it wasn't. Our adventure escalated the night that Neiman Marcus was to have a photo shoot on a Soviet ship in the harbor, with sailors as a backdrop for the models wearing furs. Peter suggested we go to see the shoot and hired a taxi to take us to the ship. A car followed us from the hotel to the dock. The men in the car asked us to enter the building with them, took us to a small room, and told us to wait there. I learned that after World War II, Peter had been a Greek partisan fighting the Communists. It flashed through my mind that that this was a problem. There was a phone in the room, and when we were alone we tried to call out. The phone line was dead.

About a half-hour later, we didn't know why, we were told to get a cab and go back to the hotel. That appeared to be the end of it, but it wasn't completely over.

At the end of the auction the head of the fur commission held a cocktail party for the fur buyers. I attended with Peter, and as I met various Russian executives in attendance, heard Peter say "black cat." He whispered to me that the headwaiter was KGB and "in charge" of the commission.

Our last day before flying to Luxembourg, and then on to Amsterdam via Aeroflot, we visited the Leningrad subway. Going down the abrupt decline I found out the subway was steep and deep for two reasons. One, Leningrad was built on water with many canals. Two, the subways were to be used as bomb shelters in case of war. The Pushkin station was so grand that I shot some pictures with my miniature Minox. Once again, Peter cautioned me. The subways were considered military installations and not to be photographed. No one stopped me, but I was a bit concerned until we landed in Luxembourg. I had requested using Aeroflot in order to experience a Soviet airline. I noticed that all the passenger planes had plexiglass nosecones. This was Soviet efficiency at work: In case of war, the planes could be easily fitted with armaments without wasting any time.

We spent a short time in Luxembourg, then flew on to Amsterdam. I called Jackie and said, "We're out," and that was exactly how I felt.

Lessons Learned

- The saying, "When in Rome, do as the Romans do," applies to all countries and unusual environments.

- Whenever in a situation different from what you're used to, let yourself be advised by an experienced person.

In the Fall of 1987, we staged one of the most extraordinary fashion show galas that Bergdorf Goodman had ever held. We were launching an exclusive arrangement with Christian Lacroix, another Dawn Mello discovery, or to be more specific, a rising star in Paris that she had recognized ahead of our competition.

Christian Lacroix salutes his fans

Printed with permission of *Women's Wear Daily*

Thinking back about all the designers we brought to Bergdorf Goodman since 1975, and the gala fashion shows we had to introduce them, we felt this should be the biggest. The first reason was that our merchandise people felt we could sell Lacroix, and the second was he, and we, were considered big fashion news. The third was, we felt that we could now justify the financial out-lay required with some support from selected sponsors.

Betsy Baron and Linda Gaunt in our public relations department and Harriet Weintraub of Lacroix came up with the wonderful idea of presenting the show at the World Financial Center's Winter Garden. This was a large, elegant, glass-enclosed mega-structure in between several newly built sky-scrapers in the Wall Street area of lower Manhattan.

Princess Gloria von Thurn und Taxis, Donald, Ivana Trump and Keneth J Lane

Amanda Burden

WWD described the location as "an eccentric choice that turned out to be a stroke of genius. It was fresh, imaginative and romantic." The dinner and dancing in the Winter Garden complete with fireworks over the Hudson—I had vetoed the fireworks, but was overruled by Dawn and our publicity department, who were right—and tango dancers on a candlelit pyramid of steps turned out to be the most outstanding fashion party anyone could remember.

The evening raised funds for Memorial Sloan Kettering Hospital. Needless to say, half the battle to have a successful fashion

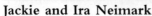

Jackie and Ira Neimark   **Blaine and Robert Trump**

show is determined by the charity that co-sponsors the event. The other half is to have a designer "of the moment." In this case the photos on the following pages from *The New York Times* and *WWD* document some of those in attendance.

I also had a great time. I not only had the opportunity to dance with my wife Jackie, but with Faye Dunaway as well. Lacroix's bouffant evening dresses quickly became the fashion sensation of the season. The dresses sold extremely well proving once again that high fashion can create great publicity and also bring about very strong sales results.

Lesson Learned

- In the retail fashion business it is as imperative to have a knowledgeable fashion director, as well as an imaginative publicity director, as it is to have "a nose" in the perfume business. Both perform a function that is unique and special and that will lead to success.

Beginnings Near the End 31

One day in 1988, I received an attention-grabbing call from Rob Smith, the son of Richard Smith, the Chairman of General Cinema. Did I have an interest in Bergdorf Goodman taking over the Spectacular space made vacant by the moving of FAO Schwartz to the General Motors Building? It sat directly across Fifth Avenue from Bergdorf Goodman.

Rob handled the real estate for General Cinema and had been approached by a broker representing the owners of 745 Fifth Avenue. Steve Elkin, then Vice Chairman, and I examined the property and concluded it presented a solid opportunity to expand into much needed space. I had always looked to the space behind Bergdorf Goodman on 58th Street for expansion, if that ever became available. My feeling was to have one large Bergdorf Goodman store. Having a separate store across Fifth Avenue made me wonder: "Will customers cross Fifth Avenue? And if they do, for what type of merchandise?" Our thinking leaned towards men's apparel.

Steve Elkin came up with a more focused answer. His logic was, we had sales of approximately $16 million in men's merchandise in approximately 16,000 square feet in the women's store, producing sales of $1,000 dollars per square foot. Moving men's across the avenue would enable us to expand the women's business into that space, with a much higher sales productivity. Even if the men's store only broke even, we would come out ahead between both stores.

With that as the guiding concept, our next step was to determine if we could build a men's business large and exciting enough to be an attraction unto itself. Our initial plan was to use 30,000 square feet on two floors. As we talked to the men's designers and shops such as Turnbull & Asser, Charvet and Hermes, however, we realized Bergdorf Goodman Men's Store would require at least 40,000 square feet of space on three floors in order to carry all the lines of merchandise necessary to create a "critical mass."

We decided to build the men's store in the latter part of 1988, with the opening planned for the fall of 1990. The interior of the store would harbor an exclusive, upscale men's club. We felt the only flaw in the real estate was the existing highly promotional jewelry and gift store located on Fifth Avenue, right in the middle of our proposed main floor. We offered to buy them out. This never happened, so we built around them. We decided that after their lease ran out in three years, we would modify the plans with a new entrance where the jewelry store existed. Before the completion of the store, the *New York Times* Sunday magazine section did a feature story by Carrie Donovan, showing the store under construction. The article went on to explain the concept and thinking behind the project in a very positive way. Carrie also told me that, riding uptown in a taxi to Barney's still-to-be-completed store on Madison Avenue, Gene Pressman said he was sorry to hear that I would be retiring after the men's store was completed. He was looking forward to "taking me on." I always enjoyed fighting competition, but I felt Barney's strong presence would only enhance uptown as a premier shopping area. Unfortunately for Barney's, financial problems held back their potential until new management put them back on track.

At this time, we all faced another challenge: the near impossibility of holding a fashion line to be exclusive. Designers had to make tough decisions as to which stores they would sell to and eventually sold to all the stores they felt that had the potential to represent them properly. (And unfortunately, some who did not.) The gathering of the exclusive fashion collections at Bergdorf

Bill Blass

**Ronaldus Shamask and
Joseph Abboud**

Goodman to create the critical
fashion mass had worked well
enough for us in the women's
store and brought us to the
point where I felt Bergdorf
Goodman had realized my
ambitions to be recognized as
the leading fashion store for
women in America, and even
for many women from abroad.

The question was, would the
concept developed for the
women's store work successfully
for the men's? Our mission statement for this new venture, con-
sciously paralleled the one we
adopted for the women's store.
The men's store was also to cater
to men who belonged to the
best clubs, went to the best
restaurants, vacationed at the best
resorts, and stayed at the best
hotels. Our intent: Create "The
ultimate store for gentlemen." In
addition to carrying the best
lines of men's clothing, furnishings and sportswear, we decided
to have a concierge to make
reservations, a waiter serving
sparkling water, cell phones
available for busy executives, A
Wall Street electronic ticker tape,
and a putting green with a golf
pro. The pro was also expected
to sell the exclusive Lacoste

Henry Kravis

Arnold Scaasi

sportswear merchandise. We also had tie cleaning. Soup at lunch? Caught in the rain? No problem. Have your tie cleaned or your suit pressed. Plus, we cultivated the best sales people, men and women, with backgrounds compatible to some degree to their customers. And last but not least, a doorman.

The "critical mass" for the proper mix of merchandise for this customer had to be screened and selected very carefully in order for that store to be very special for this new Bergdorf Goodman customer, while being profitable for the company. Major classifications, such as men's neckties, had to be presented dramatically. The two level rotunda featured neckties from Hermes, Turnbull and Asser, Charvet, Etro, Zegna and Ferragamo. Men's dress shirts were from Alan Flusser, Ike Behar, Giorgio Armani, Charvet, Turnbull and Asser, as well as Bergdorf Goodman's own line. The sportswear area carried Ralph Lauren (partly exclusive), Henry Cotton, and Willis and Geiger. Other names front and center included: Jeffrey Banks, Joseph Aboud, and Alan Flusser.

Printed with permission of *Women's Wear Daily*

Printed with permission of *Women's Wear Daily*

Marc Jacobs   **Ira Neimark and Jackie Mason**

The tailored clothing area was to be very important to the successful businessman. Brioni, requested by Donald Trump; Oxxford; Keyton; Hickey Freeman; Hugo Boss; and large shops to accommodate both Giorgio Armani and Luciano Barbera.

We introduced our new addition to the New York fashion scene with a splashy cocktail party for a thousand guests the night before the opening. Bergdorf Goodman's best women customers were invited to bring their husbands, and they did. Every fashion designer represented in the store was there. Even Jackie Mason the comedian showed up with the famous divorce lawyer Raoul Felder. The press covered the party very well, and helped to accomplish our objective: Bergdorf Goodman entered the men's business with great fanfare.

One of the things I neglected to do was invite our New York competition. I know Louis of Boston who recently opened on 57th Street and his associate (and my friend) Saul Kaplan were unhappy with me, as they should be.

Stewart Elliot of the *New York Times* wrote that Bergdorf Goodman's Men's store should be called Neimark's folly. I wrote

Janice Levin, Herbert Kasper and Ira Neimark

Sharon Klingenstein, Joan Tisch and Laurence Tisch

Bill Cunningham, *The New York Times*

**Two-story high rotunda of the new
Bergdorf Mens store**

a letter to the Times Stating: "Mr. Elliot may be a good news-paperman, but comes up short as a merchant." Within two years of opening, Bergdorf Goodman's Men's store exceeded sales of $1,000 per square foot with 40,000 square feet of selling space, with increasing profits to match. Some store, some folly!

Lesson Learned

- Whenever an opportunity presents itself, even though it may not be in the short or long term plan, examine the opportunity very carefully from every angle. Use all your best thinking, as well as the counsel of those who work with you. President Kennedy said, "I use all the brains I have, and all that I can borrow before making an important decision."

Previous to this rejuvenating launch, I learned that Dawn Mello was leaving us. After twenty years, Dawn Mello and I could practically read each other's minds regarding merchandising and fashion decisions. Dawn's opinion as to emerging fashion talent, who had hit their peak, and which designers were coasting downhill, was the best in the business. Her decision as to the order of importance of each designer in relation to the other, was critical to the launching of Bergdorf Goodman's renaissance and quoting Bill Blass, Bergdorf's was "the best shop in the world" (*Daily News Record,* June 13, 1990).

She had all this fashion insight and intuition combined with an ability to recognize and select fashion merchants, fashion directors, display and advertising talent.

Her relationships in "the market" were second to none. All together, these talents and accomplishments made it possible for Dawn to become one of the major leaders in the fashion business.

Dawn left Bergdorf Goodman for a top executive post at the Gucci Retail and manufacturing business. Could she do for Gucci what she had done for Bergdorf? It goes without saying Dawn Mello recommending Tom Ford to be the designer at Gucci was just the beginning of another great success story.

Lesson Learned

- The principal of any retail store who wants their establishment to be a dominant fashion force must realize that a professional fashion director is as important as any newspaper editor, financial director or operating officer.

Not Really the End

32

---------------------------- **1992** ----------------------------

I thought that when I reached age 70 it would be a reasonable time to bow out. I had my health and enjoyed retailing at its highest level. It would take me another year to open the men's store in the fall of 1990, and I would have one full year to work with my successor during 1991. Then I would turn 70 and feel comfortable retiring.

But it would not feel appropriate and I would not feel settled if I were to retire at the end of that year without confidence in a successor.

In most succession plans it is difficult, if not impossible, to satisfy everyone. The combination of Steve Elkin and Dawn Mello to continue what we had all started seemed the most appealing strategy. Both Steve and Dawn had made major contributions to the growth and success of Bergdorf Goodman and had a complete understanding of our goals and ambitions for the store.

Unfortunately for Bergdorf Goodman, Dawn Mello had left us in 1989 for Gucci in Italy.

Time for another succession plan.

Steve Elkin had many qualities making him a good candidate for consideration to assume the reins, but he had not yet developed the full breadth of attributes required for the job. As the financial and operating head, Steve was solid, but he lacked the market knowledge and contacts deemed essential for the job at that time. Fortunately, he developed these skills by the time he succeeded Burt Tansky.

Burton (Burt) Tansky was at the top of my recommended list to succeed me for a good number of reasons. The main one: Burt was a good merchant. He had to be, to serve for so many years as the general merchandise manager and eventually president under four CEOs at Saks Fifth Avenue. To hold those positions under merchants such as Bob Suslow, Mel Jacobs, Arnold Aronson, and Phil Miller, he had to be darned good. He also knew and was respected by all the major players in the market. This was <u>critical</u> in order to maintain the market relationships that Bergdorf Goodman had developed over the past seventeen years.

Yes, it would be Burt. He was ready to be a CEO on his own. The timing was right for Bergdorf Goodman and Burt Tansky. Even though Bergdorf Goodman was a much smaller operation than Saks Fifth Avenue, it offered what Burt always wanted, a store of his own.

Burt Tansky joined Bergdorf Goodman in 1991 as vice chairman. I remained chief executive and Steve Elkin president. I had only one admonition for Burt: "Make the store a big Bergdorf Goodman, not a small Saks Fifth Avenue." He stuck with that concept, and under his direction Bergdorf Goodman continued to grow as Bergdorf Goodman.

There were three wonderful retirement parties for me.

One was at the Plaza Hotel on November 5th, 1991. The list of attendees reflected the best of the upscale fashion market. Bill Blass, Geoffrey Beene, Donna Karan and Calvin Klein represented the designers. Terry Lundgren, CEO of Neiman Marcus; Allen Questrom, CEO of Federated Department Stores; Phil Miller, CEO of Saks Fifth Avenue—the best of the retail market. Estée Lauder and her son Leonard added great luster in addition to all the people who helped me to arrive at that point in my career. In my speech I thanked everyone in the audience for contributing to my success. I particularly paid a tribute to Jackie, and to my daughters, Janie and Robin, for their support and inspiration during my career. If I had the opportunity to do the speech again, on reflection, I would have

Calvin Klein, Geoffrey Beene, Donna Karan and Ira Neimark

Janie Neimark Lewis, Ira Neimark and Robin Neimark Seegal

Kelly and Calvin Klein

Kelli and Allen Questrom

Neiman Marcus's Terry Lundgren

Burt Tansky and Donna Karan

Ira Neimark's Family—Robin Seegal, Jackie Neimark, Russell Neimark Shattan, Ira Neimark, Janie Lewis and Dr. Michael Lewis liked to go from table to table thanking individually those guests who were instrumental in helping me to achieve success in my career. There were too many names to pay tribute to then, and the list would be too long to include in this memoir now. But it goes without saying; no executive achieves success going it alone. To all those who helped me move up the ladder, I thank you now.

In Paris on October 22nd, 1991, Caryl (nee Sherman) and Richard Actis Grande with Burt Tansky had a farewell surprise party for me that was the party of all parties. Caryl had worked with me at B. Altman as the fashion director of women's accessories. She and her husband Dick developed a buying office in Paris, representing Bergdorf Goodman, Neiman Marcus and Holt Renfrew. They were very successful and I was very proud of them for what they accomplished in the most important fashion markets of Paris, London and Milan.

The party was at the Musee du Vin (The Museum of Wine), one of the oldest and largest wine cellars from the fourteenth century in Paris. The large candle-lit wine cellar—it seemed to go on for miles—was exquisitely decorated for the party. I will never forget the beauty and warmth of that evening. The list of guests represented many of the designers and personalities from Paris, London and Milan who I had worked with since my first European trip for Bergdorf Goodman in 1975. Jackie and I were not only surprised, but also overwhelmed with the turnout. The list included Burt and Rita Tansky, from Bergdorf Goodman; Terry Lundgren, from Neiman Marcus; Caryl and Dick Grande from AGAF (their buying office); from Bergdorf Goodman, Barbara Lamonica, the merchandise manger of designer sportswear; Angela Patterson, our display director and Joseph Boitano, our merchandise manager of designer apparel; Count and Countess d'Ornano; Jean-Louis Dumas from Hermes; Karl Lagerfeld; Countess De Ribes; Suzy Menkes; Dawn Mello; Christian Lacroix; Pierre Berge, the president of Yves Saint Laurent; Marvin and Lee Traub, (he also was soon to retire); Mike Gould, soon to be the CEO of Bloomingdales; Arie and Coco

Ira Neimark and Burton Tansky

Christian Lacroix and Ira Neimark

Ira Neimark and Jean-Louis Dumas

Gianfranco Ferre and Ira Neimark

Karl Lagerfeld and Ira Neimark

Pierre Berge and Ira Neimark

Marvin, Lee Traub and Ira Neimark

Ira Neimark and Terry Lundgren

Kopelman, the head of Chanel U.S.A.; from Italy, Luciano and Rita Barbera; Jean-Franco Ferre; and Beppe Modenese.

The evening ended with my being presented with the Medal from the City of Paris An affair to remember.

Then my third party was given by Arthur Sulzberger Jr., then the Deputy Publisher of the *New York Times*, and Lance Primis, President of the paper. They held a cocktail reception honoring me and my successor Burt Tansky on January 28, 1992 at the St. Regis Hotel roof in New York City.

They should have also billed the party as a dinner because the hors d'oeuvres tables were groaning with food.

Here, too, the guests were not only industry friends, but personal friends as well. Bill Cunningham, who worked with me many years ago and went on to become the famous *New York Times* photographer, took pictures of nearly all the guests. Among them: Pauline Trigere, Abe Schrader, Barrie and Cheryl Schwartz, Steve Ruzzo, Oscar de la Renta, Isaac Mizrahi, William Lauder, Mary McFadden, Allen Flusser, and Kasper. Also included were many of our personal friends.

Arthur Sulzberger Jr. and Ira Neimark

Oscar de la Renta

The *New York Times* was Bergdorf Goodman's major advertising medium. They were very supportive in all our efforts to raise Bergdorf's profile and to get our fashion message across. Not only in the ads we ran, but also in many of their news articles, including the Sunday Magazine spread announcing the opening of the Men's Store.

This final retirement party ended my retail career that started on Fifth Avenue as the doorboy at Bonwit Teller in 1938 and ended just across Fifth Avenue, as Chairman and CEO of Bergdorf Goodman in 1992. It took many years and many experiences to cross Fifth Avenue. I enjoyed nearly every minute of it.

Lesson Learned

- Opportunity is always there if you continue to look for it. The phrase, "It is not what you know, but who you know," is only half correct. I believe, "It's what you know, and who you know," that brings success to your dreams and ambitions.

A New Career

33

Did I just suggest that my career ended with those glorious good-bye parties? There is more. I continue to this day as an advisor to companies in fashion and finance. Fashion first.

Jean-Louis Dumas, the president of Hermes, surprised me with a visit to my office shortly after I'd announced my retirement as CEO of Bergdorf Goodman. I assumed that he came to wish me well. Instead, he asked me to become a board member of Hermes of Paris, the American subsidiary of Hermes International. He explained that Stanley Marcus was retiring from the board and he would like me to replace him. I was so flattered that I instantly accepted the position, before I thought to ask basic questions like, "What is the director's fee?" In retrospect, that may have been the most respectful thing to do; I believe Hermes, being a French company, places honor before remuneration. And in truth, being able to continue my successful retail experience with another of the preeminent fashion houses in the world was indeed reward enough—until I made a contribution that justified compensation.

That came soon. In studying Hermes, I realized the high quality of their product was their number one consideration. Visiting the workrooms in Paris was an unforgettable experience. Jean-Louis strolled from floor to floor, work bench after work bench, greeting each artisan by name and discussing the leather product that each was working on. Every product had to be perfect.

On a later visit to Lyon, Jackie and I had a private tour of the Hermes factory that produced the famous Hermes ties. The artisans showed us how the prints were drawn and then printed to the fine silk. What impressed me most was the detail of the inspection at the end of the production line. It looked as though the inspectors examined each tie with a magnifying glass, rejecting any tie that did not meet their requirements.

Early on, it became clear to me that Hermes was so proud of the style and quality of their expensive products, that they couldn't be bothered with such mundane things as state of the art merchandising techniques. Hermes left decisions to their buyers about how much of each of their items—silk ties, scarves, handbags or apparel—would be carried in the Hermes stores. The buyers were also the managers of their stores.

You've heard me say this before: Leaving the buying strategy, as to how much to buy of what and when, to the buyer can only lead to too much merchandise at the wrong time. At Hermes, the buyers/store managers compounded that problem with the conviction that Hermes merchandise was of such high quality that it wouldn't go out of style.

I suggested to Jean-Louis that the weeks-of-supply program that was successful at Bergdorf Goodman could go a long way to training his buyers in the U.S. in how much merchandise to buy by classification. When it proved to be successful—I was confident there was no "if" involved—I suggested he might then expand the program to his stores around the world.

Jean-Louis agreed to this advisory project and even agreed to my consulting fee. That shows French practicality.

Without going into too much detail, I'll note simply that I explained to the Hermes buyers that, instead of their being given a set open-to-buy budget and spreading it around to cover their many classifications, they were to plan by classification, that is, how many units of each classification they anticipated selling based on their previous experience. Afterwards, they would add all that up, and the result would be their budget. In many cases, the light went on. Once again, we were off and running.

I am pleased to say at one of the recent Hermes board meetings in Paris, when Robert Chavez, the president of Hermes of Paris, made his presentation showing the dramatic rise in sales in the U.S. and the reduced inventory required to achieve those sales, Jean-Louis made a small salute in my direction and quietly said, "Thank you." From Hermes, this was a special honor.

As with the senior players at Hermes, I had known Yoshiaki Sakakura, chairman and CEO of Mitsukoshi from his many visits to Bergdorf Goodman. He had asked a number of times for permission for his people to photograph our new designer shops, since he wanted to upgrade the fashion image of Mitsukoshi, which was the largest retailer in Japan with over thirty department stores throughout Japan, as well as in Taipei.

While the announcement of my retirement was still fresh news, Mr. Sakakura contacted me through his representative, Mr. Katsu Nitta, and requested a meeting. Mr. Sakakura wanted me to consider offering my consulting services as a retail advisor to Mitsukoshi. I accepted, but this time I knew to ask questions about fees and obligations at the outset. In this case, I was predisposed to say "yes" as I recalled how much I'd enjoyed visiting Japan, first on my trip to Japan for B. Altman in the early 70's, and later for Bergdorf Goodman. We quickly cut a deal and I began my consultancy.

At the time, Mitsukoshi was the largest department store of them all. Floor after floor featured vast assortments of merchandise and sales staff unmatched anywhere for their service to customers. Fortunately, I was asked to help upgrade their men's and women's business without concern for the many other departments throughout the store.

Retail merchandising in Japan differed considerably from Western methods. In most cases, Japanese retail stores bought from distributors, not directly from wholesalers as in the U.S., and the distributors had their assigned locations in the department stores. The distributors usually sold the merchandise to the stores on a memorandum, or "memo," meaning that, at the end of the season, the retailer could return slow moving merchandise back to the distributor. With that type of arrangement, the retailer had a lower profit due to the distributor taking the risk. It became necessary for me to find those fashion collections that were not controlled by distributors and assign them "buy-sell" departments. With the challenge of buying, selling, and then having to mark down the slow or old merchandise, Mitsukoshi merchants embarked on a risk management strategy that was, literally, foreign to them.

Fortunately, once again, the unit weeks-of-supply procedure played a starring role in the transition to greater profitability. At first, the Mitsukoshi merchandise executives were anxious about following it because they recognized this as a new and worrisome step toward Western retailing. The Vendor Program was also extremely useful since I found that, even though Mitsukoshi had a large volume of business with all the suppliers that they bought from, there was no program in place to negotiate for better terms on each purchase.

The weeks-of-supply program was of particular interest to one of the young executives, Ken Shigematsu, with whom I'd worked when he was in charge of Mitsukoshi's New York office. Back in Japan, he had developed a trendy women's ready wear department called Broadway Runway. Using both the Vendor Program to negotiate better terms and the weeks-of-supply to manage his inventory, the ready-to-wear division improved dramatically. He went on to be the president of the large Mitsukoshi Ginza store in Tokyo.

On one of my visits to the men's department in the Ginza store, Mr. Taneo Nakamura stopped by. He heard me explain to the buyer of men's underwear the need to decrease his assortment from fifteen manufacturers to no more than six, the logic being that he didn't have to have every line of underwear to satisfy his customers. I told him his store should be the authority on what the best lines were for his customers. Mr. Nakamura's serendipitous visit turned out to be quite fortunate. A few years after that, he become CEO of Mitsukoshi—and a true disciple of my approach. He recited this story many times in schooling his executives.

As part of my work for Mitsukoshi, I advised them on their licensing arrangements with various design houses. When I studied the Oscar de la Renta license performance, I was disappointed in the translation of the style Oscar had submitted to Mitsukoshi from his original styles. Not only were they poorly interpreted, but the sales were also very poor.

I arranged to meet in New York with the Mitsukoshi executives responsible for Oscar's license, and the Oscar de la Renta licensing attorney. Imagine my surprise when the attorney turned out to be Jeffry Aronsson, who was also my attorney. I estimated there must be approximately 50,000 attorneys in New York, and for Oscar and me to have the same attorney was quite a coincidence. As neither ODLR nor Mitsukoshi were satisfied with the business, the license was slowly phased out and Oscar de la Renta excited the Japanese market through different selling arrangements.

Over the years I have watched Oscar grow and receive the recognition he deserves. This is all beautifully presented in his book, *Oscar*, that he kindly presented to me in one of our last business discussions. The evaluation of Oscar de la Renta from his early days in Madrid, Paris and then in America, and his rise to dominance worldwide is unique, not only from the creative aspect, but also because of his sound business decisions. During my tenure at Bergdorf Goodman, Oscar was always part of the scene, growing to be one of the major design collections of the store.

Through my association with Mitsukoshi, I was invited a number of times to speak at the Japanese Department Store Association conference. Every important retailer attended and showed great interest in what was happening in the United States. One of the points that I made, as I did in 1960 to the Frederick Atkins principals, was that discount stores in their many forms, as well as shopping malls, would encroach on their market and they must be prepared for that eventuality. My hope was that the Japanese retailers would learn from the fall of the regional department stores in the U.S. and develop the strategy required to maintain their leadership and financial health.

After my work with Jean-Louis Dumas at Hermes in Paris and Yashiaki Sakakura at Mitsukoshi in Tokyo, I got another call a year later. This time, it was from Andrew Jennings at the House of Fraser in London. In short, I trotted around the globe singing my favorite aria: The single biggest reason for erosion of profits in retailing is poor inventory management. Inventory has been, is, and will always be a drain on profits unless it is treated objectively as an investment that must bring in a reasonable return.

As with Mitsukoshi, I introduced the House of Fraser to the unit weeks-of-supply concept and to a more formal method of negotiating with vendors—whether manufacturers or distributors— through the Vendor Program. Andrew Jennings applied both programs diligently, and in addition to being a top merchant, became the successful president and managing director of Holt Renfrew, in Canada, owned by Galen Weston. In 2004, his triumph at Holt Renfrew led to the presidency of Saks Fifth Avenue.

Through recommendations, financial investors soon sought my advice about their strategies related to retail. Frederick A. Klingenstein referred me to Willem de Vogel, the head of Three Cities Research, Investors of Private Capital. His firm had invested in a retailer—not a Bergdorf Goodman or Hermes—but a prominent operation. He emphasized that I would enjoy meeting Willem, and he was right. I very much enjoyed advising Willem and his associates on certain basic principles of retailing. My main contribution to them and companies they invested in, was to convince them that, no matter what merchandise they carried, high sales and gross profit-per-square-foot productivity, held the key to profitability.

With their investment in an apparel discount chain, I had to convince them and the management of the chain that the key to discount retailing is to buy the most desirable merchandise at the lowest price possible, and then to sell it at the lowest price that is possible. Initial mark-up and gross margin goals must be dramatically lower than those for traditional retailers, I stressed.

On to Bear Stearns, where E. John Rosenwald Jr., Vice Chairman, kindly arranged a meeting with two principals of Bear Stearns, Richard L. Perkal, and Michael Doppelt. A week or so after the first meeting, Richard introduced me to their merchant Banking Senior executive, John Howard. That began a relationship of advising them in due-diligence situations, as well as introducing them to potential retail investment opportunities. More calls followed.

Most recently, Steven A. Seiden, president of Seiden Krieger Associates invited me to be a retail advisor to his executive search firm, to identify and evaluate prospective candidates. Based on my good luck and instincts building a highly professional team at Bergdorf, I felt confident in making contributions in this area, as well.

And one of my favorite executives, formerly at Three Cities Research, H. Whitney Wagner, introduced me to Howard Rimerman. He was a Senior Advisor to Quilvest, which is an investor of private capital. He felt that I could help by doing due diligence for select fashion designers looking for capital to expand their businesses.

Today I continue to consult in all of these areas and I plan to continue this work for a long time to come.

Lessons Learned

- No matter what the business, basic principles that successful executives have proven to be sound will, more times than not, lead to success.

Epilogue

34

Although I left my formal education early, I always continued learning by analyzing my way through new situations that challenged me. Even after retirement, opportunities for me to learn new things in the world of fashion have never stopped.

I wrote most of this book in 2003 and 2004. It was intended to be a memoir of my growing up in the retail business, as well as the recounting of exciting experiences along the way. It is also a detailed background on the fashion industry for much of the past half century, as well as profiles of the personalities who made it happen, as seen through my eyes.

Little did I realize that exploring what I had learned, enjoyed, rebelled against, influenced, and wondered about between 1938 and 1992 would put me in such close touch with current events. *Crossing Fifth Avenue* turned out to be not only a memoir of "lessons learned," but a lens giving valuable—and I mean valuable— perspectives on what is happening today, and I believe, what will happen in the future.

To give you a taste of this work's relevance, the following topics have turned into today's recent headlines:

Markdown Allowances Scandal: *Women's Wear Daily*, June 6, 2005: "Charge Back Crises"

New York Times, June 4, 2005: "Saks Reopens Inquiry of Deductions"

Designer Retail Outlet Stores: *New York Times*, May 26, 2005: "Mark It Down and They Will Come"

Neiman Marcus and Bergdorf Goodman Sold to Private Equity firm: *Wall Street Journal*, May 2, 2005

The Scourge of Street Peddlers: *New York Times*: May 26, 2005: "On the Streets, Genuine Copies"

"Over Inventories Causing Decreased Profits," a May 2005 article by Fred Wilson, CEO of Saks Fifth Avenue

"Selling Macy's Name", The New York Times, Saturday, August 26, 2006.

Based on all of this coverage and much, much more, it's important to stress several key points one more time.

Inventory management—or the lack of it—is and has been the single biggest reason for retailers to lose profit and often lose their businesses as well. Technology alone is not a solution to the problem: It helps those who are willing to think through their company's problems. In many cases, technology just makes it obvious how badly you're failing.

Many of the stores listed in this book will be familiar to you because of their strong retail identities—in days gone by. But they were not able to survive. Today several other major industries—the airlines and the book business, for example—are going through exactly the same transformation as the department store retailers did in the last fifty years. The retailers who are gone were too slow to adapt. They disappeared.

In conclusion, the lessons I've shared here from my life as a retailer are not just for retailers!

Index